Warren B. Johnson

From the Pacific to the Atlantic

Being an account of a journey overland from Eureka, Humboldt Co., California, to Webster, Worcester Co., Mass., With a horse, carriage, cow and dog.

Warren B. Johnson

From the Pacific to the Atlantic
Being an account of a journey overland from Eureka, Humboldt Co., California, to Webster, Worcester Co., Mass., With a horse, carriage, cow and dog.

ISBN/EAN: 9783337103293

Printed in Europe, USA, Canada, Australia, Japan

Cover: Foto ©Andreas Hilbeck / pixelio.de

More available books at **www.hansebooks.com**

FROM

THE

PACIFIC TO THE ATLANTIC,

BEING AN

ACCOUNT OF A JOURNEY OVERLAND FROM
EUREKA, HUMBOLDT CO., CALIFORNIA,
TO WEBSTER, WORCESTER
CO., MASS.,

WITH

A HORSE, CARRIAGE, COW AND DOG,

BY

WARREN B. JOHNSON.

WEBSTER, MASS.,
JOHN CORT, PRINTER AND BOOKBINDER,
OVER POST OFFICE, MAIN STREET.
1887.

Entered according to Act of Congress, in the year 1887, by

WARREN B. JOHNSON,

in the Office of the Librarian of Congress, at Washington, D. C.

PREFACE.

The world is full of books of travel, adventure and romance, which have covered almost every conceivable portion of the known world; most of which have been written by men of culture, leisure and wealth. Every land has been visited, every tribe and kindred of people have been portrayed, and the people made richer in the stores of knowledge derived from their perusal. In the accompanying pages will be found a detail of travel, novel in its character, performed by a common man, of but ordinary schooling, of a journey across the American continent, overland and on foot, accompanied by a horse, wagon, cow and dog. Perhaps, such a journey will never be taken again; especially, with a prospect of meeting with such impediments as beset his path from the nature of the roads, the means of crossing unbridged rivers, and the prospect of violence from the beasts of the forest, and the untamed nature of the Indian. In this volume, no attempt has been made to give a full description of the various States passed through, or an elaborate account of the products of agriculture, mining or manufacturing accomplished in the western wilds of the American nation. Nor has an attempt been made to eloquently describe the habits and customs of the people. The story of his travels is told in his own language, as near as possible, to make a continuous narrative. Some of his descriptions of scenes passed through are unique, told in as few common-place words as possible. Particular stress has been given to the conversations with those whom he came in contact while on his journey, and with whom he stopped over night. At the same time, he from time to time gives the reader much insight of the country passed through, that most travellers fail to get in their passage through a country while on a more fleeting excursion. He received many courtesies and attention from the people, whose hospitality was always freely given him. Some of the characters with whom he came in contact were quite original. Nowhere did he receive any insult, nor did he meet with such obstructions as might have been expected in some of the less populous districts through which he passed. As his journey drew to a close and he came into the more civilized States, he was every where welcomed and the people flocked round him in curiosity; as his mode of travelling, with such companions, was new and original and looked upon with wonderment. In fact, it was considered by some as the work of a monomaniac at least; it may be questioned if any other man would have had the courage to make the journey, under such circumstances. It required a determined will, a patient plodding along, and a constant care for the well-being of his companions. Part of his journey was a travel in solitude, and he had a chance to commune with himself quite frequently. Much interest was taken in his progress as he went along on his way, and he was the recipient of many kind wishes, and a request to send them a book if he should write such an one; to all such, he dedicates this book, with the hope that it will prove of interest, if not a scholarly production, at least a source of instruction, as well as an acknowledgement of the many courtesies received from those mentioned in the narrative.

Mr. Johnson, the traveller and writer, is an American by birth, is sixty-eight years of age, stands about six feet high, weighs one hundred and seventy pounds, is of a florid complexion, and looks what he is, a true type of the Eastern Yankee. He is a native of Connecticut, born in Woodstock, and lived there until he was nine years of age. At that time he moved with his parents to that portion of the present town of Webster, which was then called Oxford South Gore. Webster was not then incorporated as a town. Webster was incorporated in the year 1832. From that time until the outbreak of the Rebellion, he was an inhabitant of the town. In August of that year he enlisted in the 21st Regiment, Massachusetts Volunteers. In 1864, he re-enlisted in the First Brigade Band, of the First Division of the 20th Army Corps, being with General Sherman in his march from Atlanta to the Sea. He left Sherman's Army at Fayetteville, N. C., and went into the hospital at New York for treatment, where he was transferred to Dale Hospital in Massachusetts, and soon afterwards mustered out. For his disability incurred in the army, he has since received a small pension, He went to California in 1880 at the solicitation of friends and relatives, and took this means of getting back to Massachusetts, as he did not like California, and was short of means to bring himself, horse and cow back to Massachusetts by railroad, which journey he successfully made, and practically walked from the Pacific to the Atlantic, without any serious molestation. To all who helped him, in whatever shape, is this humble volume dedicated.

W. B. JOHNSON.

CONTENTS.

Chapter i.—The start, from Eureka to San Francisco.................................... 2

Chapter ii.—From San Francisco to San Jose and Sacramento........................ 28

Chapter iii.—From Sacramento to Reno, Nevada 61

Chapter iv.—From Reno, Battle Mountain, Wells to Ogden in Utah..................... 105

Chapter v.—The City of Ogden............... 180

Chapter vi.—From Ogden City to Laramie, Wyoming 189

Chapter vii.—From Laramie, Cheyenne to Omaha, Nebraska........................... 253

Chapter viii.—From Omaha, Des Moines, Davenport to Cleveland, Ohio................ 298

Chapter ix.—From Cleveland, Buffalo, Albany to Marlow, New Hampshire............. 321

Chapter x.—From Marlow to Webster and Lynn, 360

FROM THE PACIFIC TO THE ATLANTIC.

CHAPTER I.

THE START—FROM EUREKA TO SAN FRANCISCO.

On the morning of the first of June, 1882, I started on my proposed journey from Eureka City, Humboldt Bay, California, for **Massachusetts**, with my outfit, comprising myself, horse, wagon, dog and cow, with all necessary articles for the long journey—making the first day the town of Hydesville, distance twenty-five miles. In reaching Hydesville, I passed through Humboldt, Salmon Creek, Hookton, Table Bluff, Springville, Rohnersville to Hydesville.

Eureka is situated on Humboldt bay, and was first located two miles from the mouth, but this was abandoned on account of its nearness to the ocean, and afterwards located on its present site, five miles from the mouth of the bay. Eureka was planted in good soil, came up and has grown to be a fine city, not large, but enterprising, and has now a population of about 7,000. It is the shire town of Humboldt county. It has some three thousand feet of wharfage, is beautifully laid out in squares, running south to the forest, named alphabetically, and east numerically. It has five hotels. The Vance House is the leading hotel of the city, a fine house inside as well as outside. The Bay Hotel comes next, this also is a fine house. The Occidental next, and so on. There are many first-class stores in the place. Recently Eureka has been made a port of entry. She has a custom-house and port collector. Large amounts of merchandise are imported from abroad and distributed throughout the county. Many kinds of business are carried on, from the making of leather to the finest boots, and from the furness to the boot and shoe scraper. But its main business is lumber. More lumber is cut in this place than any other town on the continent, and is distributed long distances, in fact all over the world. There are seven mills for cutting lumber, five single and two double mills. They are capable of cutting from 40 to 80 thousand feet per day. Logs are cut that measure from three to twelve feet in diameter. Not many small logs are cut. It is the large ones that count. Railroads have been constructed from tide-water up into the mountains, to bring these logs and dump them into the sloughs. Then the small steamers take them down to the mills. There they lay in the mud or water until needed.

Humboldt is situated on the bay, near its entrance to the Pacific ocean, and is the oldest town on the bay. Formerly there was a fortification here, which was commanded by General U. S. Grant. Its barracks are still standing. The entrance to this bay is one of the most difficult for vessels to enter on the Pacific coast, owing to the changing character of its channel. As you enter the bay, two miles to the right, there is a high bluff. From that bluff to the neck of land which forms the bay, is a sand-bar. There was a time when the waters did not break over this bar, but time has changed things materially, for now there is a large channel, making a good inlet to the bay. It is enlarging from day to day. Over nearly one-half of this bar the waters are constantly dashing. In full tide the waters are not confined to this channel by the bar, if they were it would soon be washed away, but is covered by the waters. Its surface water passes over the bar, not through the channel as it should.

Salmon Creek takes its name from that noble fish—the salmon. In years past they were very plentiful, but of late they are not so plenty, owing to the great navigation. Its waters have become a great thoroughfare. Steamers are constantly passing up and down this creek, and make havoc among the fish. Since this time they have not troubled these parts of the bay. This town has become a great place for cutting lumber. It is one of the many places where great trees are felled. Their diameters vary from four to twelve feet. As you leave this place you leave Hookton to your right.

Hookton is situated on the southern part of the bay, and is noted for exportation. Large quantities of merchandise are brought into this place from long distances, including the southern part of the county as well as from the northern part of Mendocino county,—over the roughest of rough roads that I ever traveled. This road is called the "Humboldt and Mendocino Overland Road to California."

Table Bluff is situated on a high bluff. Reaching its summit you are delighted with its surroundings. North, south and west, are the waters of the Pacific. The bluff is not large, but level and handsome. There are three ranches on the summit. On the north side, next the bay, there is an Indian settlement. They are frequent visitors to the city, are intelligent, partly civilized, and enlightened, and make good citizens.

Springville is a small place, but enterprise stands out plainly. Indications are that this village will become one of the most delightful places in the valley.

Rohnersville.—This is a fine village. It is small but handsome. All good modern buildings, constructed of good material, one of the finest in the valley.

Hydesville.—This place is second to none in the valley. It is the termination of a line of stages to the city. All of the above villages are situated on Eel river valley, one of the richest in the state. There is more grain grown to the acre in this valley than any other in the state.

Left Hydesville June 2d and made Bridgeville the same day, having traveled twenty-five miles. On making this place, I found that there was a vast difference in roads. To Hydesville it had been good traveling. This day I found my journey had been over rough, hard and dangerous roads. After leaving Hydesville, I came to a canyon, turning short to the left, descending about four hundred feet in less than eighty rods, then turning short to the right, ascending the same distance on the opposite side. This is one way of traveling in California. Going on, I came to a large, broad river, and meeting a man with a team asked him if it was Eel river. "Oh no, it is not" said the man, "it is the Vandozen." "How is it about fording?" "Oh, it is a good ford, but the water is rather deep now, with a good hard bottom." Went on, and came to the ford; stopped, looked at it, and continued to look at it. All of this time I was thinking. My thoughts were covering a large space—from the Pacific to the Atlantic. "Can this be done?" I had struck out on a long, rough and dangerous journey—from the Pacific to the Atlantic, with a horse and wagon, cow and dog. Can it be done, can this be accomplished, all alone, no one with me? Let happen what will, I decided to try it. I approached the ford; the water was deep; I was not able to see the bottom, with a strong, swift current. There I must decide, go on or go back. If I return back I should never be satisfied. If I go on and make a success, then I have accomplished a wonderful undertaking. I there decided to go on, and did. I put my little dog on the wagon, got on myself, drove down into the river and got across all right. Went on again, coming to the same river, which I had again to ford. I did not stop but drove down into the river and across all right. Ascended the bluff, leaving the river to my right, and soon came once more in sight of the river. I am now ascending a bluff; on my right down hundreds of feet is the river; the road is just wide enough for one team only. There is a precedent established for those traveling these bluffs. It is this: on ascending a bluff, mountain or canyon, you are required to carry a horn or a bell. On arriving at any turnout, stop, blow your horn or ring your bell. Should you hear no bell or horn in answer, go on to the next turnout and stop, ring bell or blow horn, and no answer, go on as before. Should you meet a team, the one ascending is required to back down to the turnout. This mode of proceeding has become a law, and so understood by those who travel. About half-past six o'clock, I was overtaken by a team on its way from Hookton, it had been there with a load of wood. I asked the driver the distance to Bridgeville. He replied about three miles. I told him I was from Eureka city, had left there yesterday morning and was going east. Had found a good road from Hydesville, but from there to here, it was the roughest I ever traveled or had ever heard of being traveled. "Yes," he replied, "from Hydesville to Bridgeville is rough, very rough and dangerous to those who are not accustomed to such roads." Soon I came in sight of a house, then a little further on two more. I stopped, inquired how far to Bridgeville. "This is Bridgeville," said a man. "This Bridgeville?" "Yes," said the stranger. I went on, soon came in sight of a bridge, a little farther on several houses. "What place is this?" "Bridgeville," responded several men. "I was told a short distance back that that was Bridgeville." "You are not the only one they tell so. They wanted your dollar, that was what they wanted, stranger."

Bridgeville is but a small place, comprising a hotel, store, blacksmith shop and one other house. This hotel is unlike other hotels, but it is a place where you can stop over night, or get out of a rain or snow storm, and find something to eat and drink. The building is cheap, but still it has many things for the comfort of travelers. If you arrive late in the afternoon, you have got to stop or go on to the next village, a distance of twenty-five miles. You ask the hotel-keeper if you can stop over. He says yes, and leads your horse to a shed, takes him from the carriage, hitching him to a post. The traveler may have some things in his carriage that he would like to take into the house with him. He takes them in and asks for a room. The landlord says: "We have no room for you, you can lie there," pointing to a lounge. "We can give you something to eat and all the whisky you want." I was introduced to a traveler by the landlord, who informed me that the stranger was from the city of San Francisco, who comes to Cloverdale by railroad, then takes a team for Ukiah, county seat of Mendocino county, from there to Eureka county seat of Humboldt county.

Left Bridgeville on the 3d and made Blocksberg the same day; distance twenty-five miles. On leaving this place we cross the Vandozen river again. Here we cross a fine bridge built by the county of Humboldt. About 9 a. m., came to a fine plat of grass. I stopped and gave my cattle a chance to nibble it—cooked some coffee and ate my breakfast; rather a late breakfast. About 10:30 a. m., we moved on, a very warm morning; indeed the warmest I had ever witnessed while in the state. It was telling on my horse and I was afraid she would blister her shoulder. I am now working inland from the ocean, away from its cool breezes. Soon I shall be east of the coast range of mountains. To-day my road has improved, hope it will continue. About 5:30 I made Blocksberg.

On my arrival, I found that my horse had blistered both shoulders. I thought best to remain a while and heal them up before going any further. I remained five days. My treatment was cold water. I bathed them continually for thirty-six hours, with good success. Had I continued on they might have become sore and troublesome. While here I tried to get my cow shod with iron shoes, but could not. The blacksmith said: "He could shoe her as the Spaniards shoe them." "How do they shoe them?" I asked. "They sear their feet," he said. I concluded to do so, and had her shod that way. It proved a wise precaution. I traveled more than six hundred miles before I could get her shod with iron shoes.

Blocksberg is a small town comprised of a hotel, two stores, blacksmith, wheelright shop, two saloons and a few houses. Saloons are well patronized, I counted twenty-two horses at one. Their riders were inside drinking and gambling. "I asked what business they followed?" I was told that they "were wool growers, but their main business was drinking and gambling." Those that follow this business, and they are many, have nothing but gold. I have seen piles of gold on the tables. They do not appear to be afraid of each other. They do not count out their money; it is laid in piles; they go by the height. Their money consists of five, ten and twenty dollar pieces, I have seen heaps four inches high of twenties. Their money lays on the table until they get through, with their revolvers beside them.

Left Blocksberg on the 9th and made Alder Point the same day, distance thirteen miles.

Alder Point.—From Blocksberg to this place proved a very hard day's journey, the road being very rough, hard and hilly. It was hard on the cattle, wagon and myself. The road had been sideling—very much so. It was bluffs, mountains and canyons. Travelers do not go over the bluffs or mountains, but around them. In laying out this road, if it ever was laid out, which I suppose it must have been, as it is a county road, their work was crudely done. If you desire to reach a given point on mountain or bluff, say Alder Point, you start at the base and go on following the same until you have made a half circle, keeping to the right till you come to a point or plateau, you have made a mile; you then turn to the right, cross the end of the canyon, this places you on the right of another bluff, following its base you travel until you reach the point opposite where you started, thus making a second mile, and so on, until the summit of the bluff is reached. Could you have crossed the canyon at the first point two miles of travelling would have been saved. The foregoing gives an idea of the roads and the mode of crossing the bluffs, mountains or canyons in northern and eastern California, outside of the valleys. I have said the roads were sideling and they are. Over the road on which I am travelling the mail from San Francisco is carried three hundred and three miles in 36 hours, nearly 9 miles to the hour, by two horses in a wagon that weighs 800 pounds; as this team tears round the bluff it is no wonder that one rut is lower than the other. There is no money expended on the roads, only the bridges are kept in repair. I am still but a short distance from Eel river. This river is a terror to those who have it to ford. No bridge—no ferry—it must be forded. Had it not been for this river I should have started on my journey east the first of May. The rainy season had been longer in duration than in past seasons.

When I arrived at the river there was a man, with a wagon and four horses ladened with goods. He was in conversation with another person. The teamster came to me and said: "We had better get this man to pilot us across, it is dangerous for us to ford." "What does he ask to help us across?" "Two dollars each," said the teamster. "Where is the ford, I would like to look at it." "It is a few rods, just below the bluffs," replied the teamster. I went down the bluff, to the river, looked at it a short time. I then took Fanny, my horse, from the wagon, got upon her back and rode into the water, and finding it much better than I expected, continued across. Returning, dismounted, put Fanny back into the carriage, got on and drove down the bank into the river and crossed over all right. The man with the team had just got to the river. I sang out: "Teamster, come across and save your money." He dared not do it, but gave the man two dollars needlessly, to guide him across. He might have known that if I could cross with my light load he could with his heavy wagon.

I began the ascending of the mountain feeling jubilant, as the fording of this river had been a terror to me ever since leaving Eureka. About two miles from the river I met the mail stage, a heavy two-horse wagon. I was ascending. It was not a bad place to pass and I gave him right of way. The driver sang out for the road and stopped. I told him he had ample room to pass. He had but two passengers aboard. The driver said: "That he would teach me to get out of the way for the mail driver." With that he started up and came down on the rear wheel of my carriage, crushing it down. He did not stop to see what damage he had done, but went on his own way. I was vexed and felt badly, being all alone. Soon after, the man I left at the river came up; and seeing what a fix I was in, assisted me in placing my wheel back into shape, and then put my things on his wagon; we went on until we came to a sheep ranche. Here I remained two days to make necessary repairs. There was no wheelwright shop for sixteen miles. Having some tools with me, such as an axe, saw and square, I got some timber, sawing it into splints, length of the diameter of my wheel, and lashing them to the spokes of the wheel, tied them down so as to keep the disc of the wheel in its proper place. Next day I was again ready to resume my journey.

On the morning of the 10th I was up early making ready to go onward. I carry a lariet for staking out my cow. An iron pin, one and a half foot long, one end shaped to a point and the other a small ring for the rope; the rope thirty feet long. This gives the cow a circle of sixty feet in which to feed. I fastened the cow to the lariet turning the horse loose. This morning I went to my breakfast and while eating I heard a horse neigh. I thought nothing about it and kept on eating. I heard another neigh and thought all was not right. I went out, saw that the cow was quite uneasy and trying to get loose. I then thought that the horse might have slipped and returned back to Blocksberg. I left my breakfast and went in search of the horse. Looking around, I could see nothing of her. A grove of timber was between me and the house. I went in and around this grove but could see nothing of the horse. The cow had become frantic. I made up my mind that the horse had strayed back to Blocksberg. I went for the river, distance three miles. I could find no tracks on the way, yet still I was sure she had gone this way. On the river bank I found tracks of her, and was sure she had crossed over. I concluded to return back and get the man at the ranche to go after her. On returning and while on high ground, I called out: "Stop horse, stop horse, stop horse," but got no satisfaction. I engaged the man at the ranche to go after the horse, who did so. He crossed the river and went to the barn were the mail horses are kept and inquired if they had seen a stray horse? The man replied: "That early that morning he heard a man across the river hallo 'stop horse,' and at that time a horse was going by. He tried to stop it but could not, the horse starting on a good trot. He took one of his horses and drove after her. After quite a chase he overtook and caught her and led her back to his barn. She is here in the barn now." When the ranche man brought the horse back I asked him, "How much for his trouble?" He replied, "I gave the man across the river for his trouble, one dollar, I ought to have as much." I gave him two dollars. This man who went for the horse was the owner of the ranche. "How large a ranche have you, sir?" I asked. "One hundred and sixty acres," he replied. "How many sheep have you?" Four thousand or more." "And only one hundred and sixty acres?" "That is all the land I own." "Who does own all the land around here?" "Uncle Sam." "You feed your sheep on them?" "Yes." "I should suppose that these lands would be taken up by many persons, they look so handsome and good mowings." "There has been many to look at them, but I have the only spring around. South of me there is a creek, which is on my land. West there is no water, north is the river, three miles away, east is the spring which is on my ranche. Between me and the river there is feed enough for ten thousand sheep, and only four thousand to feed from it." "Are you contented to live here? I suppose so, or I should not find you here." "Yes, I have been here so long, I am contented. I do not care to leave. My father came and settled here twenty years ago. I was then ten years old. My father has been dead nearly five years. I have had charge of the ranche since his death." "How much help does it require to look after four thousand sheep?" "There are four of us; those two boys and the boy I hire." "How much do you pay that boy?" "Fifty dollars a year, board and clothes. I have three dogs. They are worth more than the boys. I leave the sheep in charge of the dogs for hours. I shall go where the sheep are pasturing soon, you may go with me and see the dogs bring them in. If you have never seen them among sheep it will be interesting for you to see them." "Do you bring in the sheep at night?" "We do every night. We don't allow them to remain out nights. The wolf and the kyote make great havoc among them when they have a chance." "You say that you have some four thousand sheep, can you get them into those four carrolls?" "Yes, there is plenty of room." "When they are in you think they are safe, do you?" "Yes, no wolf or kyote can get over that fence." "How is it about the wild-cat? I hear they are the most active of all wild animals." "They are the smartest of them all. They are very wild, but we keep them at a distance. We hunt them. Do not care to kill them, but prefer to wound them. The wolves are the most troublesome when the grass begins to dry up; then the sheep take to the canyons and the wild animals have mutton for a change. Then the sheep owners have to double the number of their shepherds or they will be heavy losers of sheep."

Wool growing has become a great business. There is more money made by it than by any other business with the same amount of capital. The owner of this ranche has four thousand sheep, which feed on two thousand acres of land, while the owner of the sheep only owns one hundred and sixty acres of land. He has no neighbors, all the land is his for use. You can see at a glance that there is money in the business.

I left Alder Point on the 11th and made the next stop at Belle Springs in the evening; distance twenty miles.

Belle Springs.—In travelling to this place I found it a fair road, some parts of it being very good, a decided improvement on the previous day's journey. After travelling about eight miles I came to a station called Spruce Grove, a place for changing horses in the transportation of the mails. About six miles farther is a dark canyon, a noted place to stop a stage for plunder. About three miles farther I came to a mountain, which I was obliged to travel around in order to reach the summit, as before described, keeping on our right or left the canyons. Some are deep, very deep, and awful to look down them. The roads are narrow, no place wide enough for two teams. Turnouts are made at distances varying from a quarter to half a mile. These occur when a change of direction is to be made. On arriving at a turnout, we are instructed to stop and look ahead, and seing no one coming we sound our horn or ring a bell and hearing no answer, go on to the next turnout. Should we meet a team, the one ascending has to back down to the turnout just left, giving the right of way to the team descending. I have had to back, or rather take the horse from the wagon, bring it around and drive back to the turnout. This is much safer than attempting to back down. This requires care, as the room for turning is very meagre. About three miles from Belle Springs I began the ascent of a mountain, the canyon and turnouts being on my left. Before reaching its summit, I saw two men sitting at a turnout; I did not like their appearance. Just below them I came to a stop in the shade, thinking it was about the time for the stage to make its appearance and let it pass. The men came down to where I was. They were Indians, half-breeds. I was uneasy and started up to the turnout and again stopped, they following me. Their attention was attracted to my dog, Bertie, in the carriage. They were talking to him. I was anxious to see the mail stage come along; after a little while it came and I spoke and said: "It is time for the stage." I got aboard my wagon, the dog beside me. One of the Indians said: "Give me that dog." I made no reply, judging what was to follow. At that moment the mail stage came along. They saw it also; one of them caught the dog by its head and was pulling him out of the carriage. At that moment I grabbed a long knife that lay beside me and made a lounge at the man holding the dog and told him to let go of the dog. Both left and plunged into the canyon. The stage had got within a few hundred feet of me, and as it came along I called to the driver to stop. He did so and asked what I would have. "Did you notice those two men as you came up?" I asked. He replied, "yes." "I came near losing my little dog. They were Indians, half-breeds, I thought, by their looks." "Yes, I think they were," answered the driver, "you would have lost your dog had I been out of sight; they are now, no doubt, in the brush." "How far is it to Belle Springs?" I asked. "About a mile or a little more." "Will you walk your horses so that I can keep with you, I am afraid of those fellows?" "Yes, fall in, I will help you out of this." I fell in his rear and went on to the next station where I arrived all right. Had I not had his company I should have lost my dog and perhaps more. On my arrival at Belle Springs I found that my horse had wrenched off one of her front shoes, tearing the hoof of the foot badly on both sides. This seemed to put me in another bad fix; I became blue and despondent. What can I do, what can be done?

First three days traveled, horse blistered her shoulders, stopped five days; next, journeyed one day, carriage-wheel crushed and horse ran away, two days lost. Next, horse wrenched her shoe off, tearing both sides of hoof. In eleven days' journey, only one hundred and eight miles. Here I am, cannot travel while horse is in this condition and no blacksmith within twenty-six miles. Doubtful if a shoe can be put on of any service. Is not this enough to discourage a younger man than I? I told the landlord, when putting up, that I should be obliged to stay a short time with him. He replied, "Stay as long as you wish." I talked the accident over with the host, told him where I belonged when at home, and where I proposed to go. "You are from the East, it seems," he said. "What State?" "Massachusetts," I replied. "I come from

Connecticut," said the landlord: "what town in Massachusetts." I replied "From Webster." "Oh," he said; "I know Webster very well, I am from Pomfret, Conn., you are from Webster, Mass.; what may I call your name?" "My name is Johnson. Allow me to ask your name?" "My name is Aldrich. You from Webster, Mr. Johnson? make yourself at home and stay as long as you can consistently with the comfort of your horse. It shan't cost you a cent, not a cent, Mr. Johnson," said the landlord.

I made myself at home, but I could not content myself. I was troubled, thinking what could be done. I looked over my project, thinking of what I had already encountered and what was before me before reaching home, if ever, and concluded to return to Eureka. I talked the subject over with Mr. Aldrich, the landlord. He said that he would buy the horse and carriage, but not the cow. He made me an offer for the horse, carriage and harness—a fair offer. The horse I raised from a colt, and when coming out here to California, I brought her with me and have become very much attached to her, my wife also. It will be hard to part with her, I had thought enough of my horse to pay a large sum of money to get her to California, and I concluded that I would not sell her, but see if it were not possible to put a shoe on her foot. I was informed that the best horse-shoer known resided at Latonville, 26 miles from that place. I made a boot for the horse's foot, put it on, and put on her a saddle and on the morning of the 23d of June took road for the above place, and walked the distance on foot, except when fording the rivers. Arrived at Latonville at 4 p. m., one hour was passed in shoeing the horse and one more for rest, and at 6 p. m., started back for Belle Springs, reaching there the next morning at 4 a. m., travelling the fifty-two miles in twenty-two hours. Going, I led the horse, coming back I rode her for the first time. From Belle Springs to Latonville the road is the worst I had travelled. It was very hilly and rocky; one place is named Blue rock, and it looked blue from top to bottom. One other place was called Rattle Snake Canyon. Here you can find rattle snakes in plenty. I did not stop to hunt them, but **saw** several; thought it best to keep them at a distance. **Fifty-two miles was** travelled in twenty hours. Twenty-six by day and the same by night. I passed through the canyon between ten and 12 a. m., and at about the same hours at night. It is a fearful looking canyon, thickly wooded, narrow roads, on each side heavy bushes. **On my right going was a beautiful creek.** I was told that there were more wild animals in this canyon than in any other in the State. They come to this creek for water day and night. This I was told after I had travelled this road three times. Had I known it at first, it might have made me quail. As it was, it only made me a little nervous. On the morning of my return from Latonville, I was considerably frightened between the hours of 10 and 12 p. m. I was on my horse, it **was very dark, so much so that I** could not see the head of my horse at times. All at once the horse stopped at some sound in the bushes. I listened, heard some rattling among the bushes. I be-thought me of my dog which I had for the moment forgot. Dismounting from my horse quickly, I struck a light so I could see, and **found the dog under the horse** trembling with fear. **It is doubtful if ever my comrades** in the cavalry dismounted more quickly than I did. **I knew that there** must be some animal in the bush or the horse would not have stopped, or the dog become frightened. I grabbed the dog by the neck and re-mounted my horse "right sharp, you bet," and urged her on her journey. Travelling on I came near the **station** house, or stable, where the mail horses are changed, I sang out "ho, ho-a." A voice from the inside answered "Who's there, and what do you want at this time of night?" I replied that "I was on my way back to

Belle Springs, and will you let me have some oats for my horse?" "Are you the man that stopped here in the morning?" "I am." "Then I will get up and give your horse the oats, and I suppose you will pay for them." "Yes, I will pay," I replied. "If you don't I will blow your brains out," he remarked, "how many do you want?" "About a peck." "A peck, h——ll, I can't spare so many, we are most out of grain." "Can you let me have a quarter?" I told him I would pay well and give him something else. "Something else, give me that first." I pulled a small flask from my pocket and handed it to him, and said "this will get me the oats." He replied, "It was pay enough, and all I ask, and when you come this way again bring the flask full, you might want some more oats." I told him that I expected to be along the day after that, if I did not get eaten up by the wild animals, the canyon appeared to be full of them. He said, I was right; he did not see how I dared to be riding at night. It was not safe either day or night, and that part of the canyon was the most dangerous. He hoped that I might get through all right. Thanking him for his good wishes I journeyed on. Nearing Blue Rock, a stage house, between Belle Springs and Latonville, which is anything but a house, I found the building brightly illuminated. Had it not been so, I should not have known that I had nearly reached the house. I wondered why the house was so brilliantly illuminated and what was going on and who were within the house. Just before reaching the house I stopped and gave my horse a drink. There was loud and boisterous talk heard from the house. I drove on, going on the opposite side of the road from the house, and had got a distance beyond, when a voice called out, "I want to ride." I passed on, paying no attention, keeping out of sight of the house as much as possible. I had gone some little distance all right, when I noticed my horse acted strangely, looking on one side and then on the other. It was getting near daylight. The horse stopped and I urged her to go on, but she would not. A few rods in front of us stood a man right in the road. I sang out "Stranger, get out of my way, the horse will not go by you, step one side and then she will pass." The man came down the road towards me and said all was right. "Stranger, what has brought you here so early this morning?" I asked. "Friend, I have been here all night. I have a flock of sheep just below here, which I am obliged to look after at night, or else they will be a feast of mutton for the wolves," he replied. "Then you have wolves in this neighborhood?" I asked. "Plenty of them," he answered: "they are getting a little shy. We put cold lead into them, but try not to kill, but wound them, so that they will keep the rest away." "Are you not afraid of them?" "We do not go out among them without our guns," he said. "You have dogs to hunt them, do you not?" "Yes, but the dogs can do nothing unless we are there with them to shoot them. We set the dogs on them, and giving them some cold lead make them afraid of us." I left this man and made the remainder of my journey back to Belle Springs without any further molestation or incident, and arrived at the house about 4 a. m., putting up my horse and giving her the usual feed. I went to bed very fatigued and slept until 10 o'clock in the forenoon. That day I made all arrangements to commence my journey eastward.

Belle Springs is a half-way station between Eureka and Cloverdale. Stages from both ways meet and return from this place at the same hours. There is a good hotel with ample accommodations. There are seven sleeping rooms, kitchen, dining room and others on the ground floor. This is kept by a Mr. Aldrich, formerly from Abington, Windham County, Conn., who proved himself a gentleman in every sense of the word.

On the morning of June 26th, after a long rest I left Belle Springs, on resuming my journey for Latonville, distant twenty-six miles, travelling over the same road I had gone to get my horse shod. Being satisfied with the manner the blacksmith had put on the one shoe, I determined to have shoes put on the other feet. The shoes were made of steel, with corks nailed at the toe, clipped back to the quarter, only four nails in a shoe. Very simple and good. I travelled nearly five hundred miles before they were removed.

Latonville is a small place, contains a hotel, blacksmith shop, store, carriage shop and several houses, all built of good material. This village is located in Long Valley, on the north side about mid-way. The valley is about fourteen miles long and one mile wide, nearly surrounded by mountains—good and fertile land, a fine river running through the valley.

Left Latonville on the 27th and reached Little Lake, my next point, the distance travelled being twenty-three miles,—travelling through the valley. After leaving the valley, for about two miles the road was very rough, until I made connection with the stage road again at Sherwood valley. From there onward the road was good travelling. A short distance before reaching Little Lake, I came to a wheat field; here I thought it best to camp. I took some of the wheat, as if it were my own, and fed my cattle. There was no one around, I could not see a house and had not passed one since leaving Latonville. I tied my cattle fast to my wagon after their supper, and got my own supper, eating some cold roast Elk venison, after which I prepared my bed for the night. Retiring, I soon fell asleep, but was awakened about midnight by the snorting of my horse. I got up, could see nothing, but my horse's ears were perched straight over her head as if in fear. I looked down the road and became convinced that there was some of those fellows around who are known as "Infernals." I went to bed but could not sleep again, so I got up, fed my cattle and made ready to go on, and started as soon as day began to break, and light enough to travel. Coming to the station I inquired of a man I saw who was the owner of the wheat field, back about a mile, saying "I went into camp there, and made use of some of the wheat and would like to pay the owner for the same." He replied "That is all right, the owner would not take anything if you offered it to him." "I would not like to have the man follow and trouble me, and am willing to pay," I remarked. "That is all right, you need not trouble yourself about it in the least," said the station man.

Left Little Lake on the 28th and made the town of Ukiah the same day, having made twenty-three miles.

Little Lake is simply a station for the changing of horses for the mail coaches, and for drivers and chance passengers to eat and drink, the thirst being the greatest every time.

About noon I was travelling a really good road, equal to a fair eastern road. I stopped, fed my cattle, made a fire, cooked some dinner and ate it all alone, no one around, not a house for miles, and had not seen one since leaving Latonville. Rested till half-past one o'clock, and then resumed the journey, passing what is known as Sherwood valley—coming to a cross-road I read on a board, "To Bartlett's Spring and over the mountain to Sacramento." So far to-day have seen but one man. I do not have a chance to ask where does this road go, or how far is it to this place or that, yet I must soon come in sight of Ukiah. Presently I came in sight of a house, and then another, and I found myself in comparatively a large town. I urged Fanny along and soon we were in the city. I call it a city, not being positive it is, but it is one of the large towns in this part of California. On arriving in Ukiah, I made for a wheelright's shop to have my broken wheel repaired. If I knew the name of that rascally driver, I would give it to show his meanness, yet doubtless he is telling the story to some of his boon companions as a good joke served on that eastern chap. I found a carriage shop and asked the proprietor if he could repair my wheel: I told him that I had, soon after crossing Eel river been run into by the stage driver, crushing one of my wheels. "Where is your carriage, let me look at it?" "It is in front of your shop, sir, I have come all the way from Eel river with those splints on the wheel, as you see." "Those splints make a strong wheel." "Yes, but what can you do to make them stronger?" I asked. "I shall have to take the wheel to pieces and glue the spokes anew." "How much will you charge me?" "I will do it for $2.50." "Can you do it this afternoon?" "Yes, this afternoon." It was then four o'clock.

Left Ukiah at mid-night of the 29th and made as far as Cloverdale that day—about thirty miles.

Ukiah is the county town of Mendocino county. It has two hotels, several stores and a variety of workshops, blacksmith, carriage and livery, which give employment to many hands. Saloons and dance houses, where both immoral men and women are congregated, are to be found in abundance, where the wildest scenes of debasement can be seen at all times. Drinking, gambling and lewdness are so prevalent that I became more disgusted with the saloon than ever before or since. The women are imported from distant large cities for the pleasure and profit of those places, travelling in the same stages as the more respectable passengers. Of course, there are some good people here, but the reckless seem to predominate. The wheelright who repaired my carriage, appeared to be a very fair man, he had done me a good job at a fair price. I called at a livery and bought a sack of grain, for which the proprietor charged me three cents a pound for ground barley, a big price. What do you think of it? Did he have to pay so much for his whisky that he had to charge so exhorbitantly for his grain?

I left Ukiah about half-past seven in the evening, and travelled until I came to a good grass spot and camped for the night. I fastened my cow, Bessie, with the lariet, and the horse, Fanny, I secured by the halter; I dared not leave her loose to give her a chance to lead me another chase after her, as she did at Alder Point. While feeding my cattle, a team with two men in it came along. One of them said, "Friend, what are you doing there?" "Stranger, giving my cattle a little grass." "What, are you travelling?" "Yes sir, I am." "Where are you going?" "I am going to Cloverdale." "Here go with me, I will do better than that, I will give your cattle both hay and grain, so come back with me only a short distance." I thanked them kindly, and they insisted on my going back with them. I told them I did not think of stopping long, would travel some during the night so I could reach Cloverdale the next day—and would it be safe for me to travel, being all alone. They answered it would, and no one would molest me, and they again urged me to go with them and have something to eat and drink with them. I told them I felt grateful but they must excuse me. So they went, but shortly after returned with hay and grain for my cattle, cold roast beef and whisky for myself, and I was obliged to eat and drink with them. I thought it best not to decline their good will. Thanking them for their hospitality, I made ready to resume my journey. They told me I was welcome and wished me good night and success on my journey.

In journeying to Cloverdale the roads had been much better, although the travelling had been hard for the cattle as the day had been very warm. I did not make this place until late in the evening. Passing now through a new county I found the weather, atmosphere and general appearance of the country was much changed, this being one of the finest counties, Sonoma, in the State; the two others being the roughest. I felt and it looked as if I were in a new world. On entering the town about 9 p. m., there was a light a-head of us. It was the head-light of a locomotive. The horse was looking at it, her ears standing erect; coming to a halt, I asked, "Fanny, what is that?" She knew as well as I, no doubt. At that moment the whistle blew and Bessie, the cow, became frightened and almost upset my wagon, but the horse stood firm. I continued onward and drew near the engine, the cow became uneasy, and I fancied the horse said to the cow, "Bessie, be not afraid, it will not hurt you." This was what Fanny said, as I understood her, and from that time I have thought that the horse and cow conversed in this fashion during our long journey. As we were standing waiting for the engine to go, the people began to gather around us, until more than a hundred people had assembled. They asked where I was from, where going, and how long I had been on the road, and many other questions. I answered them civilly and to their satisfaction, not one of them offering any insult or molestation. I asked one man where I could camp. He replied, "Come with me and I will show you where." I followed the man, who led me to a barn and told me to put my cattle in there or turn them loose yonder as suits myself. It was so warm that I thought it best to turn them loose and let them eat the grass. Having done so and given them water and grain, being very weary I made up my bed and went to rest for the night. I was soon asleep, but about midnight my horse came around where I was sleeping, her breath awoke me. "What is the matter, Fanny?" I asked. She made no answer, but went away satisfied that I was near at hand. After a while she came again, and I told her to get away as it was not time to be off yet. Daylight came; rolling up my blankets I went into the town and looked it over and returned to my camp, found all right, fed and watered my cattle, went and laid down again for awhile. Shortly the man of the house came out and came up to me where I was laying, says he, "Well, stranger, how did you rest during the night?" I answered, "Very well, as I was very tired, and now I am feeling very well." "Our breakfast is ready, come in and take some with us." I took breakfast with him; after breakfast I asked my host if I could stop there over the day, as I thought my cattle needed a rest. "Yes, I have no objections. Where are you going, if it is a proper question to ask?" "I am going to San Francisco." "How many miles do you travel a day?" I answered "About twenty-five miles." "It will take you about four days to get to the city," he replied.

Left **Cloverdale July** 1st and travelled as far as Healdsburg, **distance eighteen** miles.

Cloverdale is a fine town, beautifully laid out, and is destined to be one of the most prominent in the State. It is situated in the northern part of Sonoma county, perhaps the richest agriculturally in the State. It is the terminus of a railroad known as the San Francisco and North Pacific Railroad, owned by one man named Donahue. The distance from Cloverdale to San Francisco is eighty-three and a half miles.

My passage now is through a rich and fertile county. What a change, everything looks beautiful and enchanting. Coming from Humboldt and Mendocino counties where everything was rough, to Sonoma county, what a change. Such a contrast can scarcely be conceived. The air is bracing and healthful and gives spirit and vigor to both man and beast. I have a long journey before me, and having lost too much time already I must push on.

This has been a large grain growing county, but at this day the agriculturalists are changing to the culture of the grape. It is said that the grape crops yield more money than does the grain, and the crops are surer and more to be depended upon. To me, there is nothing more beautiful than the vineyards in this section of the golden State. See the large bunches of this beautiful fruit, look at it, think of it and taste of its delicious flavor. Is there anything more beautiful? I would like to see it. About five in the afternoon I entered the town of Healdsburg, and passing through, I camp on the banks of the Russian river for the night, just below the bridge.

Left Healdsburg on the 2nd and made Santa Rosa the same day, distant eighteen miles.

Healdsburg.—Leaving this place, I cross the Russian river, over which there is an excellent bridge and also a good ford. Instead of crossing the bridge, I preferred to ford the river. The water was about two and a half feet in depth with a sandy bottom. The morning was bright and warm. My cattle seemed to enjoy it, and I know I did, after coming down from a God-forsaken world, as we had, and finding such a change. No wonder that we felt so well. We are travelling the Russian valley, one of the most fertile and beautiful in the State. What fields of wheat! what large vineyards of grapes! they excel all. The only draw-back, the farmers have too much land. There is not the population there should be or could be supported. No neighbors; houses are too remote from each other. Should a fire occur, there are no neighbors to help put it out. East, the man that owns five, six or eight hundred or a thousand acres, cuts it up into small farms with houses here and there; has ten houses to one in this section, and has plenty of neighbors to help in case of fire. But here they would burn down and all be destroyed.

Left Santa Rosa on the 3rd and made Petaluma my next stopping place, travelling twenty miles this day.

Santa Rosa, the capital of Sonoma county, is a fine thriving town. Here there appears evidence of more enterprise than in any other place I have passed through since leaving Eureka. In this as well as other places, there are many drinking houses and many men and boys that pass their time and spend their money at the gambling tables, which to me seems foolish. I suppose to them it does not look so bad, but to me it does, as I have not been out here long enough to get over my New England education.

San Raphael.—I left Petaluma on the morning of the 4th and journeyed that day to San Raphael, a distance of twenty miles. I left about two o'clock in the morning, being anxious to reach San Raphael early in the day, there to remain till the next morning. I reached the city about ten o'clock and on my arrival I found the place crowded with people who were celebrating the national holiday. In reaching the city I was obliged to enter about the centre, coming in contact with the multitude. Guns, pistols, fire crackers were being used in no small quantities. My horse is not afraid of anything except a simple swing, and that she does not admire. As I was going around the plaza, the boys though tthey would have some sport. They opened fire upon me with their fire crackers. The horse stood it well, but the cow broke two parts of her halter and fled. The horse, seeing "Bessie" a-far off made for her. I was holding on to the horse with all my might. A man on horseback saw the cow break away and galloped after her and caught her, bringing her back to me; she was wild. On her return she came up to my horse, standing until she again became quiet. The people gathered about us by hundreds, I in their midst. A police officer came up to me saying "Stranger, what can I do for you?" I answered "please request the people to keep quiet and fire no more crackers." My request was granted. A man in the crowd came to me and said, "Take your cattle to my barn and give them some hay, they will all be safe there." "Thank you, stranger, go ahead and I will follow you." The officer went with us, and we arrived at the barn without further hindrance. The gentleman who requested me to take my cattle to his barn was formerly a resident of the state of Maine.

San Francisco.—Started on the morning of the 5th for San Francisco, distant fourteen miles. Passed on my way through St. Quentin, by the state prison to the ferry, and at half-past two I was on board the steamer for San Francisco. On passing down the bay, its entrance was on our right from the ocean through the Golden Gate. On our left is Oakland, that beautiful city of the west. On entering the city, I was charmed by its beauty and the scenery around. We entered the city about four in the afternoon. On the right is a high bluff, and on this bluff are four residences of noted men of the city—Stanford, Huntington, Hopkins and Crocker. I leave the boat about four o'clock, pass up Market street, down Fourth street across the track of the Central Pacific Railroad, at their freight depot, and drive opposite on the west, where I made my camp while in the city two years previous to this visit.

CHAPTER II.

FROM SAN FRANCISCO, SAN JOSE TO SACRAMENTO.

My stay in the city of San Francisco was much longer than I intended when I arrived, but there was so much of interest in the place that day by day passed almost imperceptibly. I was also anxious to see as much of the State as my circumstances would admit, especially was I desirous of visiting the renowned San Jose. Having heard so much about the place, I thought that if I did not visit this place it would always be a source of regret. So I concluded to do so, and travel ninety miles directly out of my way in order to see the city of San Jose.

Decoto.—On the morning of July 16th I left San Francisco for San Jose, stopping at Decoto. I left the city about 4 a. m., travelled up Fourth and Market streets to the ferry, passing through Oakland and taking the direct road for San Jose, through the counties of Almeda and Santa Clara. The latter is a very fertile one and perhaps the richest in the State; San Jose is the county town. On my way to Decoto I passed through the town of Haywards, where I made a short halt. While conversing with several persons, I found that one of the number was formerly from Hartford, Conn. Many questions were asked by both parties. About 4 p. m., I arrived at Decoto, and camped for the night.

The morning of the 17th I was up early and began preparations for another day's journey. I did not breakfast, so anxious was I to reach my object point that day, so by five o'clock I was on the move and travelled until seven; at this time I came to a farm-house where there was a fountain, from which I watered my cattle and then proceeded to the barn, and while feeding, a gentleman came and said, "Good morning, stranger." "Good morning," I answered. "Travelling, are you?" "Yes, sir, a short distance, I have heard so much of your city of San Jose, that I am going there to visit. I thought it would pay me to visit the place while so near it." "But where are you from, travelling with that outfit?" he asked. "Yesterday I left San Francisco, and thought I would visit this city before leaving the State." "Before you leave the State, what do you mean by that?" he asked. "Well, sir, I will be short; I am on my way East, as far as Massachusetts. I know that I am not on the direct road, but shall be as soon as this present visit is made. I intend to return by way of Niles and on through Livermore valley to Stockton." "How long have you been in the State and in what part have you been staying, stranger?" "I have been in the State two years and more, and resided at Eureka, Humboldt county." "And you are from Eureka? I know the place well, stranger." "How far is it from here to San Jose?" "It is seventeen miles. Come in and take some breakfast with us." I went into the house with him. Turning to his wife, the man said, "This man says he is from Eureka and thinks he must see our city of San Jose; it is the finest in California. How did you get down to San Francisco, stranger? You must have noticed a vast difference in the roads through Humboldt, Mendocino and this county." "Yes, sir, I noticed there was a great difference." "You are now travelling the best in the State. Wife, I suppose the breakfast is now ready and waiting. Stranger, take a seat and eat. Did you give your cattle all the grain they could eat?" "I think they would eat more if it were before them." "I will give them some of mine. It is very fine, as good as can be raised in the State." So they were given an extra feed that time.

After breakfast I got ready to proceed on my way to the city. As I started my host said, "Stranger, on your return, come here and stay over night with us. It is not a half mile out of your way; yonder is your road to Livermore; you will have to return to that road. Come here and tell us how you like San Jose. You will be welcome to our hospitality. How long do you intend to stay?" "But one day," I answered. About eight o'clock I left them.

San Jose.—The morning was warm, the road good, but very dusty. I arrived at San Jose about four in the afternoon, and rambled about the principle streets until I thought of a camping place. On entering the city I had noticed a place that would make a good camping spot for the night and returned thereto, about a half mile from the city. On arriving at the spot I went to the house and rang the bell, which was answered by the lady of the house, of whom I requested permission to camp in a yard near by. I told her my story, and was on my way East, but being desirous of seeing this place had rambled thus far out of my way. She gave me permission to camp as I desired. I then asked her if she would sell me some hay, grain I carried with me. "Yes," she said, "there is hay in the barn, go help yourself." Giving my cattle water, hay and grain for their supper, and seeing they were cared for, I spread out my blankets on the ground and laid me down, being very tired from my day's journey. After a while the lady came to me and asked if "I would like to go in the house and have a dish of tea?" "I would, thank you." I went in, sat down to a good supper. The lady asked, "How did I like the city?" "Madam, you have a fine town here; its surroundings are good, I have seen nothing equal to it so far in my travels." You remarked that you were on your way for the Eastern States. "How far East do you go?" "As far as Massachusetts; that State is my home." "Do you intend to take that cow all that distance," inquired the lady. "I do, that is my intention. When I came out here two years ago I brought that horse with me, she is a native of Massachusetts, so also is that little dog. The cow is a native of California. I will pay you now for the hay that I gave to my cattle, as I shall leave early in the morning, perhaps before you are about. I like to travel in the early part of the day, and rest during the hot part of the day." She replied, "You are welcome to the hay, and if you will stay to breakfast you are welcome also." I thanked her and bade her good night.

Niles.—On the morning of the 18th I was up early, and soon ready to start on my return. I left San Jose about five o'clock, intending to reach Stockton for my next stopping place. As usual with horses, she travelled faster than usual, probably thinking that she was making for her old home. It was hard for the cow to keep up to her gait. I fell back and travelled beside the cow. My presence appeared to stimulate her, as she kept pretty well with the team. She travelled lead with a slack rope. At one o'clock we reached Niles, where we halted for our mid-day meal, taking up about an hour's time. My equipage was an object of interest, and many were the questions put to me, answering all that I was on my way overland from California to Massachusetts. I travelled till half-past six and pitched our camp for the night near a wheat field, on which I fed the cattle.

Livermore.—Next morning, the 19th, I arose early, fed the cattle with wheat and as soon as it was daylight resumed my journey and travelled until 7 a. m., when reaching a creek I thought I would stop and partake of breakfast and give us all a slight rest. I gave grain to the cattle and made a fire and boiled eggs and made coffee for myself, and at 9 a. m., went on. It was a very warm morning, the road good but rolling. At six in the afternoon, I reached Livermore, stopping for the night near a saloon. Gave the cattle their feed and made coffee and ate my supper. I did not like my surroundings and thought I would go into the town, about half a mile away, but concluded to stay in camp. I spread out my blanket and went to bed, running my chances of being allowed to sleep quietly; I had not been at rest long before I was surrounded with callers—overlooking my camp and asking innumerable questions. Some were hard to answer, still I answered all civilly. I stood this bantering for a long while, in fact, until I was completely tired out. "Gentlemen," I said, "I have come a long distance to-day and am very weary, will you allow me to rest here in peace?" "How far have you come to-day, stranger?" "I have come from Niles, left there early this morning." "You have done well to travel that distance, stranger." "It has been a very warm day; I hope you will allow me to get some rest." "We will ask you but one more question, where are you travelling to, stranger?" I answered "I am bound for Stockton; I want to get there to-morrow, to cross the river so that my cattle can once more get some grass." "We don't think you can travel that distance in a day, old man. We will leave you so that you can go to sleep; come boys, come away and let the old man go to sleep." They left, but I got no sleep.

I awoke on the morning of the 20th about one o'clock, there being so much noise around that it was impossible for me to sleep. I put the horse in the wagon and quietly departed from my camp and went on my journey. It was dark, in fact, too dark for safe travelling. I lit my lantern and used it for a head-light. At three o'clock we came to a house, known as the "Midway House," located in a dreary looking canyon. Here I stopped, gave my cattle water and a light feed of grain. About this time daylight began to break and we moved on, passing through "Livermore Pass" and on up the bluff until we came to a store. Here we took breakfast, rather late, but still our morning's meal. After eating, we again pushed on our journey, crossing the railroad and entering the valley of San Joaquin. We travelled this valley for several miles, until I thought it about time to look for a camping place for the night. I left the railroad a long distance on my right and had not passed a house since breakfast, nor could I see one in sight. Still travelling on, after going some distance I sighted a house which we made for; I urging on my horse, Fanny, as she travelled as if she were very weary. We reached this house about six o'clock and stopped. I went to the door and rang the bell; a lady came in answer. I asked her if the gentleman of the house was in. "No," she answered, "he is not, I am expecting him soon: he has gone to look after some horses at pasture over the river. It is time for him to be back." "I am travelling, madam, and have come from Livermore to-day, and being tired and weary would like to stay over night. All I desire is, hay or grass for my cattle; I have not seen any grass since entering this valley." "No, sir, you will find no grass except near the river. Our last rainfall was very light and did the crops but little good. You may lead your horse into the yard, and can find hay in the barn." I took the horse into the yard, unharnessed her and gave her a chance to roll; she enjoyed her freedom very much. I went to the barn for hay, feeding it to the cattle, who greedily ate it up and then I went for more. I asked the lady for the privilege of making some coffee. She offered to make it for me, but I told her I would do it as I carry a lunch box for myself and dog—as well as grain for the horse and cow—I gave the latter hay for the third time after the supper. Spreading my blanket on the ground, I laid myself down to rest. Soon after, the husband came home and coming into the yard saw a strange company around and inquired of his wife, "What have you got here?" "This man came along, said he was travelling and had come from Livermore that morning; he wanted to stop over night and I told him he might." "Who is he, where is he from, and where is he going?" asked the man. "I asked him no questions, as I was expecting you before this," she replied. I heard the conversation and told him his wife had related the facts. "Now you may ask any questions you please of me." I had risen from my couch and was standing before him. It was not yet dark. "Stranger, who are you, where are you from, and where are you going to?" he at once asked. Answering said, "I left Eureka the first of June, came to San Francisco, from there to San Jose, and from there to this place. I am on my way home to Massachusetts where I belong." "You have answered my questions; can I believe you? When did you leave Massachusetts?" "I left in the spring of 1880, arrived in California in the month of May, the same year. Have been in this State a little more than two years." "And now you are returning home to Massachusetts?" "Yes, sir, I am." "Stranger, I am satisfied, but, O God, what a journey you have before you. I am from Ohio; came out here in 1876 and am trying to get rich by raising horses. I had a good farm in Ohio; it was small but good. I sold it, came here and here is my money. I own this house and all the lands you can see around. Two years ago I went back to Ohio, made a wife of this woman and came back and here we are, both of us home-sick and anxious to return to Ohio. Here, however, is our capital; we would sell if we could, but can not. So far, we have been unable to get a crop of wheat, owing to the drouth. We plough and sow, but no grain to harvest. When we see that the wheat is not likely to mature, which is the rule rather than the exception, we cut it for grass, and it makes excellent hay. But it is not all hay that is wanted; we need grain. Stranger, you say you are on your way east, with that outfit—horse, carriage, cow and dog. Now, I do not say that it can not be done, but I think the chances are against you—nine to one. The horse you can get through, but the cow impossible, unless you get her shod with iron shoes; then you stand a fair show. The horse you can get shod any where on the road, but the cow few can shoe. In shoeing her she will have to be confined in a brake that will hold her secure. Now, friend stranger, as soon as you come to a blacksmith that knows how to make an ox-shoe, you should get her shod if you have to build a brake on purpose, and don't you forget it. Stranger, I see you are the man for the journey. Well, wife, I want some supper. Have you been to supper, stranger?" "Yes, sir, I have; I ate my supper more than an hour ago." "Sit up and eat another with us; how is it about your cattle, have they had their supper?" "Yes, sir; I fed them with your hay, they ate it up clean and I gave them more, and they ate that up and again I gave them more." "We will go out and see if they have eaten that up, and if so, will give them more. What time do you intend to leave in the morning?" I wish to start early so as to reach Stockton." "You can't make Stockton in one day's travel; it will take you nearly two days. You will have to cross the river at the ferry, on the boat. You can not cross the river over the bridge owing to the sloughs; should you get in them, it will not be easy getting you out. Go by the ferry, it is farther, but more sure." At this, I told him that I would like to retire as last night I got no rest, having camped near to a saloon and was so disturbed that I could not sleep, so harnessed up about one in the morning and left them. So I must have some sleep to-night or I can't make Stockton to-morrow. "Wife, give me a light and I will show the traveller to a room." "Friend stranger, I sleep with my cattle every night, I will take no bed in the house. I have been advised to stay with them night and day." "You are right; you will have to look sharp at times after them."

I was up bright and early on the morning of the 21st, making ready to resume my journey,—feeding, greasing my wagon and so on. About five o'clock my kind host was up and came out to my camp and bade me good morning, which I acknowledged. "I see you mean business," said he; "you have fed your companions it seems." "Yes, sir, I intend to look out for them." "You are right; our breakfast is ready, my wife intends you should partake of it with us before you leave." After breakfast, (that was about half-past six) I was ready to move on, and turning to my host said: "Friend, how much shall I pay you for the hay I have used and for my accommodations?" "Nothing, sir, not a dime will I take. I hope you will succeed in your undertaking. You have a long road before you. Good morning, success to you." I thanked them and moved on. At one o'clock we arrived at the river and crossed over, and followed the river to Stockton. What a contrast, every thing so green and lively and the grass luxuriant. As far down the valley as the eye can reach, are many cattle feeding. I stopped, turned the cattle loose to graze and had our mid-day meal. Resumed our journey at three o'clock and at six came to a large farm-house, and proposed to stay there for the night. All around the house it was neat and trim; in front a large yard with many noble trees, most of which were fruit trees, of many kinds. I went up to the gate and seeing several persons I hallooed and made signs to them to come towards me at the gate. Two lads came; I asked permission to camp near the house. They went back and soon the lady of the house returned with the boys. After passing compliments of the day I told her of my journey, and asked if I could camp on their grounds for the night. "You say you are travelling East; how far East?" "To Massachusetts, that is my home when there." "Massachusetts is a long distance from here," said the lady. "Yes, ma'am, I am aware of it." "Yes, you can camp here." "You have any quantity of grass, would you allow me to turn my cattle loose so that they might eat grass for their supper?" "Yes, indeed, it will do them good. Stranger, I have some interest in this interview. When you said your home was in Massachusetts, I felt anxious to learn your where-a-bouts." "My home is in the town of Webster and county of Worcester." "Will you allow me to ask your name?" said the lady. "Yes, certainly; my name is W. B. Johnson." "The reason I am so anxious to learn about Massachusetts is this, my eldest son, John, is going to school at Cambridge, Harvard College, this fall. How far is Cambridge from your town?" "Cambridge is about fifty miles from Webster." The lady then said: "Mr. Johnson, our tea is ready, come in and sit with us." "Madam, I carry tea, coffee, sugar, milk and other things." "That is all right, but you will not need them, you must make yourself at home while here," she answered. After we had finished supper, I went down to my camp, turning the horse and cow loose in the grass. I spread my blankets and laid myself down. It was not long before the whole house was around me, asking a great many questions in regard to Massachusetts, and especially about Cambridge. I told them it was a fine city, about three miles from Boston and one of the handsomest in America. About nine o'clock I secured the horse and cow for the night and said to the lady: "I will show you my manner of camping at night; my horse I secure to the wheel of my wagon, and the cow opposite. I lay between them; if any one comes around I soon should know it,— my little dog is good for sleeping with one eye open." "But you are not going to sleep here with your cattle?"

said the lady. "Oh, yes; I dare not leave them. I have been advised to look sharp after them." "Mr. Johnson, there is no danger here; no one will take them." "Madam, I have a fine horse, she is a Morgan. I was offered three hundred dollars for her, but refused it." "You will stop over to-morrow?" asked the lady. "I think I will; my cattle need rest and this fine grass is tempting for them." "Mr. Johnson, you are a stranger to us; we never saw you or heard of you before. I have no reason to think you are a fraud; my sympathies are with you." "Why?" "Because you say your home is in Massachusetts and you are on your way there, also my son, John, is going to that State. He will make his home there for a time; perhaps, you will make his acquaintance there; I wish you might. Who knows what will come out of this interview. Mr. Johnson, I wish you would take a bed in the house, your cattle will be safe; I will be responsible for them. We own all the land as far as you can see; there was a time when we owned thirty thousand acres." "Lady, please excuse me; I prefer to sleep outside. California has no rainy nights this time of the year." "John, you and Charlie go into the house and bring the mattress off my bed. I will sleep in the front room to-night," said the lady. The boys fetched the mattress. "Where will you have it?" she asked. "In the rear of the wagon, madam; I see that you are determined to have me sleep on a bed." "Mr. Johnson, these grounds are quite moist, or the grass would not be so green. That river yonder makes things green; if it were not for that, everything would be dried up as you found on coming here. Well, boys, we will leave Mr. Johnson for the night; good night." "Good night, and thank you, lady."

On the morning of the 22nd I was awakened by the bellowing of a bull in the meadows. My cow, Bessie, heard him and answered. I do not know what she said to him, but I know she was very uneasy. I bade her be quiet and go to rest; I continued in bed some time longer when I heard the rumbling of a carriage. Soon it was opposite to my camp and there stopped. "Mr., what are you doing there?" asked one. "Doing, can't you see what I am doing. It is not time to get up yet, they are not stirring in the house," I answered. "Who gave you permission to camp there?" another asked. "Go on, don't ask me such a question, go on." "Yes, go on, don't stop here so early in the morning," said a voice from the window. They went on, but I had got so thoroughly awakened, that soon after I arose and turned loose the horse and cow, so that they could make a hearty repast of the fine grass. Soon after, the inmates of the house were up and all hands at work. The lady and her son, John, came down to my camp and bade me good morning. "Mr. Johnson, how are you this morning; did you have a good night's rest?" she asked. "I did; that mattress was a big improvement to the ground," I replied. "Mr. Johnson, our breakfast is about ready, come and take a dish of coffee, a bit of steak, and perhaps a boiled egg. We will go and see what we have." "Thank you, I will; I am not afraid to leave my cattle for a good breakfast." "Had you taken a bed inside last night, you would have fared better than in the breakfast," said the lady. "I doubt that; I had a good bed, the mattress was an improvement, I found." "But still it was on the ground and no springs under it," replied the lady. "That no doubt would make some difference. I will stay over another night and reverse it." "Yes, that will decide it. You can stay as long as you like. There is plenty of grass; should you prefer hay or grain, there is plenty in the barn, and what is more, you can put your cattle in as well and turn the key on them, then you can sleep with both eyes shut; you could have done so last night." "It was as well as it was." After breakfast I returned to camp and cleaned my harness and other traps. Soon I had company who staid with me until the dinner-bell rang. "Mr. Johnson, the bell tells me the dinner is ready, let us go see what Kate has for dinner," remarked my hostess. We went up and seven of us sat down to a good dinner of roast beef, pudding and pies.

After dinner and the household attended to, my hostess said, "John, harness up the horses and we will take Mr. Johnson around the farm." It did not take long to get the horses out and hitched in the carriage, and mother, son and daughter and myself were seated in the carriage, when on we went upon a tour round the farm. Riding about a mile, the team was halted and we got out. "Mr. Johnson, yonder is the river," pointing in the direction, "where you crossed on the boat. From that point to yonder barn, and as far as the eye can reach, extend our lands. Now we will get in the carriage and go on to the ranche." After riding about two miles the ranche was reached. The lady pointing, said, "From that ranche to yonder fence is the dividing line, running down to the river, where you cross the ferry are the boundaries of our farm. The land is divided into four parts or ranches. I live about the center; there are no better lands in the state than these of ours. Those meadows running parallel with the river, you can see how rich and green they look. They feed thousands of cattle every year." John turned the horses' heads homeward where we arrived having enjoyed a very pleasant ride; as we drove into the yard, my horse and cow saluted me. "Why, Mr. Johnson, your cattle know you better than I do," said the lady. "They know me as well as I know them, I am sure," I remarked. When we got back it was almost supper time. In about half an hour my hostess called me to partake of tea again with her family. "Mr. Johnson, will you stop another day with us?" asked the lady. "Madam, I would like to, but I can't, I have a long journey before me."

"Yes, indeed, you have. Do you think you can reach that distance." "Yes, I can, if I do not find many places like this. If I do it will take me a long time to reach my home." "Mr. Johnson, mother seems to manifest a deep interest in your welfare," said John. "Yes, indeed, I do, Mr. Johnson. It is because my son is to go to school in your State. How far did you say you were from Cambridge?" the lady remarked. "About fifty miles from Webster." "Mr. Johnson, I hope you will hunt him up and make his acquaintance; call on him as he may become home-sick and wish to return home, I hope not, however; what time will you leave us in the morning?" "I intend to begin my journey about six o'clock. I would like to stop a short time at Stockton. That is a fine place, I suppose?" "We call Stockton a smart city, with a population of 15,000; our best flour in the State is made there," replied the lady.

On the morning of the 23rd I was up early, as usual, and about my preparations for the day's tramp, when a voice called from one of the windows of the house, "Mr. Johnson, are you about ready to leave, won't you stop and have breakfast with us?" I took the mattress in my arms and went to the house with it; on entering I met the lady, who bade me good morning. "You are about to leave us, I did not wish you to go so soon. Kate is a little late with the breakfast, but the coffee is ready, and it will but take a moment to broil a steak. Take a seat at the table; I will soon be with you." Having partaken of a good meal I said to the lady, "We met as strangers, but as such we do not part; allow me to thank you for your kindness and generous hospitality, it has been a strange meeting." "It has," she answered. "I do not know what to think about it. John is at the bottom of it," I replied. "I bid you a reluctant good-by." "Good-by," I hope you will succeed in making your long journey. Can it be possible you have to travel four thousand miles to reach your home commented?" the lady.

Stockton.—Left Mansion Ranche at seven o'clock and I reached Stockton about 10 o'clock. On my arrival, I gave my cattle water and grain and while they were eating I rambled about the city. It is not a large city, but is solid and compact, with a population of 15,000, and is pleasantly laid out. About five o'clock in the afternoon, I left Stockton on my way to Sacramento. Travelling about a mile I came to a fine patch of grass where I stopped for the night, turning the animals loose and giving them a chance to select their own feeding. I gathered some fuel, made a fire, cocked some coffee, made my supper and made ready for the night. The cow had eaten her fill and was quietly at rest. It was not so with the horse, she continued to eat the grass. I secured the cow and went for the horse but she would not be caught, I was unable to get near her. Went back to my camp, the horse continuing to eat, I took no notice of her. Soon she came around and I got up to secure her, but no, she would not let me. I got some grain and gave it to the cow, and quickly she came for her share. I said to her: "Fanny, you know about as much as your master."

I arose quite early on the morning of the 24th. It was not yet day-light, I turned the cattle loose for grass and returned to my couch on the ground. In about an hour after I called them in and fed them with grain. While they were eating, I packed up my bedding, greased the wagon and made all ready for continuing the journey. It was about five o'clock when we left camp. On my left went the road, and still further to the left flowed the Sacramento river. We travelled until nine o'clock when we halted for water and a light feed. For myself, I had some cold milk and crackers. At noon we reached a store, stopped and watered the horse and cow, and I inquired the distance to Galt. "It is about fourteen miles; are you going to Galt?" asked the stranger. I answered in the affirmative. "Where are you from?" "Stockton." "You have come past the road to Galt; you should have taken the right-hand road about five miles back," said the man. "Must I return back to that road?" I asked. "You must." "That is too bad; why do you not put out a shingle so that a stranger can't miss but take the right road. This makes me ten miles extra travel, on such a hot day as this, too." I turned back to the road indicated, and then travelled until I came to a fine-looking ranche. I stopped, went up to the house and as I was about to knock, a man came out. I passed the compliments of the day, told him my story and asked permission to camp on his premises, telling him that I had grain and hay for my cattle and some grub for myself. He asked, "Where was I from and where are you going to?" I answered, "From Eureka to Sacramento." "Yes, you can stop if you like. Turn into the corral; you can sleep on that straw, it will make you a first-rate bed," said the man. "Now, for some hay, if you please, sir?" He went to the barn and commenced throwing down some hay. "Is this for me?" I asked. "Yes, how much do you want?" he asked. "You have thrown down twice as much as the cattle will eat," I replied. "Give it to them; let them have as much as they like; it won't hurt them," he answered. I then asked permission to make a dish of tea. The man took me to the house and remarked to his wife, "This man is a traveller; has come from Humboldt county and wants to make some tea, if you have no objection. I told him to come in; did I say right?" "Yes, of course. We have travelled too much ourselves to object to such a thing. You have come from Eureka; how far are you going?" she asked. "To Sacramento," I replied. "You need not make any tea; ours is about ready and we have plenty of it, you will sup with us," said the wife "When did you leave Eureka, stranger?" "The first of June last. "You have been a long time on your way, stranger." "Yes, I have; I stopped in San Francisco nearly two weeks; I came down the overland road to the city. I had travelled only one hundred and eight miles, when I was obliged to stop fifteen days on account of my horse having wrenched one of her feet, which caused me an extra tramp of fifty-two miles to get her shod." "Well, stranger, you are a plucky old fellow. There is scarcely a young man who would have undertaken such a journey, you must come to the table and have a dish of tea." Having done justice to the supper, I retired to my camp, looked to my sleeping quarters and arranged my bed and laid me down. I had scarcely got settled when a voice said: "Hello, traveller, have you retired for the night? My wife bade me to tell you to have a bed in the house." "Please say to your wife that I thank her very much, and that I have a better bed here than she has inside. However, friend, I will pay you for the hay I have used, as I shall start on my journey early in the morning, and perhaps before you are around." "I charge you nothing for your supper nor for that of your cattle, and the same if you will stop and have breakfast with us in the morning; which I think you will do if you dream of it over night.

On the morning of the 25th I was not as anxious to be travelling as usual. My good fare and that of the cattle no doubt made me feel indolent so that I slept longer than I intended. I was watering my cattle and giving them some hay when the man of the house came along saying, "Good morning, stranger; did you sleep well during the night? I did not expect to find you here; I thought you would have been half way to Galt by this time." "The last words you said to me last night, were the first that came to me this morning, and having over-slept through weariness, here I am." 'Come in, our breakfast is ready." We went in and turning to his wife he said: "I found him in bed, he seemed to care but little whether school kept or not." In answer to her greetings, "I told her that I had rested well, and over-slept, or should have been eating breakfast in Galt instead of there. I thanked them for their hospitality, and asked them to show the same hospitality to the next traveller like me." "I was welcome," they said, "but thought they would have to wait a long time for such another traveller." Good-byes were uttered and I drove off on my journey.

Travelling along, presently we came to a field of melons; I stopped, went into the field and appropriated four of the best I could find, and then continued on our journey. The morning was fine and very warm, about eleven o'clock we arrived at Galt. Here we crossed the railroad; after crossing, I stopped for dinner. We rested two hours and then resumed our journey, at this time I passed through several wheat fields. They are about two miles long; several machines were at work cutting the wheat. I stopped to watch the working of one of the machines; it was drawn by six horses. As they came round near where I was I inquired, "How many bushels to the acre do you thrash?" "About eight bushels," was the answer. Only eight bushels. I passed on; I was very hot, not a shade to be had, the full burst of the sun on our heads. Travelling further, I noticed to my left a ranche, for which I made. I went to the house, in front of which was a fine, large, live oak. Two ladies were sitting under its shade. I bade them good day, which they politely returned. "Ladies, I have been travelling since early this morning; it has been a hot day, would you allow me to stop awhile under this tree, it makes a fine shade, I have seen nothing like it to-day." They answered, "I might with pleasure." I got permission to use water from the well with which I refreshed both man and beast and then spread out my blanket and laid down. The ladies soon retired and I continued to lay under the tree in the shade. After a while one of the ladies came up to me and said, "Stranger, will you excuse me for offering you some refreshment; you must be weary travelling on so warm a day. Here is a dish of tea and some refreshments; please accept them." "Thank you, madam, It has been a very warm day." Before eating I asked the lady, "If she could accommodate me with some hay for my horse and cow." She answered "Yes, I think so. My husband will be home soon; you can have some, whether he comes or not." "Shall I wait until he comes or not?" I asked. "No, it is not necessary; you can help yourself, it is in the barn," she replied. I went for some and gave it them, and they ate it as if they were starved. When it was done, the lady said, "Your cattle were hungry; you may get them more, give them all they can eat; the hay is good and cheap." "I think it is wheat hay," I said. She answered in the affirmative. "Madam, this is a good place to camp, if you have no objection I will remain over night; I always travel early in the morning and will try and reach Sacramento to-morrow," I remarked. "Mister, you are a stranger to us; we like your appearance and think you are all right. But should my husband come home as he does some times, you might be roughly handled; if you will run your chances, we will ours. I am satisfied that you are what you appear to be; we don't go to bed without our doors being all bolted," said the lady. I asked the lady for more hay which she allowed and I gave it all to the cattle. I milked the cow and gave it to the lady, who was pleased to accept it, as she said at that time they had no cow; the cow yielded about four quarts. "How much a quart do you ask for the milk?" she asked. I answered, "Nothing, to you. But how much for the hay I have used for my cattle?" She answered, "Nothing, to you." About eight o'clock the owner of the ranche came home and put up his horse and went directly into the house. Shortly after he came out and made directly for my camp, and said: "Good evening. Are you the man who stopped about three miles from here and inquired how much wheat to the acre?" "Yes, sir; I am." "I thought you were. Where are you travelling to?" "I am going to Sacramento; it has been so warm through the day that when I got here I thought I could go no further, and seeing this fine shade-tree I asked permission to stop and am still here and have fed my cattle on your hay and given the milk from my cow to your lady. Have I done right or wrong?" "You look like a man that would do right every time, you have done as I should have done; any-how, I will let you pass. Won't you go in the house and take a bed, stranger?" "I prefer to sleep under this tree, I think no harm will come to me, good night." "Good night, sir."

Live Oak Ranche.—The morning of the 26th was bright, so I arose early and attended to my travelling companions. As I was watering them the proprietor of the house halloed, "Stranger, do you think your cow would give us some milk for coffee this morning. There is plenty of hay and grain in the barn, give them all they need." "Friend, my cattle have been well cared for since camping here." "What I was driving at was to give my wife time to get the breakfast ready and have you partake of it. It is not the milk but the joke I am after," said my host. "I see it; give me a pail and I will get you the milk." After milking the cow and giving it to the lady of the house, I was invited in to breakfast, which I accepted. After the meal I got ready for my day's journey; on doing so I bade them good-bye and thanked them for their hospitality. I left them amid wishes for my success. It was about six o'clock when we started on our way for Live Oak Ranche, and travelled until nine, when we halted from over-heat and weariness. Not a shade tree to protect us from the rays of the sun. "Well,

Fanny, we must go on, it will not do to stop here in this blazing sun." We passed on until we came in sight of a line of railroad; when near the crossing we came to a swamp of timber. Here we succeeded in getting from under the burning sun and remained here the remainder of the day. The cattle had but a sparse feeding ground for grass. Grain and food for myself I had always with me.

Elk Grove Station.—The morning of the 27th we started on our day's work as soon as it was light enough to see our way, crossing the railroad at Elk Grove station. The sun was getting high, not a breath of air, very hot and sultry; a good road, however, but dusty. "Well," addressing my horse, "where is our shade tree for the day, we shall need one soon, it is too hot to travel." After tramping on a while longer we sighted a ranche, with a house built in a modern style and in the rear was a fine shade tree. There did not appear to be any thing to prevent my use of it for rest; so I went to the house and rang the bell, which was answered by a lady. I said to her, "Madam, I am travelling with a horse and carriage, leading a cow. It is very warm; I would like to stop for a while in the shade, that myself and cattle might get from under the rays of the scorching sun. I see you have a fine shade in the rear of the house, would you allow me to use it for a time?" "Where are you from?" she asked. "I am from Eureka city." "What, with that cow from that distance?" she questioned. "Yes, ma'am; just as I am, with that horse, carriage and cow." "Yes, sir; you can give your cattle the benefit of the shade, it will be a luxury to them this hot day," answered the lady. I led my cattle around to the rear and hitched them there, giving them water. I spread my blankets on the ground and laid myself down on them; it was delightful. While lying down I fell asleep; I do not know how long I had slept, but the lady of the house awoke me and said:

"Stranger, would you like some dinner; it is now ready, come and sit down and have a dish of tea, you are cordially welcome." I accepted her offer and went in and sat down to an excellent dinner. After we were through with dinner I asked the lady to sell me some hay for the cattle. She told me they had plenty in the barn and go and help myself to all I wished. I did so and fed to them a good quantity of wheat hay, which my animals ate with a keen relish. "Madam," I said, "It seems as though I was providentially cared for; coming here this hot day and finding such a pleasant shade and sharing your hospitality. I appreciate your kindness and I know that my cattle do; I thank you, and as the sun is getting low I will resume my journey, as now it will be much more comfortable travelling and I can reach the city this evening." The lady said she would like to know my name. "My name is W. B. Johnson, of Webster, Mass." "You are an Eastern man, from Massachusetts, it seems. I thought you used New England language; we were formerly of Springfield in that State. How long have you been in this State?" "Two years and over." "You are not returning back to Massachusetts?" "I am." "What, with that horse and carriage, leading that cow?" "Yes, just as I am." "My husband is in the city attending court as a juryman. He would be glad to see you or any one from Massachusetts. How long do you intend to stop in the city?" asked the lady. "Two or three days only." "Where will you stop?" "I shall camp out in some convenient place, but, Madam, I must be going, it is four o'clock. Good-bye." "Good-bye; I hope you will arrive safely in old Massachusetts."

Sacramento.—About seven o'clock I reached the city. On my way I noticed a fine patch of grass, and at the time thought that I had better stop there and camp for the night. However, I travelled on to the city and then thought it best to turn back and camp on this green spot. I did, and turned my cattle loose to graze for themselves. There was a house a short distance away and I went there for water. As I came near to it I noticed a gentleman and two ladies standing in front of the house; I stepped up to them and addressing the gentleman bade him "Good morning," which he acknowledged. "Sir, I am travelling, and in passing here to the city I noticed your fine grass and have returned to camp and rest for a while. Can I have your permission so to do, also water from your cistern?" He answered, that I might have all I wanted, he had no objection. I took water and gave it to the horse and cow, they were very dry and needed an extra watering. After seeing their wants supplied I spread out my blankets and tried to sleep. The cow I had fastened with her lariat, the horse I allowed to ramble about, as I knew she would not leave the cow.

On the morning of the 28th, I passed into the city of Sacramento, and upon reaching a fountain I stopped to water my cattle; while doing so, a man came out of one of the stores near by and said: "Stranger, is that cow for sale?" "No, sir; she is not," I replied. "I would like to own that cow; I like the looks of her. Stranger, I will give you a good-price for her." "She is not for sale," I answered. "How far have you come with her, stranger?" "I started from Eureka, came down the overland route to San Francisco, and from there to here." "Where are you going with her, stranger?" "I am on my way East." "How far East, stranger?" "Well, sir; my intentions are to cross the continent to Massachusetts." "Massachusetts, the devil you are, stranger?" "Yes, devil or no devil, I am." "Are you going to take that cow with you? she won't travel half that distance. I will give you a big price for her, stranger." "What do you mean by a big price?" "I mean that I will give you one hundred dollars for the cow, stranger." "Sir, I do not want to sell her this morning. I would like to stop somewhere in this vicinity where I can turn my cattle out among some good green grass." I had noticed a little way back some fine green fields. I had seen no such grass before reaching Stockton, since leaving San Francisco. "What is the cause of this change?" "Stranger, I will tell you the cause. Yonder is the American river, pointing east; yonder is the Sacramento river, pointing west; the American river flows into the Sacramento at the north. The city is about three-quarters encompassed by these two rivers. The American river is not so large as the Sacramento, but has more fall. It empties into the Sacramento. The Sacramento has been badly used. Before hydraulic mining was known, it was a very fine and navigable river. Large steamers could then come up to the city and some distance above. Now it is hard work for steamers to sail up, owing to the mud deposited on the bed of the river from the mining on its banks. There is but thirty feet fall to the ocean. Since the introduction of hydraulic mining, the river bed has gradually filled up, until now there is only a depth of about fourteen feet. This became a source of alarm to the city. Not only to the city, but to the land-owners in the valley as well. The river banks do not confine its water, but at times are overflowed and the low lands are submerged and continue so for some time, which the farmers do not like. I have said that the city is nearly surrounded by these rivers. The earth is so saturated with these waters, it gives us green grass the year round. Now, what we fear is this; some day the American river will cut through and spoil our city and us too." "I would rather have it come in the day than in the night," I remarked. "Oh, well, you are a Yankee, I will bet the beer," answered the stranger. "You are right, I am a Yankee," I replied. "Now, stranger, just see what those d—d hydraulic miners have done with our city. I wish they were obliged to dredge the river; we have already expended tens of thousands of dollars with but little good. There is but thirty feet fall from here to San Francisco, about one hundred miles, only think of it. We have a fine city, but those d—d miners are fast spoiling it. Think of it: they have compelled us to commence filling some portions of our low lands, and now we have to fill some sections from five to fifteen feet. Look yonder, and see how that house sets up from the ground; a new house just built. That yard has to be filled up eleven feet. Go up to our State House and see what has been done there. It is one of the finest buildings on the continent; already its first story has been buried, which lays now underground. The time is not far distant when we shall have to fill up our streets; when that is done our first stories will be under ground, all owing to those hydraulic miners. Just think of it, you Yankee." Turning to my good-natured informant, I said to him, "I would like to stop here two or three days, can you tell me where I could get grass for my cattle?" "I can give your cattle grass. That lot yonder, or the other adjoining, take your choice, stranger." I went to look at both lots; there was no difference in them, except one had a large shade tree on it. I concluded to take the lot with the tree, as it would make a fine shade for myself and companions. I asked the man how much he would charge me per day for the use of the west lot, as I preferred that on account of the shade it affords? He answered, "Stranger, turn in your cattle into either lot, I will not charge you anything, not a dime, either one or more days. Stranger, come in and get all the beer you wish, it will cost you nothing." I thanked him, but I refused the beer; turned my cattle loose into the field and camped under the tree. Remember, that it was the last day of July, the mercury up to 127° in the shade, and you can imagine what a luxury a good shade tree would be in that part of the State. It was now about eight o'clock in the morning and as yet I had had no breakfast. About six rods from my camp was a house made with hands, to which I went with my coffee-pot in hand, to see if I could get some coffee made, telling her that I was camping for a few days in the lot opposite her house. She answered, "Yes, sir; I will make it for you. I saw you drive into the lot with a horse, carriage and cow, and I think you are the man." The coffee was soon ready and I returned with it to my quarters. As I sat eating my breakfast, the lady accompanied by two others, came out to my camp, and said: "Stranger, bring your basket in the house and eat at our table. How long do you intend to remain here?" "But two or three days; I was permitted to come in here one or ten days free of charge." "Was it the man that lives in yonder block?" she asked. I answered in the affirmative. The next question was, "Where are you from, and are you going to remain in the city?" I answered, "I am from Eureka, and am passing through this State on my way East, to Massachusetts." "Do you mean me to understand that you are travelling to Massachusetts?" said the lady in astonishment. "I do." "Why, Mister; that is a great way from here." I told her I was aware of it. As she left me she said, "As long as you are here, come in to make your tea or coffee or anything else you need, you will be welcome." After breakfast I went into the town, looking for a blacksmith's shop, as my horse needed shoeing. Finding one, I returned for the horse and had her shod on all her feet. It was a good job; the cow I could not get shod. The journey through Humboldt and Mendocino counties was very trying to my carriage, the wheels were light and the tires were of iron and also light; I thought it was best to get the tires reset and make the wheels more dishing, in order to make them stronger. I took the carriage to the blacksmith and had the tires reset at a cost of four dollars.

The blacksmith remarked that the tires were not fit to be put on, they were so much worn. I told him to put them on and afterwards took the carriage back to the camp.

On the morning of the 29th, as I was going down town I called on the blacksmith, when he said, "Stranger, you made a mistake in putting on those old tires on your carriage wheels, you ought not to have done so, you should have put on good steel tires. They would have made a good strong wheel and do you good service." "Blacksmith, they are on and paid for. How much will you charge to put on steel tires, make your figures small. I have just paid you four dollars, that must be partially thrown in?" "I will put on good steel tires for ten dollars." "Those are your best figures? I will give you eight dollars for new steel tires, which with the setting of the old ones will make twelve dollars. If you will do it, I will bring the wagon down after dinner, that is if you will put them on this afternoon, will you do it?" "I will put them on for nine dollars, that is as low as I can afford," answered the blacksmith. "No, I will only give you eight dollars." I stopped for a moment, not a word was said, I then started from the shop and was on the sidewalk when he said: "Bring your wagon down, I will give you the dollar." I went back to the camp and was about to take the wagon to the blacksmith, when my lady neighbor came out and invited me in to her house for dinner. I excused myself on the plea of taking the wagon to the blacksmith's, but she pressed me so that I took dinner with her. While eating, many questions were asked around the table. They learned that my home was in Massachusetts, and I learned that their former home was also in that State. After dinner I took the carriage to the blacksmith's and about five in the afternoon he had re-tired my vehicle and I returned to camp all ready to leave early on Monday morning.

On the morning of the 30th, Sunday, a milkman came along and stopped in front of my camp and said: "Stranger, you have a fine looking cow there. Where is that cow from?" "From Eureka," I answered. "Where are you going with her?" he inquired. "I am going East, to Massachusetts." "You don't say you are; are you going to old Massachusetts?" he asked, incredulously. "I do; do you belong there, Mr. Milkman?" "I do, when I am at home, and I have a mother there. I come from there, or just over the line, in New Hampshire." "What part of Massachusetts are you from?" asked the milkman. "From Worcester county, the town of Webster." "I know all about the State. I have been to Worcester many times. Are you honest about going to Massachusetts?" he asked. "Yes, sir; I am." "And going to take that cow along with you? Friend, you can't do that much; such a thing is impossible. Why, sir; neither she nor any other cow could live to travel that distance." "Milkman, I propose to try it; I may fail in the attempt." "You have a fine looking horse, she looks as though she could stand the test," said the milkman. "I brought that horse from Massachusetts two years ago; now I am returning back in this manner. I came out by rail." "You are from Worcester, you say?" "No, from Webster. Friend, what do you think of that cow?" I asked. "Friend, stranger, I think she is a fine looking animal, so handsome; she is a beauty. I wish my wife could see her, and you too. She would like to go East with you, she does not like here; I think I shall return East next Spring, if we can sell out and not lose what little we have made. We don't like; never have done, and I do not think we ever shall." "How far from here do you live?" I asked. "About three miles," answered the milkman. "Go home and bring your wife here, perhaps she would like to see us all." "It would make her more discontented, she is so anxious to return East and would start to-morrow if she could." "Do you think the cow will come in soon?" I asked. "She does not look as if she would come for some time," said the milkman. "If I mistake not her time is now out. This morning's milking yielded two quarts." "I think she will not come in for four weeks, sure. When do you leave here?" inquired the milkman. "I intend to leave in the morning. To-morrow is the first of August, I left Eureka the first of June. I have travelled but five hundred miles in that time. It won't do to kill time in this way." "Should I not see you again, I hope you will succeed in making your long journey. Yes, you will find it a long journey before you reach old Massachusetts; good morning," said the milkman. "Good morning; give my regards to your lady, I would like to see her," I said in parting. About sixty rods from my camp, on the other side of the railroad, there is a very large grove that will accommodate a large number of people, who are at this time, assembling in the grove. A band has just commenced playing, so I thought I would go that way to see what was going on. The music was very fine, I stood in the road or its limits, near the entrance to the grove. I saw a carriage coming from the south towards the grove, a gentleman with two ladies drove up to where I was standing; of course I did not know them. I was not thinking about the milkman that I invited to call on me. No, my attention was wholly taken up with the music, it was very good. The gentleman reined up his horse and stopped near me. This I noticed, but still I did not know the man, but he knew me. He got out of the carriage and coming up to me said: "Stranger, I know you very well, perhaps you don't recognize me. I am the man who was talking to you this morning about going East. I judged you did not know me. You asked me to bring my wife to visit you and the horse and cow. She is in the carriage yonder." We went to the carriage. "This is my wife and daughter, Mrs. Wood; I do not know your name, so will call you, stranger," said the milkman. "You have called me stranger, but hereafter call me W. B. Johnson." The lady said, "When my husband, Mr. Wood, returned home he told me that he had had a long talk with a man who was going to Massachnsetts, with a horse and carriage, leading a cow; I said that I must see him. He told me to get ready and they would go and find you; I hastily made ready, did not even stop to crimp my hair, so anxious was I to see the man who was courageous enough to cross the continent with such an outfit as yours. I wish Mr. Wood would sell his farm to-morrow and go with you. We have a farm about three miles from the city. We call it a farm, others call it a ranche. I am anxious to see your horse and cow." I requested Mr. Wood to drive his lady to my camp and I would follow him across the railroad and be at the camp as soon as they. I made the camp first and opened the gate that they might drive into the field under the tree for shade. As they arrived the cattle were at rest under its shade; they quietly gave it up for the visitors, but soon returned and took up a part of the shade. "Mr. Johnson, what a fine cow you have here, how handsome, how beautifully she is marked. Has she a name?" queried the wife. "She has, I call her Bessie." "Does she know her name?" "She does." "What a fine looking horse, what is her name?" asked the lady. "Fanny." "And here is the dog, what is his name?" inquired the wife. "Albert, I call him 'Bert' for short." Here you are, horse, cow, dog and self, all going to Massachusetts. Oh, that we were going with you, Mr. Johnson; I have been so sick of living here and I am so to day, that I am afraid I shall not live to see the East again. It troubles me very much, I wish I were going along with you. Mr. Johnson, do you think you can make this long journey?" spoke the wife. "Yes, I do." "I hope you will succeed, but that cow, I think you will never succeed in getting her through," said the wife. "If I can get iron shoes on her feet, I have no fear in the least, but what I can get through; if she falls on the way, I can't do more than leave her. Perhaps, I may have to stop awhile on my way." "When do you leave?" was the next question. "To-morrow morning." "I wish I was going with you." "You may," said the husband. "I want to get back to my old home, once more; I hope to see that time. When a person gets the California fever, they will never be satisfied until they know it from experience. I am satisfied that there is more solid living in Massachusetts than in California. Here it is all climate and nothing but climate; but I think it is all drouth and nothing but drouth," the wife remarked. "I am feeding my cattle to-day just the same as I would in winter, and only the first of August. But a short distance this side my ranche, the grass is green; if my farm was one mile nearer the city it would be worth three times as much as it is where now located," said the milkman. "What is the cause of this change?" I asked. "It is owing to the two rivers, American and Sacramento. You can readily see how low and flat the lands are; we are almost surrounded by these rivers. The American river is a powerful one; when its waters get down to the Sacramento, its banks being low, it overflows and the land becomes thoroughly saturated, and holds the moisture for a long time," said the milkman. "Mr. Johnson, you leave to-morrow; I sincerely hope you will arrive safely in old Massachusetts," said the woman. "Thank you, both of you; I hope I shall accomplish the journey. Friends, should you come East, hunt me up and make me a call, it will pay all of us." We bade each other good-bye. It had got five o'clock in the afternoon, supper time. While I was eating supper, the man who gave me permission to use the lot came to the camp, says he, "Stranger, do you leave us in the morning?" "Yes, sir;

I intend to do so," I answered. "You had better sell me that cow; I will give you one hundred dollars in gold for her. Here it is, stranger; you will be obliged to sell her where you will not get so much for her." "Friend, that may truly happen; she may die on the road and my horse also, but I must take the chances." "I hope you will succeed in your undertaking; should you, truly it will be the greatest thing on record. You will have attained a round on the ladder of fame." "Will you not take pay for what my cattle have subsisted upon?" I asked. "Not a dime; I said the other day you might turn your cattle in for one day or ten, I would not charge you a cent, stranger." "Friend, I am greatly obliged to you, and would like to pay you in some way for your kindness." "Good-bye, friend." "Good-bye," I replied.

On the morning of the first of August, I was up early getting ready for an early start. As I sat eating my breakfast, I saw a man coming across the lot and when near my cow he started on a sharp run, as for dear life, the cow after him. At once I left my breakfast and went for the cow. The cow ran but a short distance and turned back. I went directly up to the cow; what did I find? In the tall grass I found a little "Bessie." It was not the man the cow was after, but his dog. I went back and finished my breakfast but did not leave the city as I intended; I informed the man the cause of the delay and told him why the cow ran after him. "It was not you she was after, but your dog," I said. "I thought she was after me, I did not know that my dog was with me, stranger." "That is not all, the cow had occasion to run for the dog, she had a little calf in the grass and did not care to have dogs around at that time in the morning." "Is that so; then she has a calf. I did not think she would come in so soon, did you, stranger?" "No, I did not; I shall have to remain here longer, I can't move at present," I said. "Stay as long as you wish, you are welcome, stranger." "Friend, I will sell you the calf when it is six days old." "I would like to have the cow with the calf, it will bring the cow to her milk. Friend, I am going to make you a big offer; I will give you one hundred and twenty-five dollars in gold for that cow and calf." "Friend, I do not want to sell the cow; your offer is more than she is worth. I will sell you the calf for ten dollars when it is six days old. That will be on Monday the seventh." "I will give it you, here is the money, stranger." "I do not want the money now." "I will pay you now, you won't run away with the calf; I will take my chances," said the stranger. "On the morning of the 7th I will leave the city and the calf also. I prefer to leave the calf rather than have you take it from its mother. I think it will be best," I remarked. "Suit yourself and you will suit me," he answered.

Sacramento is situated on the river of the same name. The American and Sacramento rivers make a junction with the city between them. It is about one hundred and twenty miles from San Francisco. When that golden gong sounded in 1848 there was no Sacramento city. Eastern immigration made the place. Navigation up this river to the present city was good for large steamers, and smaller ones could sail up a much greater distance. High in the mountain valleys are the mining camps, some of which have become towns, such as Auburn, Marysville, Grass Valley, Nevada city and many others, all of which sprang into existance at the time of the gold craze. Many kinds of merchandize were taken there, even lumber from the State of Maine was imported to Sacramento. While this was going on, the city was growing and now is the second in size and commercial value in the State; her population is nearly 30,000. It is a fine city, beautifully laid out with fine streets and boulevards, well shaded.

Shaded, did I say; yes, Sacramento is a warm city and those shades were made for her. She does not get the cool breezes that prevail in San Francisco. Neither does she get the storms that other cities get on the Pacific coast.

CHAPTER III.

From Sacramento to Reno, Nevada.

On leaving Sacramento, it was my intention to follow the Central Pacific railroad to Ogden, so that should anything of a serious nature happen to me, I should have ready access to the railroad.

I was up early on the morning of the 7th and made ready to continue my journey. Several times I left my camping ground on pretense of leaving and left the calf, so as to get the cow used to the absence of her calf. By so doing, on my last departure the cow would not miss her calf so badly. When all preparations were ready I started and travelled until I came to the bridge that crosses the American river, which is about a mile from the city. Here I stopped and looking around I found my cow missing, she having broken her fastening to the wagon and had probably returned back to her calf. I was sure of this, so retraced my steps to the camp I had so recently left. On my arrival I found the calf had been taken away, nor did I see the cow. I secured my horse to the tree and returned back in search of the cow. I called "Bessie," but no answer. Then the horse would neigh; very soon I heard the answer from the cow, the horse answered back and then the cow came running down the road, making for the lot where she had left her calf in the tall grass. There was no calf. Oh, how I felt for the cow, and how must she have felt. I took the horse from the carriage and turned her loose, when she immediately went to the cow. Reader, I verily believe that the horse understood the matter, as well as the cow. I concluded to stop here and have my breakfast and then try to make a start once more. I gave my cattle some grain and made a dish of coffee which I drank, but I could not eat anything. When all had been eaten up, I again made ready to start on my journey afresh, and travelled over the same road to the bridge. This bridge is made of very heavy timber and some day its great weight will carry it down in one of the freshets. As I leave the city I take the road that puts the railroad on my right. On crossing the bridge I enter on a fine and extensive valley; on my right was a vast plain. In front, a long distance a-head, was the Sierra mountains; to my left are the mining hills of California. I am now travelling in the Eastern valley. On my right and left are many trails, no doubt leading to many ranches. There is no main road; when you come to a trail, there is not anything to tell you the way to this or that town. Knowing that the railroad was on my right, I could take the right trail every time. When the trail took me across the railroad, then I would bear to the left. About one o'clock I came to a ranche; here I stopped, giving my cattle grain and water and eating a lunch myself. About half-past two I went on and came to a creek, I drove down into it and stopped for a short time, the horse and the cow enjoyed it very much, on account of the day being very hot. I travelled until near six o'clock in the evening, when I came to the village of Rocklin. Here I was permitted to turn my cattle into a field of wild oats, which gave a satisfactory pasturage for them. I remarked to the owner of the field, that I should leave early in the morning and desired to pay him for my cattle's supper then. "I shall not charge you a dime," he replied. "You are welcome, stranger." I thanked him.

On the morning of the 8th I left Rocklin. It was a very fine morning, but extremely hot; I passed through the town of Auburn and reached Clipper Gap, where I rested. Just before entering Auburn I had the pleasure of witnessing a scene that I had often heard off, but never before had a chance to see. Coming down the mountain, I saw three men on horseback, driving a herd of cattle; they were on a dead run, and were driven into a corral—opposite to which I then stood. In this herd were two wild bulls, which the men had made many attempts to lasso, but up to this time had failed. This corral was about eight rods square, with a large rock in the centre. The herd was driven into the corral followed by the men, on a keen run, who at every chance threw their lassos at the bulls. I was an onlooker, watching the manœuvre with the lassos, as they scampered around the carrol several times without success. One of the men rode up to me and said: "Stranger, you are in great danger, standing there, as the herd is liable to go through the corral and come for you." I at once started on and went some distance with my cattle from the corral. After securing them, I returned to see the fun. After many attempts they at last succeeded in capturing one of the bulls. As soon as the bull was thrown, the cattle were driven out of the corral. The bull commenced to bellow and kept it up for some time. The cattle returned back and commenced battering the corral down. The bull was still lying on the ground; they took a stick of timber, about seven feet long and four inches thick and fastened it to the bull's head, in front. I asked why they did that, and the answer was, "That timber is to prevent the bull from going through the corral. Now we will give him a chance to get up and show himself." All this time the bull kept up a great bellowing. "What is your next operation?" I asked. "Our next operation will be to cut his throat after he gets cooled off." "This is something new to me, I never saw the like before," I remarked. I left the carrol and reached Auburn, as it was called in 1848, and now known as West Auburn. There is also another village situated on the railroad and called East Auburn. It is a place of considerable enterprise, has handsome modern buildings, finished and in course of erection. Between the two villages are good roads and some fine residences; none such have I seen on my journey, so far. I passed through until I came to a fine patch of grass, where I stopped for the night, allowing my cattle to roam for their supper; after giving them grain I spread my blankets and retired for the night.

I arose early on the morning of the 9th, turned my cattle loose so as they could get their breakfast of the grass, and while they were feeding, I went up to a house a little ways off to see if I could make some coffee, but I found no one around and returned back. I had not been back long when a man came out of the house down to where I was. We passed the compliments of the day. He went up to my carriage and looked into it, I watched him but said not a word, but was thinking. "Stranger," said I, "Can I assist you in looking into my wagon?" "I have a peach orchard over there, and thought you might have found it and filled your wagon; but it seems I sold myself this time," he answered. "Stranger, I came here last night, saw this grass and concluded to stop for the night. I am travelling and came down from Eureka, going East," I said. "How far East?" he questioned. "To the Atlantic; I started from the Pacific and intend to reach the Atlantic ocean, or Massachusetts," I said. "Excuse me, stranger, for being so impertinent. Go up to the house and get some breakfast with me, you will be welcome," he said. I went to breakfast with the stranger. On returning to my camp my host came down to the orchard and stopped; as I was about to move on he called out, "Stop, stranger, I will be there soon with a basket of peaches." He was not long before he came along with a strong half bushel of fine peaches. "Here, friend stranger, take them for my insulting you; I was mistaken for once. If you come this way again I will fill your wagon," he said. "Thank you, it is doubtful if ever I pass this way again, good morning," I replied. "Good morning, success to you," was the reply as I left him. In order to reach Gold-run, I passed by several stations—Applegate, N. E. Mills, Lander and Colfax stations. Colfax station is a first-class station, and a fine town for this part of the world. A hand railroad comes in here from Grass Valley and Nevado city. Here I had an interview with the postmaster and others in regard to getting through the mountain passes. I was told that it was impossible to get over with my wagon. They advised me to go to Grass Valley, then take the old Marysville and Virginia city turnpike over Henness Pass, coming out at Reno. I did not know what to do; keep on, go back or around as advised. I thought, perhaps, I could get through where others might think it impossible to do so. I further reasoned, that I had already accomplished what others would not attempt. Well, here I am, is it to go on or go back, I can't stay here long, it won't do. I concluded to press on and did so, reaching Gold-run all right. Here, I again made inquiries as to the possibility of going over the mountains, or some other way of reaching Reno, telling them that so far I had followed the railroad. "Stranger, when you were at Clipper Gap, you should have gone on to Emigrant Gap; there they would tell you whether you could get over the mountains or not. It is very doubtful if you could with your wagon, the snow is so deep in many places where you would be obliged to travel with your carriage. Last week, a party made the attempt, but could not get through and were obliged to return, and go the way you had better go.

Stranger, you had better return to Colfax, from there to Grass Valley, and take the Henness trail to Verdi. "Mr. Teamster, where can I get grass for my cattle, I would like to stop here to-night. My cow has recently come in, I would like to sell her milk being short of money," I remarked. "Stranger, where are you from and where going, perhaps I can assist you a little?" I answered, "I left Eureka, Humboldt county, California, the first day of June, for the East." "Stranger, are you insane; such an idea, travelling across the continent with a horse and carriage and a cow. Across the continent, you must be insane. Come along with your cattle, which do you prefer, hay or grass, you can have either if you wish. I have some tip-top hay, try some, if they won't eat that we will turn them out to grass," said the teamster. I gave them hay and they ate it right greedily, being very hungry. "Now, stranger, come with me and we will try some hay too. You going to Massachusetts; what a man you are. Well, stranger, when you get there, drop me a line, will you?" I told him I would. "Come in, stranger, we will take something on this occasion, what shall it be?" "Mr. Teamster, what have you, sir?" I queried. "I have some good California brandy and wine, and also some good, old bourbon whisky, made down East somewhere," he said. "Friend, I will try some of your California brandy." I knew nothing about the brandy, I took the decanter and a small tumbler, poured out about two teaspoonfuls and drank it. "I thought you were insane, now I am quite sure you are, stranger." "Well, now, what makes you think so?" I asked. "Your taking such a heavy drink, stranger." "It was enough to test it, that was all I wished, merely to test it. Now I will taste your wine." I took the decanter, pouring the tumbler about half full, putting it to my lips and tasting it. It was good, I filled the tumbler and drank it all, filling again, drank all of it and filled again several times until the decanter was emptied. "There, stranger, I thought you was insane, but now have changed my mind, I will risk you on your journey East, don't you forget it. Well, stranger, our supper is about ready, after partaking of it I can tell whether you are good for a long journey or not." After supper I asked the man for a pail to milk in. Said he, "We will go down and see if the cattle like the hay." We found that they had eaten it up, so gave them more. I milked the cow and when through had filled the pail to the brim. "Stranger, you have a good cow, tip-top; too good to lose on your journey. I will buy her from you and will give a good price for her. She is worth one hundred dollars in gold; stranger, what do you say will you sell her for those figures?" "I can't sell her to-night; I know you offer large figures for her, but I prefer her milk and company rather than the gold."

I rose early on the morning of the 10th, fed the cattle and got ready for an early start. Went to the house of the teamster and asked for a pail in which to milk the cow, after milking I gave it to him saying, "You are entitled to it for your kindness to me. It is the best I can do, I am short of money, having been obliged to pay out much more than I expected." "Friend traveller, how much money have you?" I took out my portemonnaie and counted the money I had, and found that there were just twenty dollars and twenty-eight cents, which must last me until I got to Ogden. "Your cow will support you on your way; after you leave Reno you can get fifty cents a gallon for your milk and when you get to the cars you can get double that amount for it," said the teamster. "Friend, you talk as you think and I think as you do, and the cow will almost support us on our way; I will do the best to get her East and think I shall succeed." "Stranger, breakfast is ready, come in and get some hot coffee; will you take something before you eat?" "No, thank you; coffee will do me more good than wine." It is about six o'clock and I am ready to retrace my steps back to Colfax. I bade the teamster good-bye and thanked him for his kindness and interest in me and started on my day's journey. Returning, my horse travelled much faster than usual, which troubled my cow to keep up with her. We reached Colfax at about ten o'clock, having come a distance of eleven and a half miles in four hours. We rested until one o'clock and then took the road to Grass Valley. This road was a good one but very hard. The material of which they are composed is about the color of bricks and about as hard. On my right and left millions of yards of dirt have been handled by the gold diggers. This style of mining is called surface mining. About four o'clock in the afternoon we came to a fine creek, about two rods across; the water about a foot and a half deep, with a bottom as red as burnt brick. As I sat in my carriage, mid-way of the creek, a short distance on my left, I spied a fine plat of grass. My first thought was to stop here over night; my second, that it was yet too early to do so, and thirdly, it was a good chance for my cattle to partake of a good feed of grass and the rest was essential to the cow, so I crossed the creek and went into camp for the night. Turning the animals loose, I gathered some fuel and made a fire, made and ate my supper, after which I spread out my blankets and went to rest myself.

On the morning of the 11th I was up before daylight, being very restless, having omitted to wind up my watch, which had run down; I thought, however, it must be near morning. I gave the cattle liberty to graze among the grass; made a fire, boiled me some eggs and coffee and ate a hearty breakfast. It was a good early meal, you bet. By this time day was beginning to break. My cow I milked twice a day, getting my can full at each milking.

I am fond of milk, but it does not agree with me so I sell it when I can, when I cannot, I give it or throw it away. This I have done very many times. It is about four a. m., when I start on this day's tramp, and I will make the next town at about seven o'clock. I travel around the hills, bluffs and mountains. My road is good but very crooked, the road-bed very hard; so hard that the rains do not penetrate, make gullies or washouts. I am in sight of the town, the sun is up about one hour. It must be nearly six o'clock, a little later I am in the town and making my way to a pump at which I stopped to water my cattle. Leaving them, I went around the town until I came to a house with the sign "Hotel." I did not like the looks of it so went on and inquired for a first-class hotel. I was told to keep on down this street, turn to my first right, go on, turn to my left and keep on and I will come to the best hotel in town. I went as directed, and on reaching the hotel inquired for the proprietor. A lady came in answer. "Madam, I inquired for the proprietor, are you the proprietor?" "I am, sir, what can I do for you?" "I am travelling with a horse, carriage and cow; she is a fine looking cow and fresh in milk. She has not been milked this morning and I would like to exchange the milk for something to eat." "Where is your cow? I would like to look at her?" said she. "Just around the hotel, will you step there or shall I bring her here?" I asked. "I will step around with you," said the landlady. She went with me and saw the cow. "My dear sir, what a fine looking cow! Where have you and that cow come from?" said the landlady. "I have come from Eureka, Humboldt county," I answered. "I know that place very well; have been there. Have you come from there with that cow?" asked the landlady. I replied in the affirmative. She commanded me to take the horse and cow to the barn and give them what hay and grain they needed, and invited me in to breakfast as it was waiting. She seated me at table and said: "We have beefsteak, pork steak, sausage and boiled eggs, with tea and coffee." I took some beef and pork steak with fried potatoes. As I was eating she questioned me. "You said that you came from Eureka city; which way did you come?" "I came overland, down through Humboldt and Mendocino counties to Cloverdale; from there to San Francisco, from there to San Jose, back through Livermore pass to Stockton, Sacramento; from there following the Central Pacific railroad to Gold-Run, back to Colfax and from there to this place." "Why, stranger, has that cow come all that distance. Where are you going to?" said the lady. "You see I started from the Pacific and am going to the Atlantic Ocean." Having answered many questions, I left the table and went to feed and milk the cow. Having done so I carried it in, together with the last night's milking, which she tested and pronounced good, and I gave it to her. "How long do you intend to stay here?" she asked. "I would like to stay to-day and to-morrow; the cow needs rest and I don't care to crowd her along too fast as she is not strong." "Will you sell me the cow; I will give you a good price?" said the lady. "How much is a good price?" I asked. "You have got me now," she answered. "Madam, I do not want to sell her, it will take more than five of those twenties to buy her; in fact, I don't care to sell her. I may be obliged to do so before I can get through my journey." "How long have you been in the State of California?" she asked. "A little more than two years." "Where did you come from, what State?" "From Massachusetts." "I am from the State of New York, you are from Massachusetts and are returning home, it seems," said the lady. "I am, I prefer the East to the West every time." "We are strangers to each other; now, sir, I wish to say a few words with good and pure motives. They are these: I think you will be unable to get your cattle East; you will lose your horse or cow, or both. They will be taken from you; being alone, you can't help yourself; two men can take from you all you have in spite of your resistance, and should you resist your life will be the cost. I have heard and seen so much of this kind, that I feel anxious for you. For instance, you have a fine looking horse, you meet two men on horseback, they stop, saying, 'Hello, friend, do you want to trade horses?' 'No, I do not,' and you start on. 'But stop, hold on, I want that horse, you can take mine,' he says. Now, suppose you come in contact with two such men, what would you do?" said the landlady. "I will tell you what I would do in such a case; before I would trade horses in that way I would talk to them, and would say, strangers, here I am three thousand miles away from home, myself, horse, cow and little dog. I have a tip-top horse, one that I thought so much of as to bring her from Massachusetts to California. I do not like California, and am now returning back to my home. To accomplish this it will require nerve and some considerable time. I have it and the horse has it, she will take me through, when no other will. Now, gentlemen, please consider the matter a little and under these circumstances will you insist on my trading horses with you; I believe you will not?" I answered. "Stranger, that is all very well, but I think your preaching would do no good with that class of heroes. I sincerely hope you will succeed in your undertaking; make yourself at home as long as you stay and take good care of your cattle. Give them all they can eat; I wish you would sell me the cow. If you should lose her you will remember my offer," said the landlady. "I will remember you whether I lose the cow or not." "Will you excuse me if I ask your name?" said the lady. "Yes, indeed I will. My name is Johnson, Warren B., of Webster, Mass." She invited me in to dinner but I declined, having breakfasted so late I was not hungry. When evening came I milked the cow and carried the milk to the landlady, when she seeing the large quantity said, "I do not blame you for not selling the cow, what a large mess of good milk she gives." She invited me to supper and I sat down at table as the bell summoned the others for supper. The table was soon filled with visitors, having taken my seat the landlady said: "Mr. Johnson, let me make you acquainted with Mr. and Mrs. Jones and family, of San Francisco." "Mr. Johnson, our landlady informs me that you are travelling East, and came down from the north-western part of the State. Eureka I know very well; I have been there many times, know all the leading men of the town, such as Vance, Carson, Jones and many others. I learn that you are going East with a horse and carriage, leading a cow; is that so, Mr. Johnson?" "Yes, sir; it is." "How long have you been in the State, Mr. Johnson?" "Two years and more." "When you came out, how did you come, Mr. Johnson?" "I came by railroad." "You will find a vast difference in the time of travelling; you think you can make that distance, do you, Mr. Johnson?" "Yes, sir; I do, and know that it is going to take a long time to perform it, but think it can be done." "I am inclined to think if the thing is possible, you are the man to do it; how long do you intend to stop here, Mr. Johnson?" "I will stay over another day as the cow needs rest. While in Sacramento the cow gave birth to a fine calf and I left there too soon. She was not as strong as she should have been." "Well, Mr. Johnson, I hope you will succeed, should you do so, we shall have to make a President of you some day." When we were through supper, I went to the barn and fed my cattle, made up a bed beside them and went to rest. About nine o'clock the lady of the house came out and called, "John, John, where is Mr. Johnson?" "I don't know who you mean by that name," answered John. "Why, the man with that horse and cow, his name is Johnson," said the lady.

I heard them and answered, when the lady and John came to where I was lying. "Are you here, Mr. Johnson?" she queried. "I am, and have retired for the night." "Come into the house and take a bed; don't lay out there when you can have a bed inside," said the lady. I told her that I preferred to sleep with my cattle, that being my custom, and begged her to excuse me. She answered she would, but it did not seem right to sleep with the cattle as there were plenty of beds inside.

On the morning of the 12th I was up early as usual, I gave my companions hay and water and went back to bed again. I intended to stop over another day, therefore, I would make it a day of rest. About six in the morning they were stirring in the house. John was up and around feeding the horses. He came where I was lying, saying, "You are in bed yet, shall I feed your cattle?" I told him they had been fed, but he might give them some hay if they had none before them. John said the landlady had told him to look well to my cattle and let them have all they could eat. About seven o'clock the bell for breakfast rang, I thought I would wait and take the second table; the lady came out, asked where I was and came to me saying, "Our breakfast is ready, come in, I will give you a fine dish of coffee, it will be good and we have some fine cream taken from your milk," said the landlady. I went and sat down to a fine breakfast; when through, I remarked that I was going to make the day one of rest. "You are as well as usual, I suppose," said the lady. "Yes, I am as well as usual, but we all need rest; I know that the cow does." I returned to the barn to my cattle and went to bed. At noon the bell rang for dinner. I went in and said, "Madam, excuse me from the dinner table, I am not fit to appear at the table." "Mr Johnson, we know you are travelling and furthermore, will be more or less dirty; it can't be otherwise, but we will excuse you," she said. I did not care for any one that might be at the table, except Mr. and Mrs. Jones. They I hoped would be late for dinner. I was through before they came in. After dinner I went straight to the barn, fed the cattle and went to bed. About four o'clock I got up, ran out my wagon and looked it over to see if it needed any repairing. As I was looking it over the landlady came along and said, "I think you are preparing to leave us, are you not?" "No, ma'am; not to-day, but think it well to look things over to see if any weak places can be found and make them strong when you are where you can. I think I will leave you in the morning. I am giving my cattle a good rest, it is what they needed. To-morrow about five o'clock I intend to leave you." About six o'clock I milked the cow and took the milk into the house for the landlady. "Why, Mr. Johnson, what a large mess of milk you have taken from your cow. Ah, that is too fine a beast to be taken from you when you can't help yourself," said she. "Madam, please keep track of me, you will learn my whereabouts through the papers, no doubt," I answered. "Tea is ready, you need not fear about your looks, if you only behave yourself." The tea bell rang and I took my seat as before. After supper I returned to my place with the cattle and gave them a good feed, made up my bed and retired for the night. About nine o'clock the landlady, with Mr. and Mrs. Jones, called on me. "It is rather late to make calls," said Mr. Jones, "but our landlady tells us you are going to leave us early in the morning. I have come to give a good-bye and wish you success with it. I hope and pray that you will make a success of your journey." "Mr. Jones and lady, I believe I have your sympathies and thank you kindly. Should I succeed in reaching home in Massachusetts, I should like to meet you on my arrival." "You will not leave in the morning until you have eaten your breakfast?" asked the landlady. "Thank you, but I expect to breakfast in Nevada city. It is my custom to start early in the **morning, and** I can thus make a day long or short, as I choose.

On the morning of the 14th I was up early, had fed my cattle and was getting ready to leave, when I heard a voice say, "Kate, get up, Mr. Johnson is leaving." I knew from whom the command came, the others were already around. I went in and asked Kate for a pail in which to milk the cow before I left. Having milked, I carried it to the kitchen for the landlady. "Mr. Johnson," said she, "you are doing more for me than I have for you, and we are up earlier to give you a good breakfast before you go; come in and have some beefsteak, boiled eggs, fried potatoes and coffee, come and be seated." I accepted the pressing offer and did justice to it. After eating I said to the landlady, "Madam, I reluctantly leave you, and thank you for your hospitality and the interest manifested in my behalf, I thank you and bid you a long good-bye." "Mr. Johnson, if I have said or done anything that has made your stay with me a pleasant one, I am glad. You are cordially welcome to the hospitality given you, and I pray that you may successfully travel your long journey; good-bye." "Goodbye," said two voices from the window above. "Goodbye," I answered and left.

On the morning of the 14th I left Grass Valley for Reno, travelling the old trail known as Henness Pass, which passes through Nevada city, North Bloomfield, Graniteville, Jackson's Ranche, Webbers Lake, Sardinian Village and comes out on the old turnpike, by Silver Peak mountain to Reno. About six o'clock I reached Nevada city, a distance of four miles. I passed directly through making no stop.

Nevada city is the county town of Nevada county. It

is not a large town; I well recollect the court house, it is situated on a high bluff. I was directed to take the right-hand road, and leave the court house to my left. After ascending a hill, I turned sharp to the right and went on. About ten o'clock I came to a house and stopped, I gave my cattle water and grain; while eating, a man came up to me, who after passing the compliments of the day remarked, "You seem to be travelling. You have a fine-looking cow there, and horse also; where are you from? Excuse me from asking that question." "I am from Eureka," I answered. "I know that place very well; that is, I have been there; it is a great place for lumber. You say that you have come from there?" "I have," I said. "I think you know something about the East by your talk, you speak as. I did when I was at home; where is your home?" "My home is in Massachusetts." "I knew as soon as I heard you speak that you was a yankee; I am from Connecticut," said the man. "Stranger, how long have you been out here?" I asked. "I came to this State in 1852, and was in the mining business for several years, but could not get rich at it. I have a mine on this place, but it's all work and no pay. Friend, go into the house, my wife would like to see you, as you are from Massachusetts." We went into the house and he introduced me to his wife, saying, "Wife, this man says he belongs to Massachusetts, and is now on his way there." "Do you belong in Massachusetts when you are at home?" she inquired. "I do, when at home," I answered. "How came you out here?" "I had heard so much about California that I thought I would come and see it." "How do you like the country?" "Very well; it is a large empire, and will hold all China." "I am afraid all China will be here; but what brought you out, have you relatives here?" "I have, my family are all in the State." "You are going back East, don't you like this State?" "I do not like well enough to live and die here, but still, I might before I get out of the State; I hope not, however. What part of Connecticut are you from?" "We came from New London," she answered. "You like here, do you not?" "Yes, we like here the best of any part of the State, and have lived many years at this place. During all this time we have intended to return East, but have now given it up. Do you want to sell the cow?" "No, I do not." "What are you going to do with her?" "I am taking her along for her milk." "Will that pay?" I was asked. "It does pay; I have the milk and her company, that pays well. I must go on, I am making too long a stop, I have so many miles to make per day." "How many miles a day do you travel?" "When I travel ten hours, I make twenty-five miles; when but eight hours, only twenty miles; in this way I know the number of miles." "Stop and have some dinner with us." "Thank you; it will make a small day's journey, I dare not travel in the night it is so hilly, I have no brake on my carriage. When I have a hill to descend, I block the wheels with a rope." "You have one hill to go down, about six miles from here, that will make you shake. You have got to get down into a canyon; don't miss tying both wheels, should your harness break you would go where we don't know; going down is worse than coming up." "Our dinner is ready, it is early, but some hot coffee will do you good," said the wife. I sat down and ate with these good people of Connecticut. It was eleven o'clock when good-bye was said on both sides. About three in the afternoon I met the stage, with six horses; it was a strong double-brake Concord coach. The driver stopped and said, "Stranger, chain your wheels before you go down the mountain, and be careful, you are a stranger to these parts, I think." "I am, sir." In descending the hill to the first turn, I did not chain my wheels; at the turn I chained both and continued down to the bridge. I paid my toll and went on, up the opposite side of the canyon, which has but one turn. A faint description of this canyon is about as follows: From the water at the bottom, at the bridge, to the summit of the mountain, is twelve hundred and sixty-two feet. In descending, you have to make four turns. This elevation is inside of one mile of travel; from the first turn to the second, is about one-third of a mile; from the second to the third, about one-quarter of a mile; from the third to the fourth, is nearly a half mile. In travelling this canyon the road is wide and good; two teams can pass at any point. When you have made the descension, and stand on the bridge looking east, to a stranger, the sight is most wonderful. My toll for crossing the bridge was thirty cents, for horse, carriage and cow. In ascending, after leaving the bridge, you have but one turn and this is to the left. I think this part is the most dangerous. The road is much travelled as there are many mines in the vicinity. This county is noted for its extensive mines. I have seen sixteen horses attached to one wagon. To this wagon three others were attached. These are eastern built wagons, made of the best of timber and have double brakes. All the large teams have iron shoes made expressly for travelling these canyons. Even the stages are provided with them; they dare not depend on the brakes. You will remember the stage driver cautioned me not to go down the canyon without chaining my wheels. He knew I was a stranger and it was thoughtful of him in giving me the warning; I shall ever remember him for his kindness, and should he by chance ever get this book, he will remember me by my cow. About six o'clock I reached North Bloomfield. Just beyond the hotel, to the left, I pitched my camp by permission of the landlord and gave my cattle water and hay. There was no grass for "Bessie." It is hard, but cannot be helped—grass one day, hay next, does not give good satisfaction to the cow.

North Bloomfield is situated on a high elevation. It is not much of a town for business or population; it is a stop-over place for the teamsters, and about mid-way from Grass Valley to Graniteville. The hotel is about sixty by fifty feet, two stories high and fronts the east. Its proprietor is a gentleman about sixty-five years old. In front of the building is a store, saloon and one other building. I think there is also a blacksmith's shop, which constitutes the town. Standing in front of the hotel, looking east and south, you can see nothing but hills, bluffs and mountains. To my left, in full view, are the Sierra mountains; to my right are numerous mining districts; in fact, they lay all around. There is an immense amount of freight brought here from around the country, which requires a good road, and they have them. But the way they transport merchandise is a surprise. Sixteen horses harnessed to one wagon and three other wagons attached, making a long train. To me, this was something new, but I found it a common mode of transportation.

The morning of the 15th found me up early, making ready for my day's travel. I went to the hotel and found only the lady of the house up; I asked for a pail in which to milk, promising her the milk. I gave it to her, saying she was welcome to it, on which she said, "Stranger, please sit down and I will broil you a bit of steak." In about five minutes she brought in steak, potatoes, hot biscuit and coffee. This I did not expect, but did ample justice to the repast and thanked her for the same. I left on my journey about half-past five o'clock; on leaving this place I took the road to my right, by so doing I saved about four miles of travel, and came into the same highway. The road to my left would have taken me to a large mining town; at half-past eleven I came to the main road. Here was a small pond, of which my cattle drank heartily, I gave them grain and had a lunch myself; I rested a little over an hour and at one o'clock resumed my journey. The road we are now travelling is tip-top, during the rest of the afternoon I crossed several bridges over small rivers. In crossing one, off to my right, I noticed one stream rushing along with great power. Here I met a four-horse team and asked the driver how far it was to Graniteville. He answered, "Not quite three miles." "Where does this water come from and where does it go?" I asked. "It comes a great distance, some twenty-five miles, and goes on below North Bloomfield. Where are you from?" "I am from Grass Valley." "You came through the canyon, did you?" "I did." "This water goes to South Eureka through the canyon, and on until it is used up. This is a great water for hydraulic mining, one of the greatest in this State." "I thought hydraulic mining was not allowed in this State." "It is not in some sections. Near the American and Sacramento rivers no dirt is allowed to get into those rivers, within so many miles of Sacramento city; it has spoiled navigation on those rivers." About six o'clock I reached Graniteville, I stopped opposite the hotel and inquired for the proprietor. "I am the man that stops here; what can I do for you?" "I am travelling East, just as I am, horse, cow, dog and myself, I would like to go into camp near here and would like hay for my cattle. I have grain and a lunch-basket which contains my own grub." "I can accommodate you with hay, I suppose you have plenty of gold." "I am not cold," I remarked. "I said gold, you understand. That cow is a fine one, I see she has a noble bag; but where in h——ll have you come from, that's what I want to know?" "I started three hundred miles north of the city of San Francisco, Eureka, came down to the city and from there here." "Where are you going to haul up, I would like to know that?" "I don't like to tell the whole of it." "Why not?" "Because you will think that I have a lot of gold to carry me that distance. Now show me a good place to camp with my cattle to-night, give them some good hay and I will milk the cow to pay for the hay; will you do it?" "Yes, I will, and better than that by you; come on with your cattle and follow me. I will give you a good camping place." I followed him, when coming to a lot he said: "How do you like this place for sleeping to-night." "First best. Lend me a pail in which to milk." He found me a pail and I milked the cow and handed him the pail with its contents. "Come to the house and get your pay for this," he said. I went in and took a seat on being told to do so. "Wife, what do you think of this from a cow that has travelled most a thousand miles, eh?" "That is good, where have you come from?" asked the wife. I told her. "Get this man a supper, he is worthy of it; I told him to come in and get his pay for the milk. Now pay, and well too, don't be stingy. Take a seat." I sat down to a good supper and enjoyed it much. After supper I went to look at my cattle and found them all right. I returned to the hotel and inquired for the Post Office, and on being directed went thereto. I accosted the postmaster, saying, "Do you know a man by the name of Sherwood, a miner, who owns his own mine, if I mistake not?" "I do, sir." "Where does he live?" "He lives about three miles west of this place, down in the canyon, on the road to North Bloomfield. Follow the road about a mile and you will come to a small creek. A few rods this side the creek, on your right, you will find a trail follow this trail to the creek, on crossing the creek you will find yourself in the canyon; continue along this trail and you will come to some tall grass, go on and soon you will reach his cabin. For a stranger, this is the simplest and easiest way to the canyon. There is a trail much nearer, but a stranger would be troubled to keep the right one, as there are more than one," said the postmaster. "I belong in Massachusetts and am on my way East. Before leaving home a lady called on me and said, "Johnson, I have a brother in California, by the name of Sherwood, he came to this State before my recollection; I have never seen him, but have corresponded with him ever since he left home. His address is Graniteville, Nevada county, Cal.'"

On the morning of the 16th I was up as usual, feeding the cattle, milking the cow, greasing the wagon, doing this and that, looking here and there, and I came to the conclusion that Graniteville was a smart, lively, business town. It has a hotel, two stores, livery stable, two saloons, two blacksmith shops, a market and many houses. When the right time came I carried in the milk, presenting it to the lady. She looked at it and said, "You must have a good cow that gave such a quantity, and good at that. Our breakfast will soon be ready, come in and take breakfast with us; make yourself at home as long as you are here." The bell rang, I went in and the lady gave me a seat at the table and was my waiter. I remarked to her that I was going west about three miles, to the canyon in search of a man named Sherwood, and asked would my outfit be safe with them. "I will keep a lookout myself, I think they will not be disturbed; how long would you be gone?" queried the lady. "I hope to return by noon, and think I will." I started for the canyon, taking the road for the creek and finding the trail as directed, crossing the creek and on towards the cabin. Going up to the cabin door I knocked and listened, but did not hear anything; knocked again, listened and heard a noise inside. I gave a louder knock, when a voice answered, "Who is there?" "No one who will harm you," I answered, "I want to see Mr. Sherwood, is he not at home?" "He is not, he is up at the mines." "Where is the mine?" "Up in the canyon." "My home is in the far East and I am on my way back to Webster, Mass. I have come a long distance to see Mr. Sherwood, and don't want to go away without seeing him. I have a message from his sister, whom he never saw, that lives in the town I come from. Now dare you open the door?" "Yes, when I hear the name of Webster." The person came and opened the door and said, "You from Webster?" "I am, and know those whom neither you nor your husband ever saw. Mr. and Mrs. B——, by me send their most sincere love to you and yours; this is why I was anxious to see you." She sounded a horn, and soon after a young man came in, to whom she said: "Go up the canyon and tell your father a man wishes to see him." It was not long before a man came to the cabin, when the woman said, "This man came to the door and knocked three times before I dared to open it. Had he not said he was from Webster, Mass., and had a message from Mr. and Mrs. B——, I should not have dared to let him in." "You are from Webster, Mass?" "I am, sir." "You know my brother and sister, B——?" "I do." "When did you leave Massachusetts?" "In April, 1880." "How long have you been in California?" "Two years, I arrived at Eureka on the 28th of May, 1880, and have been here ever since that time." "You are on your way back to that State?" "I am." "I think you do not like California by returning so soon, is that so?" "I think this, that there are those who are responsible for the deception that has been sent abroad in regard to California. So much has been said on paper that brought out thousands who are not able to get back, who would if they could. I have heard many say that much. Oh, such a climate, so warm and pleasant and so beautiful. I will admit that the months of December, January and February, to Eastern people are most agreeable, that is, in regard to heat and cold. But in April and the summer months, till December, everything is dried up, except what irrigation has kept green. If you are located on the river valleys you are all right, but these are scarce. I have seen the sands blow like our eastern snows. I prefer snow to sand every time, when the wind blows. No rain is expected until the month of December. In the northern sections you may get some rain in November, but seldom. After the first rain things change; when the second rain comes, should it prove a good substantial one, say, so many inches, you put in your seeds and in order to get back the value of your seed and labor, you must have so much rain, or so many inches of rain-fall in order to warrant a crop. Now during the months of December and January, these two months, the rains come. The best months are the first four. In April, things begin to dry up; May is dry, June is very dry, in July you are trying to get your sheep to the mountains. Can wait no longer, and you have to be smart to get them there or they will perish on the way. It is not yet August and don't expect rain for several months. August, September, October, November; four months, all dried up. Think of it; ten months out of twelve, no rain. You get up in the morning, say five o'clock, the sun is just up, not a cloud to be seen. The day advances; nine o'clock, hot; twelve at noon, very hot, not a cloud to be seen. No, no rain to-day—no showers to lay the dust—all dried up. I prefer living where it is cold, warm, hot, with showers occasionally, to lying down in the hot burning sands, to bring out the rich colors of the shrubbery and make nature grand and sublime. A smart thunder-storm that will burn up the nitrogen and gives us in place a healthy oxygen, that is what I admire."

Graniteville I left on the morning of the 17th and travelled to Jackson's Ranche that day, distance, twenty-five miles. On this morning I arose early as usual, and got ready for my day's journey, having had a short rest which had done myself and the cattle much good, all of us being well cared for. Before leaving, I went to the house and called out, "Landlord, get up, I am ready to leave you." He came out and up to my camp. "Well, friend, are you going to leave us this morning?" "Yes, sir; I am now ready to start, give me a pail that I may milk the cow. He went and got me a pail. Having milked, I handed the pail to him and he took it into the house, saying to his wife, "How is this for high, good ain't it? This man is going right off, how soon before he can have breakfast?" "As soon as I can broil a steak; not more than ten minutes," answered the landlady. "How much must I pay you for your kindness?" I asked. "Kindness, what have we done that we should charge you for?" said the landlord. "You have fed my cattle with hay and myself with good steak. I have given you in return only the milk." That is enough, I am satisfied if you are; the breakfast is ready, sit there," answered the landlord. I seated myself at the table, before me was a good breakfast of which I partook heartily; after breakfast I prepared to make a start, and said to the landlord, "Friend, I feel gratified to you and your lady for your hospitality, you have shown it in its fulness." "Stranger, when I first set my eyes on you, I said that you are an honest, old man, and fully qualified to travel any where among men that are civilized. No man will harm you. As you leave here your road will be a rough and hard one for about seventy-five miles, which will be through a wild mountainous country. You will have a chance to see some wild game, and big ones at that; so you must be ready for them. What kind of a gun have you, shot or rifle?" "My dear sir, I have no firearms whatever, neither shot, ball or revolver, nothing but an axe, hatchet, knife and that hay fork you see there; those are the only weapons I carry and no others." "Do you expect to get through this long journey without fighting something. If you do you will be the first man, and a lucky one you will be." "Good morning," I answered. "Good morning, I hope you will get along all right, but look out for yourself, you are getting into a wild country, with wild animals on every side. You may reach Jackson's Ranche to-day if you have luck; make it if you can, for there you will be safe." We bade each other good-bye.

It was six o'clock when I left Graniteville; could I have taken the left road I should have had a good highway to travel, but being obliged to travel to the right, I had wild mountainous roads, with timber in abundance on every side. On my right I hear the roar of a waterfall. About nine o'clock I met two men with guns. Passed the compliments of the day with them and said, "Strangers, I hear the roar of water on my right, what does it mean?" "Soon you will come to a lake or pond; the roar is from the water taken to supply the canal and carried many miles for mining purposes," they answered. "I must have crossed this canal in coming from North Bloomfield to Graniteville, did I not?" "You did." I had noticed with what a rush the water ran in this canal. "Strangers, what time is it?" (I carry the time, but always ask when I have a chance, I do this for a blind.) They answered about ten o'clock. I left them and in a little while came to the lake and taking the left-hand road followed it close to the water. A large amount of money has been expended in and around this lake; the road having been set back to the mountain-side. I was informed that twenty-five years ago, this lake was a deep canyon, with a small creek running through it. On the right, looking east, is a heavy mountain with snow still on its summit; on the left is the road. It is said that this canyon was very deep. At its outlet on the west, it is almost surrounded by solid rocks, with only space to let the water pass through. The mining companies have taken in the situation and built a dam to store the waters. This dam makes a deep lake, in some places nearly three hundred feet deep, and covering a large surface of land. About half-past eleven I came to a nice patch of grass, here I halted, unharnessed the horse and let her and the cow loose to pick a feed for themselves. I gathered some fuel and made a fire and got hot coffee for my dinner. About one o'clock we moved on until four, when coming to another grass lot I made another stop; our rest here was short but sweet. I have still six miles to travel to reach the ranche. Coming to a creek I crossed over and a short distance further came to a field of excellent clover grass and was tempted to stop there for the night, but having been advised to get to Jackson's Ranche pushed on towards that place. In a little while I came to a house, from which two men issued with pails, evidently for milking. I called out. "Strangers, is this Jackson's Ranche?" "It is, sir." "Can I camp here for the night. I was told at Graniteville to reach Jackson's Ranche, and suppose this is the place, as I have seen no other house." "You can stop anywhere you choose; you can feed on grass or hay, either will not cost you anything." "After fording the creek I noticed some fine grass; would it have been safe for me to camp there, I would like to, as there is some fine feeding? I ask this because at Graniteville I was told that there was large game both sides of the creek and was told to be on the look-out." "Well, stranger, there are some wild game on this road; there is not enough of travel to make them afraid. All who have guns, should they see any game will blaze at them, hit or miss." "Well, I will try my cattle on hay, but I do not think they will eat it as they have had grass, unless they are very hungry." I gave them some hay but they refused it, so I returned to the plat near the creek and camped. I turned the horse loose and fastened the cow by the lariat and allowed them thus to eat at will. I gathered fuel and made a big fire, got my supper and went to bed. About nine o'clock in the evening, two men and a boy came along with guns. "Friend, don't be afraid of us, we have come to see how you are getting along and always carry our guns with us, so that we are ready should we come across any game. This is a great place for deer, they feed near here at all times of the day. There being but little travel in this trail they are very tame. No doubt, should we go down to the creek, but that we should find some grazing." "How is it about the wolf and wild cat, and that kind of game, are there many of them?" "Well, I suppose there are many of them. You came past one place that is noted for that kind of game; it is a good place for camping, but a wild spot for all kinds of game." "Think I stopped there and fed my cattle on the grass, I thought that was a good place for deer; they are great on feeding." "Will you go up to the house and stay over night with us?" "I prefer to stop here, if it is safe to do so." "You will be safe here, but more so at the house." "If I remain here my cattle will be fed for the morning, and will enable me to make an early start, so I will stay here." "You may have one of our guns if you wish, and think you had better take one of them; you can stop at the house in the morning, leave the gun and take breakfast with us." "I will, thank you." "Good night, you had better keep your camp fire burning, it will keep the animals away, they will not come very near you." About midnight I was awakened by a loud talking that did not come from any two-legged animals, there appeared to be many of them by the noise. The cow was lying down and the horse was standing near her. The horse left the cow and came up to me, the cow could not come as she was fastened by the lariat. I arose at once, renewed my fire and then went and drew the pinion and brought the cow nearer the camp, my dog was in the carriage, so that we all were now together, ready for any emergency. Our disturbers were to the left of us, and were evidently quarreling among themselves, or they would not have made so much noise. I put the horse in the carriage and made for the ranche, thinking that would be more satisfactory to all of us, and it was, "you bet." It was just half-past twelve as I fastened my horse to a post; I made up my bed again and laid down but not to sleep. At half-past three o'clock I returned to the creek to give my cattle an opportunity again at the grass, and on my arrival found a herd of deer feeding there; they left as soon as they saw me. As it was breaking day I was surrounded by many coyottes, who were sending forth their melodies. They were not very near us, say about forty rods away. I am not afraid of this kind of game, as they do no harm but to the sheep. At five o'clock I again left for the ranche, on my arrival I found them still in bed; and called out, "Friends, if you want me to breakfast with you, for my sake get up. It is now half-past five and the sun is up." "John, get up and make some good strong coffee." It did not take long to get the breakfast ready and all hands partaking thereof. I related to them my experience of the night and my disturbance, saying that the landlord at the hotel told me that I should find plenty of game and big at that, and asked what weapons I carried. I told him I had neither ball, shot, or gun. "Stranger," says my present host, "have you no firearms with you, not even a revolver?" "Not anything of the kind," I replied. "What are you thinking about, travelling in this wild part of California without a weapon of any kind. No one here thinks of going out without a revolver; here you are in the midst of a wild country, without anything of the kind, you can never get as far as Reno, if you do I would like to know of it." "If I do you shall be informed of the fact; you of course, read the papers?" "I do when I can get them." "Get them and keep track of me," I said. "I will, you bet." "Stranger, your hospitality to me is such as I have received daily on my journey. It seems as if people could not do too much for me; I appreciate it, but I must leave you and make Webber's Lake to-day, how is the road thereto?" "From here it is a much better road than from Graniteville." "Friends, good morning." "Good morning, I hope you will succeed in getting through, such an undertaking is not to be read of in books; success to you." Thanking them I left on my journey.

August 18th, I left Jackson's Ranche for Webber's Lake, which I made the same day, travelling a distance of twenty-five miles. Having been disturbed in my rest I did not feel so fresh as on the previous days.

Webber's Lake.—In reaching this place, about mid-way is an old log cabin, built of handsome timber, the logs of which it is composed are dove-tailed at the corners, making a very strong and durable building. When the stages formerly ran over this road from Virginia city to Marysville, before the Central Pacific Railroad was built, this trail was a good road, but since the building of the railroad this, as well as many another good road, has been neglected, especially that part running through the Sardinian Valley, a distance of seventy miles. About two miles distant from this log cabin is the summit of the mountain, which rises from the lake to a height of two thousand feet. The scenery from the summit is lovely, in fact everything around was beautiful, while on my right are the Sierras covered with snow. In travelling along, the lake is on my right going east, on my left were many buildings, one was large, and evidently an hotel, situated directly in front of the lake. The road passed between the lake and the buildings; from the hotel to the water was only about four rods. The length of the lake is one mile; the width about a half mile, many boats were on the shore. On my arrival, I asked for "Dr. Webber." A tall man, about seventy-five years of age, answered me, saying, "My name is Webber, I answer to Doctor Webber." "I stopped at a hotel about four miles from Grass Valley, and the proprietor gave me this note to give you on my arrival, here it is." The doctor read aloud:

"This traveller called at my hotel and said that he was from Eureka, with horse, carriage and cow going East, to Massachusetts. I told him to follow the old Fermis trail to Reno, and on reaching Webber's Lake, to stop and give this note to Doctor Webber.

From,   JOHN CLARK."

"Stranger, walk into my office; sit down. You are from Eureka and going East, to Massachusetts, your old home, and with that outfit; it will take some grit." "I am." "Don't you like California?" "I like the East much better." "How long have you been in the State?" "About two years, or a little more." "Have you been in Eureka all that time?" "I have, sir." "I do not wonder that you do not like that part of California, where the sands blow like the snows of the east. No wonder you are anxious to get back to old Massachusetts; I know all about this State, having travelled it all over. I think I am situated here the best of any one. Look at my surroundings; look at that beautiful sheet of water; look at the green grass; we do not have to pump water on our lands to keep them from drying up. No, not a bit of it. Look on yonder mountain; see those white caps, they are white by night as well as day; they are white from the first of August to the first August the next year." "Doctor, you have here a delightful situation, I would like to stop with you over night; here is good grass to which my cattle will testify, I shall soon be where there is none; am I not right?" "You are; when you get into Nevada you will often think of me; what can I do for you?" "I would like to picket my cattle where the grass is short and sweet, not where you intend to cut for hay. I suppose you make hay of that tall grass?" "I do; yonder is a good white clover patch, take your cattle there, turn them loose if you dare do so; they will do no harm. Our tea will soon be ready and come in, perhaps you will find something you do not carry. Do not refuse when one asks you; travelling as you are, accept the invitation, you are right welcome." I went to see that my cattle were all right and having their supper and returned to the hotel for my own. After supper I got a pail and milked the cow, and carried it to the doctor saying, "My cow sends this pail of milk to you in return for the grass she has and is now devouring; please accept it." We sat in front of the house talking on every subject, when two hacks with four ladies and gentlemen drove up from Reno, who were coming to make a visit of three or four days at this pleasant resort. The doctor turned to his visitors and said, "Gentlemen, this man is from the northwestern part of the State, Eureka city, and is going to Massachusetts with a horse, carriage, cow and dog; a long journey." "Yes, a very long journey; do you think you can make it?" "I do." "You will never be able to take that cow all that distance; if you do, you will stand on the top ladder of fame." "Sirs, if I can get the cow shod with iron shoes, I shall succeed; but if not I am afraid I shall not succeed. I have not been able to get her shod as yet. I have had her feet seared four times and they are getting small." "What do you mean by getting her feet seared?" "Take a flat piece of hoop iron, heat it red hot, then take up the foot and rub the red hot iron over the bottom of the hoof; that is the way the Spaniards shoe their cattle." "Now, friend, I will tell you where you will get your cow shod. But a few days ago, when passing a blacksmith's shop in Reno, I saw the blacksmith shoeing an ox; this I know, for I saw it done.

When you get there you can have your cow shod with iron shoes." "How far is it to Reno?" "It is about forty-five miles." "It will take me two days to travel thereto; what kind of a road is it?" "It is a good road. When you get to the four corners, take your left and you will have a good road to the valley. Do not keep straight on as that is the old trail; when you get there you will come into the turnpike that leads to Truckee, as you strike this road turn sharp to your left." "Doctor, are you troubled with wild game at night?" "There are some around, but seldom come near here. If we kept sheep we should have them around continually; the coyotte and wolf are terrors for sheep." "How is the wild-cat?" "The wild-cat is the smartest animal we have; they will drive the wolf away every time, they are not as heavy but very quick and active; I have seen the wolf and cat fight. The cat will jump on and off the wolf and the wolf does not care to be scratched to pieces by the cat." I now left the doctor, went to camp and made ready for the night, securing my cattle and went to bed.

Webber's Lake I left on the 19th and travelled twenty-eight miles to Silver Peak. This morning I got up early as usual and made ready to move another stage on my journey. Having had a good night's rest, I feel tip-top and am anxious to reach Reno to-morrow. There I hope to be able to shoe my cow, if not, I do not know when it can be done. It is just half-past five and all ready to start. I went to the hotel to see if the doctor was up and told him I was ready to start but he would not let me till I had had some breakfast. "I do not wish to offend you, but am very anxious to cover as many miles to-day as possible," I said. "You stop and get a good breakfast and you will make more miles," he replied. I reluctantly stopped and requested a pail and went and milked my cow and handed him the milking. "You have a fine cow, she will more than pay her way," said the doctor. I sat down to a breakfast of beef and veal steak, boiled eggs, fried potatoes, biscuit and hot coffee, which I thought was well worth stopping for, and turning to the doctor I said, "Doctor, I have been well paid for the stopping, good morning." "I knew you would be; good morning. I hope you will make a success of your undertaking." It was just half-past six o'clock as I left the hotel. My road was a good one, on a down grade. Travelling a little ways I came to where four roads crossed and took the left-hand road. About eleven o'clock I came to a ranche where I stopped, giving my cattle a ration of water and grain. I then went on and after travelling about two miles came to another ranche, where I again halted for a short rest. Travelling still further, I came to a valley and passed through a timber lot which had been felled and the logs were scattered in the road and all around. This timber was handsome, not large but a good size for use— say, about two to four feet in diameter. I am still but a short distance from the Central Pacific Railroad, not more than two miles. It was with great difficulty I got through the timber lot, and when through I emerged into the turnpike for Reno. This is a very good road, I have had none like it so far on my journey. I am travelling in the rear of a large flock of sheep and can not get by them. On my left is a deep canyon, and on my right is a high bluff or mountain. I asked the herdsman where they intended to camp? He said, just this side of Silver Peak, but a short distance further. At six o'clock we came to a saw mill. At the left of this mill the herdsman turned in and drove down into the canyon. I was informed that there was good feeding, but did not go down to see. I pitched my camp opposite the mill where there was a good feeding of wild oats, which my cattle readily devoured. They were the first wild oats on which they had fed. I made a fire, wood being around in abundance; made a dish of tea and ate my supper and laid down for a while. About nine o'clock I got up and after securing the cattle for the night I again laid down, but could not go to sleep, on account of the sheep bleating for their young, there being about six thousand of them in the canyon. About half-past ten o'clock I heard the report of a gun, then another, and another. I called out, "What is the matter down there?" "Matter enough, the wolves are after our mutton, the canyon is full of them. We dare not set our dogs on them as they will be killed, so we blaze at them." "Come up here and get some milk, I have some and you can have all you wish." The man was soon at my camp who said, "I have come for that milk, thinking it must be worth coming after." "But what have you to carry it in?" "Oh, the d—l. I did not think to bring anything. Can't I take the can, I will bring it back; what is it worth?" "I paid a dollar for it in Sacramento." "Will you sell it, I will give what it cost you and more if you say so." I let him have the can at cost and he gave me a dollar. He wished to pay me for the milk also but I declined to take it. "What is the matter among your sheep?" I asked. "The wolves want mutton; they were as thick as rabbits when I came up, I could hear them in the brush after the sheep; they can smell a sheep a long way off. Our sheep are hungry, still we dare not let them feed at nights; they must wait till morning and then the dogs can take care of them," said the shepherd. "In what kind of a place are your sheep to-night?" "They are in a kind of oblong square, and there are six thousand of them; they will cover about two acres. On one side we have three camp fires, on the other are six dogs and four men with guns." "Do you fear the coyotte?" "No, we do not, we set our dogs on them, but the wolf would kill a dog mighty quick. When the wolves show themselves we quickly blaze at them, we try not to kill but to wound them. If a wolf is badly wounded we are not troubled with others for some time." "You was not afraid to come for the milk?" "I should not have dared to come had I not had this lantern, it is enough to keep any wolf away from me." "Do you think they will make an attack on me?" "They will not trouble you as long as the sheep are there, if they were not around they might attack your cattle; but you need not fear." Bang, bang, bang, went three guns. "I must go back, there may be something for me to do; they may have a strong army and if they attack us would make a clean sweep of the sheep. Stranger, you have been passing through a wild country; have you not been troubled by these infernals during the night, if not, you are remarkably lucky?" "At Graniteville I was told that I was entering a wild region and should be ready to meet them. Since then I have been on the look-out, and to-night the varmins are plentiful around and should be handled with firmness."

I left Silver Peak mountain on the 20th and reached Reno that day; journeying fourteen miles. It was about midnight when I left my camp; I concluded it would be safer to move on than stay there with all those wolves around me. I filled my lantern with oil and moved on; after travelling about a half mile I found that I had a big hill to descend, it was very dark and could scarce see my way. I roped my wheels and descended the hill with bated breath, not knowing what might happen; I could see on my left a deep canyon, the road was apparently wide and good. Having made the descent safely I breathed more freely; on going some further distance I came to a house, which I approached and knocking at the door a voice answered, "Who is there?" "Get up, friend, I would like to ask a few questions." "Go on, I can hear you without coming there," was answered. "I won't harm you, I am travelling and from Eureka, three hundred miles from San Francisco." "You from Eureka?" "I am, sir." "You talk as I used to do at home; I left Maine for Eureka, in 1868. I am a Yankee as evidently you are by your talk?" "You are right; I am. I came by way of Grass Valley, on the Henness trail, by Webber's Lake. When I reached the turnpike I was in the rear of a herd of sheep and could not pass them and was obliged to travel in their rear until we came to the old saw mill on the hill where they turn into the canyon, while I camped opposite the mill. There seems to be any quantity of wild animals in that canyon; the herdsmen kept firing away all the first part of the night, I went to bed but dared not sleep, and became so much excited that I broke camp and came on here, running my chances of safely reaching Reno early in the day. How is the road thereto, is it safe to travel at night and is there much timber on the road?" "From here to Reno is twelve miles and the road is both good and safe either night or day; there is no timber on the way." "How far am I from the railroad?" "Not more than a half mile. This is Verdi, you will not pass the depot, as it is to your right a few rods. Stranger, you have been passing through the most dangerous part of California; no part being so dangerous as the last hundred miles you have come so far unharmed, and so far you are a very lucky man, I hope you will succeed as well on your longer journey, good morning." It is two a. m., as I leave this house and travel on until sunrise when I came in sight of Reno. At six o'clock I came to a good grass patch where I stopped for my companions to get a nibble. At seven I journeyed on and entered the town of Reno at half-past eight o'clock, passing through and halting about eighty rods west of the town. Having secured my cattle I went in search of a blacksmith to shoe my cow; I inquired of several but did not find the right one, but was told that such a man could shoe her; I went there and inquired for the proprietor, of whom I asked,

"Can you shoe a cow for me; I am travelling East with a horse and carriage, leading a cow. I have travelled about seven hundred miles and have not been able to get her iron shoes; I have had her feet smeared three times which have worn very small." "I have never shod a cow, but have shod a great many oxen and think I can shoe her." "How much will you ask me to put iron shoes on her?" "My price for oxen is four dollars; if you and I can do it, I will charge you but two dollars." "When will you shoe her?" "After dinner; where is she?" "But a short distance from here." "Lead her down after dinner and I will see what we can do," said the blacksmith. About one o'clock I drove down to the shop with my horse, carriage and cow. I had not said a word to any one but the blacksmith, but on my arrival there were scores of people to see the cow shod. Many were the questions levelled at me, which I patiently answered with as little show as possible. "Stranger," said the blacksmith, "lead your cow around into the brake, we will see what can be done." I untied the cow from the carriage and led her around the shop to the brake. The horse was very much troubled at seeing her led away, but on coming in sight of the horse she was all right again. I am in the habit of talking to my cattle and think they understand much more than we give them credit for. "Come, Bessie," I said, "get into that brake, it will not harm you." I went into the brake ahead of her and she followed me without any further trouble. A strap was put under her belly and she was raised from her feet; this was more than she would stand, so I asked the blacksmith to let her down again, which he did. I then went to my carriage and got some rope; putting a rope around each hind-leg, and bringing her feet back under her rear parts, I took up her forward foot, telling the blacksmith to make it fast, which he did. She tried to get loose but could not; in the meantime, I had taken the horse out of the carriage and fastened her beside the cow, telling the blacksmith to make a good job. He answered, "That he would do his best." About this time the whole town had assembled to witness the shoeing; many questions were asked and answered at leisure. The blacksmith had commenced nailing on the shoes; he would strike on the nail, driving it in about one-third of its length, or until bending, then drawing it out and taking another, drive that in further, and so on, until the whole were driven and the shoes securely put on; the hardness of the hoof causing many of the nails to bend. Her feet having been seared three times, made them hard and flinty. While all this was being done, "Bessie" behaved herself bravely. Two nails were driven that made her flinch; these nails were marked, so that should they trouble the cow they could be removed. On taking her from the brake she could scarcely travel; we got her back into the brake and had those two nails drawn and replaced which made quite a difference. The blacksmith said that the soreness would wear away. He charged me not to take the shoes off, but keep them on and remain here for a few days until she could travel again. Should I take them off I should be in a very bad fix. Without shoes, I could not get her along, and now they are on good; wait until she can travel. It may be three days, perhaps five or more, but be contented; I am sure you will be the gainer by so doing. Turning to the crowd I said: "Gentlemen, you see the condition in which I am placed; being obliged to stop a few days, where can I get grass for my cattle, I prefer grass to hay as they have been fed mostly on grass during my journey?" "Stranger, I have grass and a grass cutter, and you may have all your cattle can eat as long as you stay and I won't charge you a dime." "Friend, where is your grass?" "One house this side of where you stopped this morning; I will show you." I led the cow by the halter, but it was no use, she could scarce walk, and she laid down; I got a pail of cold water and poured it upon her hoofs continuously for several hours. About six o'clock, I took my horse and carriage and went to the man's lot for grass, but had not been there very long before the cow came into the yard. "Well, Bessie, you have done finely; did you think that we had left you? No, we only came for grass for you and you shall have some," I said to the cow. I gave her the grass, which she ate greedily as she lay down. I continued to pour cold water on her feet, rubbing her ankles and legs occasionally. The whole town knew where I was and in what condition; many came to see me and learn my intentions. Ten thousand questions were asked and answered. The time had arrived for milking, her bag was hard-full, I got a pail and went to the cow, and said "Bessie, you must be milked, then you will feel more comfortable; get up and let me milk you." She got up and I milked her, filling the pail "Good, Bessie; you have done well, lay down and I will bathe your feet." She lay down and I bathed her feet. All I said to her she understood, she could not talk but made motions that I understood. I carried the milk into the house and offered it to the lady; she was reluctant to take it, saying that she did not know what to do with so much milk. Just then the gentleman came in and the wife said, "Frank, come here; here is the milk that this man traveller has brought to me in return for the kindness he has received from us." "Stranger," he answered, "it is about time for the express train from the East, it will be here in about ten minutes, take this pail of milk to the depot and when the train arrives, go and sell your milk. Wife, have you a tin dish that will hold a little more than a pint." She got such a dish. Taking the cup from his wife he continued, saying "This cup full is worth ten cents, even change every time, the value of a dime. It is now ten minutes after eight o'clock, I will go with you and we will see the depot master, he may have objections, if so, you can sell it on the highway, don't stand on the platform and call out milk." We went to the depot and saw the depot master, my friend saying: "Mr. Chamberlain, this man is from Eureka, Humboldt county, on his way East, to Massachusetts, he stopped here to get his cow shod. In doing this the shoes are put on so tight she can't travel, and so this man is obliged to stop here a short time. The cow is a fine one, and here is her milk. I told him to bring it here to sell; will you allow him to do so on the trains?" "How long do you intend to stop here?" asked the depot master. "But a short time, I hope to be able to travel in three or four days at the longest," I answered. "It is strictly against our rules to allow peddling in or around the depots, but situated as you are, I will allow you to sell any where around the depot." When the train arrived I went aboard the cars and sang out, "I have better milk than any of you have had since leaving Omaha, don't take my word for it, but try it." One man said, "Bring some here, pour it into this cup." I filled it, he tasted, saw it was good and had it refilled. Then the man said, "Ladies and gentlemen, it is the best milk I have tasted since leaving Massachusetts." "Are you from there?" "I am." "So am I and now on my way back; I belong in Webster when at home. This milk I have got from a cow that I have led from California to this place, more than seven hundred miles and which I intend to take to Massachusetts, I may fail, but intend to try." "Stranger, we hope you will succeed," was answered. I entered the cars with two gallons of milk and came out with one dollar and thirty-five cents in return. I went back to my camp and commenced to bathe the cow's feet. About half-past ten I went to bed and slept till about midnight, when I awoke and gave her another wetting and more grass. I went back to bed but could not sleep, so soon got up again; I examined the cow's feet and found them very hot and feverish, so I bathed them most of the remainder of the night.

On the morning of the 21st I felt very anxious about Bessie's feet, as they were very hot and feverish, and thought there must be inflammation or they would not be so hot. I mowed down some grass and gave the cow a large quantity, throwing water on it so that it would be cold for her to stand on. This morning, there were two trains from the west—an emigrant at half-past five and an express train at seven. My camp is but a short distance from the railroad track, less than five rods, and about thirty rods from the depot. I was milking at half-past six, when the emigrant train came along, due here at half-past five. Being late, it had to stop until the express had passed, due at seven o'clock. Many of the passengers came where I was milking, and bought the fluid as fast as I got it from the cow; this time I did not have to take it to the depot. It was all gone before the other train arrived. I got ten cents a cup, a little more than a pint; for this milking I got one dollar and five cents. My milk being disposed of, my breakfast also, and the cattle well cared for I went into the town and called on the blacksmith and told what I had and was doing. He said I was doing the right thing, he was afraid that I would take off the shoes. You must make her travel and get used to them, she would soon be all right. About twelve o'clock I went back to my camp and found all right and gave them their mid-day meal. At three o'clock I took the cow by the halter leading her around where it was soft, that she might walk as comfortable as possible. I noticed that there was improvement so took her down town to the blacksmith and said, "How is this for high?" "Ah, friend; I see you understand things, keep on doing as you have and you will soon leave us. I have adopted a new plan, that is, while the cow is in camp she stands on grass well wet with cold water, this softens up her hard hoofs. I returned to my camp and prepared to meet the train so as to sell my milk. I sold fourteen cups which brought me one dollar and forty cents. The three next days were a repetition of the two first. The incidents were, the meeting of the trains, selling the milk and the care and exercise of the cow; the overhauling of my wagon and seeing that everything was ready for a move. While here, the people were kind to me. I wanted the blacksmith to reset my wheels, but on examination he advised me not to have them touched. I had him make me several bolts as my whiffle-tree and transient-pin were well worn, so that I should have others when they gave out. While I was here, I was interviewed by the local reporter who said, "Stranger, I wish to ask you a few questions, if you have no objections?" "I have no objections; go on, sir," I replied. "Where are you from with this outfit, horse, carriage, cow and dog?" asked the reporter. "I am from Eureka city, Humboldt county, California." "About how many miles have you travelled?" "About seven hundred and fifty, to reach this place. From Eureka to San Francisco, is three hundred and eighteen miles; from San Francisco to San Jose, is forty-seven miles, and from there through Stockton, Sacramento, Gold Run, back to Colfax, Grass Valley, Nevada city, Graniteville, Webber's Lake to this place." "But you have been nearly three months in getting here," said the reporter. "Yes, but I have not travelled half the time, I have stayed over more days than I have travelled." "About how long will it take to accomplish this great undertaking?" asked the reporter. "About six months." "You think you can make this long journey, do you?" "I do, sir; and time will tell." "You are the man to do it, if any one can," said the reporter. "How soon will you leave this place?" "I intend to leave to-morrow morning, early." "Will your cow be able to travel so soon?"

"Well, I am going to try it; if I see that it is too much for her I shall rest again. From here to Wadsworth is about thirty-four miles and I will take two days to travel there." "I suppose you have your road marked out before you?" said the reporter. "I have; I intend to follow the Central Pacific Railroad to Ogden. I do not intend to leave it any distance, in case any serious accident should occur to me, I shall have the railroad to fall back upon." "Well, stranger, I hope you will succeed; if you do, you will stand on the top ladder of fame. Good-bye," said the reporter. "Good-bye, sir," I replied. I returned to my camp, fed my cattle, got my dinner ready and ate it; I put the wagon together, tried the bolts and found everything in good order, ready for my start next day. In the evening I allowed the cattle their liberty, but they did not wander far, and kept their eyes on the picture; by which, I mean my wagon. About 6 p. m., there were a large number of the citizens of the town around, asking me many questions, all appeared anxious about our journey. One said, "Friend traveller, when do you leave us?" "I propose to leave to-morrow morning, early." "Since your arrival, and knowing your intentions, being obliged to remain here on account of your cow, you have given us something to think and talk about when you have gone. This is a new and wonderful undertaking; a man of your age, journeying from ocean to ocean, from California to Massachusetts, with a horse, carriage, cow in the rear, and dog jumping in and out of carriage at pleasure, and yourself a man of sixty-five years, or thereabouts; I repeat, it is a most wonderful undertaking. I, for one, will daily look in the papers to learn of your whereabouts; I hope and pray that you may be safely carried through, you will need a strong arm of protection, and hope you will be protected night and day. Stranger, you appear to be a man of strong nerve; if you falter in the least you certainly will fail in this undertaking." A man in the crowd sang out, "Three cheers for the man from California going East to Massachusetts," which were given with a will. "Strangers to me you all were, but now friends. On my arrival I at once made for a blacksmith's shop, so anxious was I to get shoes on the feet of my cow. On my way I had tried to get her shod, but could not. I was told at Webber's Lake, that here I could get her shod. Therefore, I was anxious to reach this place. Now she has iron shoes on all her feet, I hope she will be able to wear them out; to-morrow morning I intend to leave you. Ladies and gentlemen, I believe your sympathies are with me. I believe this, for you have been kind to me and befriended me in many ways. To you, stranger, in particular I feel grateful, and I am sure my cattle are, for the grass you so kindly offered me for them, so accept this small token of my regard. There is another person to whom I wish to express my gratitude, but I do not see him here, I mean the depot master, for allowing me to sell my milk to passengers on the passing trains, to him I give my thanks and thanks also to you all, farewell."

CHAPTER IV.

From Reno, Battle Mountain, Wells to Ogden, in Utah.

I left Reno the 24th of August, and reached Wadsworth on the 25th, a distance of thirty-four miles. It was about four o'clock in the morning when I left. In journeying to Wadsworth, we follow the railroad and the Truckee river—river on your right and railroad on your left, with carriage road on both sides of railroad right and left. The river is very crooked, especially as it winds through the canyon. Both rail and carriage roads are on the north side of the river. The railroad crowds the highway in many places. The river here takes a heavy bend to the left close up to the bluff. The old trail used to be between the river and the bluff; the railroad took possession of the bluff, throwing the carriage road more on the mountain; at another place, where the river ran close to the bluffs the railroad was obliged to cut back into the bluff to make room for the highway. This cost the railway company a large sum of money, and it may yet cost them much more. This is a dangerous place and should there ever be a collision in this narrow pass, the cars would surely be thrown into the river and prove a complete wreck.

Reno is one of the most promising towns in the county. It is situated on a high elevation, on the Central Pacific railroad, in the county of Washoe, State of Nevada. As you enter the town from the west, you pass through a broad street; on your right is the railroad and on your left are many fine houses. In front is the depot, a large fine building, comprising both depot and hotel. About twenty rods from the depot there is a sharp bend in the road to the right, which carries you over the railroad and then it bends again sharply to the left. On the right of this road are two long brick blocks, which contain a number of stores in which all kinds of merchandise can be found for sale—dry goods or wet, hardware or soft, whiskies and lemons, etc. All teams have to pass this point and in passing I stopped, there was plenty of room to give others the right of way. Having a time table in my pocket I looked at it, and found that the morning trains had all passed and the trains in the afternoon were late. There are but four trains per day over this road— two from the west and two from the east, one express and one freight each way. You are able to see but a short distance up or down the road, the roads being so winding. The road lies between the railroad and the river mostly, especially in the canyon. In front, is a bend in the river, there I am obliged to cross the railroad to my left. I went on but a short distance before I re-crossed—being now between the railroad and river. Going further, I came to another sharp bend in the river to my left; here I crossed the railroad and my route then lay over the mountain. Having crossed over I went into camp and fed my cattle with grain, I made up my bed and lay down to rest but could not sleep as there were too many wild animals around for comfort. I kept a good fire burning all night.

On the morning of the 25th I broke camp early, and travelled until I came to some grass where I stopped and gave the cattle a good feed from it, after which I made for Wadsworth.

Wadsworth is an old town, and when the emigrants used to come overland through this great American desert, the sight of this place was most cheery after weeks of hard travelling. Since the building of the railroad the town has considerably improved; there is a depot on a large scale and the town has a population of twelve hundred. The railroad corporation has established a machine shop here for the repair of their rolling stock, which gives employment to many hands. It has two hotels, several stores and many saloons; drinking and gambling are very common in this place. In an interview with the superintendent of the railroad about my route, he advised me to buy two ten gallon cans, fill them with water and carry them with me, also giving me introductions to the station agents on the road, asking for water for my cattle. This was magnanimous; for hundreds of miles water is transported by the railroad and deposited in tanks at the several stations from Wadsworth to Ogden for drinking and cooking purposes.

I left Wadsworth on the 25th and made Mirage the same day, a distance of twenty-five miles. After leaving Wadsworth, the first six miles was through deep, heavy sand, the wheels sank into it about six inches, which made hard pulling for the horse. I also had a heavier load than usual; there was a sack of barley for the horse, and a sack of bran for the cow, each 100lbs.; ten gallons of water, 85lbs.; in all 285lbs.; besides my common outfit, such as clothing, bedding, provisions and other things say about 200lbs. more. My carriage is light, about 300lbs.; making a total of about 800lbs. Fanny had to haul through this six miles of sand. I had been informed of this heavy road before starting. About nine o'clock I reached the desert; just as I was reaching the bottom of the bluff on the desert, the express train from the west passed me. I stopped and gave the horse a can of water, but did not give any to the cow although she wanted some. About two miles further we came to a second station, I stopped and looked around but saw no one; I looked for the water tank and soon found it below the surface of the ground, I lifted the lid and found there was water, I got a pail and tested it and found it fair. I gave both horse and cow as much as they would drink and filled my empty can and then went on; it was about ten in the forenoon. I had not gone much further, when on looking round saw the freight train from the west approaching. All hands on the train knew me, as they had bought my milk. At this time I was travelling on the great desert, a better road I never saw; a hard smooth surface, rather too hard for Bessie's feet. I am now on the left of the railroad, my direction is to the east. In front of me are some buildings, which proved to be salt works. About three o'clock I met the freight train from the east, and at four reached Hot Springs. Here I made a stop and introduced myself to the agent, showing him my card in regard to water. He told me that I could have all I wished. I gave the cattle water and grain and refilled my cans, intending to do so at every station. It was fair water, brought from Wadsworth from the Truckee river. "Where are the Hot Springs?" I asked of the depot master. Pointing, he answered, "They are yonder, you will see where to turn in at the trail, it is only a short distance to your right." I went to see the springs and found a wet, dirty, nasty, mud-hole. The water was warm, not hot as I had supposed. I thought myself sold, as others before had been on this place. I travelled further and about six o'clock met another train from the east, but could not see much express about it, as stops were made at every station, running at the rate of a mile in three minutes. It was about half-past eight o'clock when I reached Mirage. I took Fanny from the carriage and fastened her to the left rear wheel, the cow opposite and gave them water and grain, made up my bed between them and laid down and was soon asleep. Some time in the night I awoke, my watch having run down I could not tell the time; all around was still. On my left at a long distance, I heard the cry of a coyotte. I thought it was morning, still I could not see any signs of the sun having risen. I laid down and thought to sleep but could not. I spoke to my horse, "Fanny, are you asleep?" she at once got up and I gave her some grain, this brought up Bessie, she wanted some too, so I gave her some and both were busily eating. Looking eastward, I was sure I saw a light and thought it must be morning and so made ready for moving forward. The light I saw was only about the width of my hand.

I left Mirage very early on the 27th and made Granite Point that day, a distance of twenty-eight miles. It was one of the finest mornings I ever saw, and my road was a good one and I journeyed with good cheer. About half-past six o'clock I saw smoke in our front, and spoke to my horse, saying "Fannie, go on, we will soon have breakfast." We shortly came to a station called White Plains. Here was a good house not painted brown like others, but white; there were several men around and as I came up bade them good morning. One of the men answered, "Where in h—l are you from, and where are you going; you must have come from the East some time?" "Yes, I came from the East" "But where are you now from?" "I am from California and going East." "Yes, I know you are travelling East, but where do you intend to haul up?" "In Massachusetts." "The d—l you are, with that outfit; that cow will never see Massachusetts." "But where are you from, and what are you doing with that derrick?" I asked. "I am from New York and came here to make an artesian well," was answered. "I want a pail so that I can milk my cow; you can have the milk. By the way, I don't suppose that you have any hay that I can get for my cattle?" "Yes, I have some hay, you can have some of it for your cattle. Perhaps they would not eat it, but we will try them." The hay was placed before them and they seemed to relish it very much from the greediness with which they ate it. I got a pail and milked the cow and giving it to the stranger, said "Will this pay for the hay?" He answered, "Yes, and more; go into the house and get some breakfast." So I partook of breakfast with him. "How far have you come this morning?" he asked. "From Mirage," I answered. "How far did you travel yesterday?" "From Wadsworth, about twenty-five miles." "Now, stranger, you say you belong in Massachusetts and going home; do you honestly think you can make that distance with that cow?" "I do, why not; you see she has iron shoes on her feet, and I think she will stand the journey as well as the horse. She has nothing to do but walk ; I think she will make the journey." "Stranger, I hope you will ; if you do succeed, just make a book of your journey." "I will, and you may get hold of one of them." "I should like to meet you somewhere down East ; I would give more to see you that Barnum's big show." "Well, friend, I must be going on, I have got to tramp every day, and make big days at that before I reach the Eastern States." "Well, stranger, I hope you will get safely through ; good-bye." It was about seven o'clock when I left him ; I kept the railroad on my left. At eleven o'clock I came to another station, called Brown's Station. I made but a short stop at this place, just long enough to water and feed. This is a telegraph station ; only two buildings, the depot and a house. At half-past twelve I left and journeyed with the railroad on my left, and as I travel the desert is left behind me, my course now lying through Humboldt valley, the river of that name being on my right. I intended to reach Lovelock's, but my trail led me so far to the right that I was obliged to return to the railroad, so made Granite Point instead. This station is nothing but a house for the Boss of repairs and a shanty for his Chinamen. I took the horse from the carriage and fastened her as usual, with the cow opposite, after feeding I made my bed and laid down, being only disturbed that night by a passing train.

It was four o'clock when I left Granite Point on the morning of the 28th, and made thirty miles in reaching Rye Patch. I was at Lovelock's Station at seven-thirty. On leaving Granite Point I found that I was travelling as it were in a new world ; such a change? Fields that had once been cut were again ready for the scythe ; wheat, oats, barley, were in the fields ready for thrashing. What is the cause of this sudden change? I have stated that I had got through the desert and was travelling the Humboldt valley near the river. The change is caused by the system of irrigation. A short distance above the station, the owners of the land adjoining have built a dam across the river; ditches about three feet wide, are also constructed to run on each side of the road, which are kept full from the dam; other ditches are constructed at right angles, dividing the flat lands into plats about twenty rods long by sixteen wide, from this dam and ditches the land is thoroughly saturated with water and is preferred to overflowing as practiced at Reno and other places. I remember when crossing the Savannah river, at Savannah, S. C., that the lands for miles were level and cut up with ditches, filled with water, which made the best rice grounds in the States.

Lovelock's is quite a place, two hotels, two stores, a post-office and many houses, such as they are. The surroundings look rough. There are many Indians. I went into the post-office and had an interview with the Postmaster, telling him where I was from, where going, and asked him if it was safe to travel among such people as were there—Indians in particular. He said I need not fear their people or the Indians; I need only fear the tramps and those who are put off the trains at such stations as this, who travel to the next to steal a ride and be put off again. "Had I met any of them?" he asked. I answered, "That I had met many of them; they ask for something to eat or drink and I have often given them bread and milk. Some have offered to pay, but as yet I have taken nothing from them." "You had better feed them, it will be the best way to get along with them." "But I am afraid they will want something that I should not care to give them." "That will be the trouble, but look sharp at them. If you want anything that I have, sugar, tea, coffee, bread or cheese, take it along with you," said the Postmaster. "I would like a small piece of cheese and some crackers, I have plenty of sugar, tea and coffee." "You have a wagon and a good looking horse, who will draw a good large load." A large piece of cheese, about 5lbs., a large box of crackers, four cans of salmon, a bottle of vinegar and a small bottle of bourbon, all for nothing. "He that giveth, lendeth, etc." I think of this proverb many times; it is good to think of, but better to practice. I thanked the Postmaster and we bade each other good-bye, he expressing a wish to hear from me. At twelve o'clock the express train passed me from the west. At one o'clock I crossed the Humboldt river over a bridge, about a mile from Oreana Station. The river is on my left, the railroad on the right. I stopped here and gave my cattle water from the river and a feed of grain. At two p. m., I resumed my journey and did not stop at the station, but left it to my right, as I was anxious to get to Rye Patch this night. The good road has left me and I am now travelling a road of sand, sage and ravines. At three o'clock the freight from the west passed and at four the express from the east passed, I signalled for them to stop, but they kept on as though I was nothing. At half-past seven I reached Rye Patch; on arriving I inquired for the station agent. A large noble-looking man answered my inquiry. "Are you the agent of this station?" I inquired. "I am, what can I do for you?" "I am a traveller, come a long distance and have a great distance still before me; this cow is anxious to have her milk taken out of her bag, will you find me a pail in which to milk her." He brought me one and I sat down and milked her in the presence of several persons, and then gave it to the depot master, saying, "I would like some hay for my cattle, if you have any?" "I have both hay and grain, and you can have a dish of tea also if you wish." Myself and cattle were then well cared for. The Depot master then said, "Come in, stranger, take a seat and tell me all about you, where you are from and where going, I am anxious to know." "Landlord, I will call you, you have a fine commodious hotel building here. When the railroad corporation erected this building they must have had something large in view for such a building in a desert." "Yes, they had; it was intended for a hotel, where the cars should stop and time be allowed for passengers to take meals here, which was done for a time, but it was changed so as to stop at Humboldt station, eleven miles above this place, the change made Humboldt a busy place every day in the week. When you reach this place and see the handsome trees planted in the grove you will be delighted and will want to stop over a day or two. But, stranger, tell me where you are from and where going to?" "Well, landlord, I belong in Massachusetts, I went to California in 1880 and resided in Eureka, I left that place the first day of June on my way back to Massachusetts, and have got so far." "Well, stranger, I think you are a man of great nerve. It will take all you have got to cover that distance; you surely cannot do it with that outfit. The cow will not go half the distance. It is a fine looking cow, too good and handsome to throw away; you had better sell her at the first chance." "Now landlord, let us reason together; here I am with horse and carriage, cow and dog; both horse and cow are females; you say the horse may go through, but the cow may fail. Sir, my observation is that a mare is worth more than a horse in the market, so what reason can you show that the cow will fail before the horse; she has on iron shoes, so has the cow, both are well shod. The horse has the load to haul, the cow none; there is the difference in the two. Now, I really think the cow will come out the best of the two; time will tell, however." After supper I said to the landlord, "I shall start in the morning before you are up, shall I feed my cattle before starting?" "Yes, look well after them, there is hay and grain, give them all they can eat."

Rye Patch I left early on the morning of the 29th and made Humboldt, a distance of only eleven miles. I arose early as was my custom, got a pail and milked my cow and left the milk with the landlord, who wished me to stop for breakfast, but I declined, and took "something else," after which we shook hands on parting. It was four o'clock as I left the place. I was directed to cross the railroad above the water tank and follow the river to the second right hand trail, as it was the harder and better road to Humboldt station, and no sand for nine miles. I left this morning in high glee, every thing bright and cheerful. Travelling on the river bank, on my left is large quantities of grass, but I have no time to stop, so about nine o'clock I reached Humboldt Station. On approaching the station I met the freight from the East; all the hands knew me and passed signals of recognition. Driving up in front of the station, there was not a person in sight. I sang out for the proprietor, and a man came at my call saying, "What is wanting, sir?" "I want to turn my cattle into that grass and let them feed all day; how much will you charge me?" "You may turn in your cattle for two dollars." "That is a thundering big price, as big as that hill yonder." "You are a Yankee, I'll bet." "Yes, I am a Yankee." "Where are you from?" "California." "Where are you going?" "Going East, to Massachusetts." "What part of California are you from?" "From Humboldt Bay, Eureka city." "And going to Massachusetts?" "Yes, that is where I belong when at home." "Take your horse out of the carriage, turn into that mowing, the cow also," he commanded. I did so with a will. When the time came around to milk, I did so and carried the milk to him, giving it to him, who on seeing the large mess, said "Come with me." I went with him into the house, when he said to the steward, "Give this man a good supper." When morning came, I again milked, giving him the milk, and getting my breakfast in return for the same. After breakfast I spoke to the proprietor, telling him I would like to stop another day as my cattle and myself were faring sumptuously and it would do us all much good. "You can stay if you desire. I will not charge you anything." I remained there a day longer than I intended.

Humboldt is the station of stations; all trains stop here. The express train from the west arrives at 12:50 p. m.; freight and emigrant at 4:45 p. m.; express from the east arrives at 3:15 p. m.; freight and emigrant at 8:15 a. m. A fine dinner is furnished for one dollar. A passenger from the east said to one conductor, "How long do we stop here?" "Thirty minutes," answered the conductor. "Thirty minutes, who can eat a dollar's worth in that time; I want more time than that. Say, conductor, can't you give us a little more time, I am not in the habit of taking my dinner in my hands?" "Yes, I will give you ten minutes more, as you are a down-east Yankee," answered the conductor. This station is situated between two mountains, one on the right and one on the left. The one south, is but a little distance away, and is a splendid looking fellow, so noble, so grand, scarcely such another to be found between the Pacific and the Atlantic. There has been more money laid out on this station than on any other on the road. From whatever point you approach this station you will think you are entering a fine grove. The buildings are completely hidden by the trees. As you stand on the platform and look around, you must be pleased with the surrounding landscape.

It was midnight of the morning of September first, as I left Humboldt station and at six I reached Mills City station, a journey of thirteen miles by railroad and fourteen by trail. This morning's walk was very invigorating, a good road and fine weather, even the coyottes' call was melodious. My thoughts were interesting and spread over the continent from the Pacific to the Atlantic.

Mills City is a station on the Central Pacific Railroad, consists of a hotel and store in one, house for the boss of repairs and one for his Chinamen—in all, four buildings, making the city. My stop was short, just one hour in feeding the cattle and myself. As I was leaving, the morning's freight and emigrant train passed me. At this place I was advised to take the left hand trail to the river, as it was the better road and more travelled, and freer from sand, which I did. I was still but a short distance from the railroad; on the left the river and on each bank an abundance of grass, but now, nearly all were fenced with barbed wire. About eleven o'clock I came near the river, and at this place there was a break in the fence; I went in and gave my cattle water from the river and fed them with grain and the grass. I detached the horse from my carriage giving her liberty, which she enjoyed by a series of rollings; she did enjoy it. The cow luxuriated on the grass. About half-past one o'clock I resumed my journey, returning to the road through the break in the fence. During the afternoon the expresses from the east and the west passed me. About five o'clock I saw some men hauling hay. I spoke to my horse, as I frequently do, saying "Fanny, we will soon turn in for the night." I travelled on until we came around a knoll of land on which was a stack of hay, along side of which I drove, giving my cattle a chance to eat as much as they wished; presently some men came with another load, when I said to them, "Gentlemen, excuse me, and I think you will when you know my story." There were four of them, and the elder, a man about sixty-five, who replied: "Stranger, what is your story, you look as if you had one?" "Well, sir; we are both strangers, I am a traveller and have come a long distance, three hundred miles north of San Francisco." "What place, so far north?" "Eureka city, Humboldt Bay." "What, with that cow?" "Yes, just as you see." "Well, stranger, where do you intend to fetch up?" "I intend to fetch up in Massachusetts; I may fail, there is abundance of room for that." "Yes, I think your chances of slipping up are very good, but you look the man to perform the journey if it can be done by any one, and you are about the right age too. Will you allow me to ask your age?" "Sir, I was 63 years of age the 11th of July." "I was 68 on the 4th of May last." "I came from Humboldt station this morning, and I want to stay over night here, as it looks a fine place for my cattle, I have to look well after them, so that I can have a chance to accomplish my great undertaking. I carry grain and feed them three times a day; hay is something I can not always get." "You can stay here and welcome. I live in Winnemucca, and am going there to-night." "How far is it to there?" "About ten miles." "It will take me four hours to reach that place, I shall start early in the morning and get there at six o'clock." I gave the cattle water and grain, greased my carriage and got everything ready to start in the morning.

I left Rose Creek early and reached Golconda, a distance of twenty-seven miles. It was two o'clock when I broke camp to resume my journey; it was a fine and lovely morning. The road was very sandy, especially the last two miles in reaching Winnemucca, which place I reached at six o'clock. Here I rested, giving the cattle water and grain and took a bite myself. At this place I replenished rations both for myself and cattle; my stop here was just two hours.

Winnemucca is an old town for this section of the country; settled long before the railroad was thought about, since it has become quite a business centre. Large amounts of merchandise are brought to and left at this station. It has extensive connections with Boise City, Carterville, Idaho City, Silver City, Washington and many others. I left this station at eight o'clock, sharp, and at nine o'clock fell in with a band of Indians, sixteen in number, most of whom were young and well-mounted on fine horses. I travelled about six miles in their company; they could talk good English. The elder Indians kept in the advance, while the younger kept near me. I conversed with them on the road, asking where they lived, what kind of labor they did and how much they got a day. They said they had been cutting hay for some weeks, and were paid a dollar per day and board. "I asked them if they were satisfied with the white people?" "Oh, yes, no trouble with the white folks." "How do the older Indians like them?" "Some of them no like, no good, some very good," was the answer. Two of the Indians, with their wives kept with me, the others kept ahead of us. One of the Indians I asked if he had any whisky; he said he had—would I like some. He stopped and took out a pint bottle, which was full and handed it to me; I took a small drink and passed it back to the Indian. He took a drink and then gave it back to me, I again tasted and then went to my basket and got my flask, took a small drink and passed it to the Indian, calling his attention to the quality of the two; he noticed the difference. "How far is it to Golconda?" I asked. "About eight miles," he answered. "What is the time of the day?" "About noon," he answered. I stopped and took out my water can and gave the horse and cow its contents to drink. The Indian said, "You carry water?" "Yes, I have two cans, I keep them full all the time." "You good traveller, you carry water." After a while they left me with their good-byes, and were soon out of sight. About four in the afternoon I arrived at Golconda; here I got some hay for my cattle. I asked the landlord if he would take milk in exchange for the hay. "Yes," he answered. After milking, I carried it to the house and gave it to the landlady, saying, "This milk is for the hay my cattle have had." She replied, "My husband won't take anything for the hay." "Please take the milk, I would like something for my supper that I do not carry." "You can have supper with us, you will be welcome." At this time the landlord came in and she said, "This man has brought in a can of milk to pay for the hay; I told him you would not charge for the hay, did I say right?" "Well, I don't know about that." "Well, there is the milk, he says he can not do anything with it, we can. I told him to come in to supper." "Well, stranger, you seem to be a traveller, where are you from?" "I am from California and going to Massachusetts." "Massachusetts, you are a fraud." "Do not say that; how do you know but that he speaks the truth. He appears and talks well," said the landlady. "Yes, he appears well and talks well, and that makes me think he is a fraud." "Well, landlord, come with me and see my cattle, you, landlady, come too. I will try and convince you I am not a fraud. Landlord that horse, carriage, cow, dog and myself left Eureka city, Humboldt Bay, the first of June last, and have made all that distance; this is true and no fraud." "I will take back the fraud, but you are crazy." "Well, I can stand that much better, but I can stand both." "Stranger, I think you are a Yankee." "I am, and I think you are also." "Yes, I am from the State of Maine, and you from Massachusetts, you say. Wife, go in and get supper ready and we will be in soon." After a little while the bell rang for supper and I went in and sat down to a hearty meal. After supper I got every thing ready for an early start and went to bed. About ten o'clock I was awoke by two men who were passing near my camp. "Hello, stranger, what will you have?" I asked. "Nothing, we are only passing to a herd of sheep. You are from the west; we saw you when near the river some three miles back, as we were feeding our sheep. Where are you going?" "I am bound east; where are you going?" "We are going down to the south part of Utah," was answered

I left Golconda on the morning of the 3d at four o'clock, and journeyed as far as Stonehouse, a distance of twenty-eight miles. In travelling to this station, I was advised to take the left-hand trail for some six miles, crossing the river when I came to a bridge, by so doing leave the mountain pass and Iron Point, then follow the river until coming to a carroll on my right; then take the right-hand trail until I came to a house, there they would give me the trail to Stonehouse station. In travelling this trail you pass around the mountain, instead of going over, and it is about three miles further, but an easier road. It is as good a country road as you can find. I followed the road as advised. Since leaving Lovelock's I have travelled near the river Humboldt to this place, but here I have to cross and follow it to my right for two miles, to Iron Point. About eight o'clock I halted, took my cans and filled them with water, but it was a difficult job as the bank was rather steep, yet I always keep a full supply. I watered my cattle and gave them grain and took a lunch myself, eating my breakfast on the bank of the river. My dog was beside me, the dog growled and on looking around I saw a man on horseback coming towards me. As he came up he said, "How do, sir?" I replied, "How are you, my friend." He was an Indian, with a gun and game on his back, I offered him a bite of some bread and cheese. He took it and thanked me. I found he could speak good English and I asked him many qeustions. I requested him to show me the trail to Stonehouse station. As soon as I was ready we started, he leading, passing the house

I had been directed to take. Keeping on the right of the river, and shortly turning directly down a heavy bank on to a flat mowing, and running at a right flank, till coming to the river, which we forded, still bearing to the right until coming to the railroad. Here he left us. I got the flask of whisky and after tasting myself, handed it to him. He looked at it and tasted, but the drink being so small I handed it back to him again, and then we bade each other good-bye. At this point I was twelve miles from Stonehouse station; and after making five miles more I stopped and milked the cow, giving both the horse and cow their grain. As I was milking, the horse started along and the cow would follow. This provoked me so, that I stepped forward to the horse and took hold of the bridle, and then gave it a jerk, causing her to back; the cow being directly in the rear and being fastened to the wheel, and the horse backing crushed in the wheel completely. This was done about half-past five o'clock and seven miles from Stonehouse station. I had nothing to fix it with. I got a short piece of board that I use when greasing the axles of my carriage to raise it up. I lifted up the axle and put the board under, thus keeping the carriage in its proper position and left it for the night. I secured my cattle to the sage bush, made up my bed on the ground as usual and laid down, but could not go to sleep. In this way I passed several hours; about half-past ten, the train from the west came in sight. I was about a mile to the west of the railroad. All around was quiet, except the call of the coyotte. Morning came, there was no light to be seen and the sun had not yet risen, but it was at least three o'clock. I left my all and went to the next station, Stonehouse. On arriving about five o'clock, there was no one to be seen around. I went to the station and called out at the top of my voice, when a man appeared at the window and asked, "What did I want at this time in the morning?" "Want, I want many things, but at this time more particularly, I want a piece of timber 2x4, fourteen feet long. I am in trouble, my carriage broke down about eight miles back, one of my rear wheels being crushed. I want this timber so that I can bring my wagon here; come out and see if you can find something that will answer my purpose." He came out and after looking around, said "Stranger, there appears nothing suitable around the station. Over there is a corral, I think you may find something there." I went to the corral, saw what I wanted and went back for a saw, and then returned and cut out a piece of timber that I thought just the thing for my purpose and went back to the station. I said to the man, "This timber I took out of the corral, and I purpose to make one end fast to the rocker, letting the timber run under the axle to take the place of the wheel; I would like you to come and assist me." "How far are you from Iron Point station?" "I think about half way. I will get the boys up and we will go and help you." "How far are you from the railroad?" "About a mile, perhaps not so far." "Stop and get some breakfast before returning." "Thank you, I am anxious to get back to my cattle; some one may borrow something I do not care to lend." "You need not fear that, there is scarcely any one passes by." I would not stop, so I took the scantling on my shoulder and returned to my outfit; but the road back seemed long and on my arrival I found everything about as I had left it. For more than a mile I could see the horse, and when within less than a half mile I called her and she came scampering towards me; I had been five hours away from them. I gave them all the water I had in my cans, and fed them with grain. I fixed my wagon as best I could, the way I have already intimated, and had travelled some distance to my right when I saw three men on a hand-car, coming in my direction, who proved to be the station master and two others—when opposite they struck across the lots and came up to me. The station master returned with me and the others went back with the car; we got to the station all right, where I remained all the rest of the day. The station master and his wife were from New York State. They made my stay with them most agreeable. I asked at what time the freight and express trains would arrive, and could I ship the heaviest part of my outfit to Battle Mountain. I thought I would do this as it would be a very hard job for my horse to pull the wag n with only three wheels and a shoe for the fourth. I found that the freight was due at 11:15 p. m., and stops for water and put off freight. I got the articles ready and sent them by the freight. I then made ready for rest, gave the cattle their rations and went to bed. I rested all night only being disturbed by a passing train in the night.

Stonehouse I left early on the morning of the 5th and travelled to Battle Mountain, a distance of nineteen miles that day. The lady of the house was up getting the breakfast ready, I milked the cow and took it into the house. "This milk is a great luxury to us," said the lady. "It will make the coffee much better; we have to use condensed milk, but there is a taste about it that I dislike very much." She called her husband up, telling him that I wished to start off early, and saying, "John, get up, I have some extra good coffee." He got up, saying "I am in for some good coffee." We sat down to a good breakfast, very good to me, and as I start I thank them for their hospitality. They replied, "You are welcome, would like to do it again. Good morning, we hope you will get along when your wagon is repaired, without any further difficulty." It was just half-past five when I left and reached Battle Mountain at half-past twelve o'clock. In reaching this place my road has been good, being hard and solid, the day very fine and hot. On my arrival I went direct to the depot, where I found the freight I had shipped from Stonehouse. I then went to a carriage shop where I found two men at work, one at the forge and the other at the bench. I asked for the proprietor and the man at the bench was pointed out as the person, so I went up to him saying, "Are you the proprietor?" "I am, sir." "I am in a bad fix and would like to be helped out of it. I am travelling and come from California on my way East, and have broken one of my wheels and not able to go any further until it is repaired." He asked where my wagon was, I told him and fetched it so that he could see what was needed. Then I asked him what it would cost to repair it. "There has got to be fourteen new spokes, seven dollars; setting tire, two dollars; painting, one dollar; the job will cost you ten dollars," he replied. "I am in a tight place, all the money I have is eleven dollars and forty cents; you want ten dollars, will you do the job for nine, under the circumstances?" "No sir, not a cent less." "Will you repair the wheel without painting for nine dollars?" "Yes." "When can I have it?" "To-morrow morning," was the reply. The morrow came, I was feeling anxious, blue, and everything looked discouraging. I did not like the place, nor its surroundings; I passed up and down the street, stopping in front of the shop. At noon he had not touched the wagon, but I thought best under the circumstances to keep mum. About four o'clock he commenced work and finished the wood part, the setting of the tire was not done, so I could not start on my journey as I intended and was obliged to remain. I held my temper—said not a word—my horse and cow I kept continually in my sight. While obliged to stop, a reporter came up to me asking many questions, where I was from and where going, which I answered most respectfully. After he had got through with his questions, I thought, perhaps he might befriend me; so I told him how I was situated and the amount I was to pay for repairing my carriage. He answered, saying, "He is a mean, contemptible scoundrel, in taking advantage of a man in this manner; why, he ought not to charge you half that amount." I told him I had but eleven dollars and forty cents, and could not get more until I arrived in Ogden, where I expected to get a check that I had ordered to be sent and retained until my arrival. "Having given you the full particulars I would like your consideration?" He answered, "Come with me." I went with him and he introduced me to a person who he said was a Deputy Sheriff of the county, and related my circumstances to him and how I was being treated by the man who was repairing my carriage. "When does he say it will be done?" asked the sheriff. "He agreed to do it yesterday, but it is not done yet, the tire is not set." "What does he say about it?" "I have not said anything about it, I dare not." "When he gets it done, do not pay him, let me know and I will go down with you; we will talk this matter over with him, I think he will make a reduction; at any rate, we will see what he has to say about it." "It is now about half-past nine o'clock, I will go down and report soon," I said. I went to the shop and asked him if the carriage was done, he said not, but would be soon. About this time there was considerable excitement among the people; the reporter had told it around that there was a man in town who had come from Eureka, California, with a horse, cow, carriage and dog, on his way East, to Massachusetts, which caused the people to gather around, Indians as well. This town is a great place for Indians. (There was another railway running through this place, and the Indians ride free on all the roads.) At this junction they gather in large numbers; I saw more here than in any place on my journey. You remember I have told of an Indian lunching with me on the banks of the river two days ago. This same Indian came to me while

here, saying he had seen me at Iron Point. I did not
recognize him, he being dressed up in such a fine suit of
clothes. He wanted me to get him a pint of whisky,
saying for an excuse, "They would not sell an Indian
any." He gave me the wink to follow him, which I did;
on getting out of sight he handed me a pint flask with a
dollar in silver, telling me to go to such a place and there
I could get it. I did not let any one know about this at
the time; after I had purchased and delivered the whisky
to him, he told me that there was a heavy fine for any
person who should sell or deliver whisky to an Indian; so
you see how shrewd the Indian was, while I was ignorant
of the law. After this I went to see if the carriage was
done, and finding it ready I went to the printing office
and informed the reporter. He, with several others, went
to the shop with me. The reporter went up to the man
and said: "I want to speak to you. You have been doing a job for this man and are charging him ten dollars
for it; if I were having the same done you would not
have charged me more than half that price or less,
you are doing very wrong with this man. He says he has
but eleven dollars and forty cents, and he told you the
same. It is all he has or can get until he arrives at
Ogden. Now, let us come to the point; will you rob that
man and take his money, or half it with him?" The
wheelwright turning to me said, "Give me five dollars,
that will do for this time; when you come again bring
more money; further, if you will stay until to-morrow morning I will paint the wheel for you and charge
nothing for it." I agreed to stop-over and returned with
the reporter; on the way I had to "smile" with him and
others. I was pressed with a thousand questions, which
I answered and became quite familiar with the people and
was frequently pressed to "smile" with them. I expressed anxiety to be with my cattle, or some one might want
to borrow and forget to return them. I was told I need

not fear, I was too old, too honest, for any one to harm me. I was a noble man, and a man of great courage to undertake such a journey as I was on. They hoped I would get through all safe, and if I did, to let them know. A hat was passed around and the contents given me, nine dollars and fifty cents were counted out. Some one in the crowd put in fifty cents more, making ten dollars. I think the above incident is worth recording and give the credit to the boys of Battle Mountain.

On the morning of the 8th I left Battle Mountain, about three o'clock, intending to reach Beowawe the same day, travelling a distance of thirty-three miles. On leaving Battle Mountain I followed the railroad to my right for over a mile, then following the river for some ten miles, when I again came to the right of the railroad to Shoshone station. In making Beowawe I pass two stations, Argenta and Shoshone. I travelled twenty-three miles in nine hours, making only one stop, the road being one of the best. On arriving at Shoshone, twelve miles, I introduced myself to the station agent, who was a boss of repairs, as a traveller from California on my way home. "Where is your home?" "My home is down East." "Where in the name of all that is good is down East?" "Why, way down to Massachusetts, that is down East." "I should think it was; you are one of our Eastern Yankees, are you?" "Yes, I am." "And going to take that cow with you?" "Yes, I intend to." "But you can not do that much, she can not stand it." "But she has, much better than the horse, and will I think." "I am from New York and have been here three years." "You like here, do you?" "It is a good place to save your money, no way to spend it. I get seventy-five dollars a month and board, and no where to spend my money. Stranger, take your horse and cow and turn them into the grass, give them their dinner and come in and take dinner with me, and when you get home, you can say that you dined with John Briggs, of Shoshone, formerly of New York city." I did not wait for a second invitation. Our dinner consisted of bacon and eggs, bread, butter and coffee; you will remember I have always milk with me. After dinner we talked awhile, his Chinamen went to work. I inquired the distance to the next station. He replied, "It is ten miles to Beowawe. About a mile from here take the right trail, leading you over the mountain, it is a less distance, and you will not have to ford the river, which is more mud than water." I left him with good wishes and went on. On coming to the trail I hesitated whether to go over the mountain or ford the river, but concluded to cross the mountain. When about half way up I stopped, I left my horse and went to the top, came back and said to the horse, "Fanny, can you get up this hill with your load; it is a hard pull, but let us try." We went about four rods further, then halted, and then made one more pull for the top which we accomplished. This saved some three miles and we ran no chances in fording the river. The descending was much easier; making the descent we cross the railroad, and from this crossing to the station the road is good. The course of the railroad from Wadsworth to this mountain is north by east. Then turning to the right, making three-quarters of a circle, in reaching Beowawe, a distance of ten miles, where I arrived about six o'clock in the evening.

Beowawe I found on arrival consisted of a depot, section house for the boss of repairs and a Chinaman's house or shanty, and a very respectable house for the entertainment of any travellers. I called on the proprietor of this house, introducing myself as a traveller from the west, bound east, saying "I would like some hay for my cattle and the privilege of camping near by, will you grant my request?" "I will, sir, with pleasure." "That cow I am obliged to milk twice a day, will you take the milk in exchange for something I can eat; I have plenty of milk, tea, coffee, sugar and bread, but crave for something different. I want some cold meat and potatoes, or grub of that kind?" "Follow me with your cattle, I will give you a good place for the night, or you may have a bed in the house if you like." "I prefer to sleep with my cattle, should any one come around in the night my horse and dog tell me of it, sure." After securing the cattle we returned to the house, and after a wash we sat down to supper. On being bade to take a seat at the table, the landlady said, "We have no cold meats, but some hot meats." "This is better; I asked for cold meat as it is much less work to get than hot." Our supper consisted of ham and eggs, hot biscuits, butter and coffee, a first-class supper. After supper the landlord said, "Well, stranger, I am anxious to learn your story, you must have something interesting to relate." "Yes, I have, and I will tell you it if you desire." "I do, very much." "Well, where shall I begin; I am from Eureka city, Humboldt Bay, California, three hundred and thirteen miles north of San Francisco, which I left June 1st, 1882, with a horse, carriage, cow and dog. We came down to San Jose, from there hereto, following the railroad most of the way, nearly 900 miles. I belong in Massachusetts, when at home, and have no other." "That cow; have you come that distance with her?" "I have." "That is ahead of anything of which I ever heard, and going to Massachusetts; you must be crazy, or something else." "You are right, we will call it something else." "But how can the cow travel that distance, I should suppose she would have worn out her feet several times?" "My dear, sir, I have iron shoes on her feet, I could not have got her along so far had it not been for her shoes." "But how have you got along all alone. I should think you would have been torn to pieces by the wild beasts. Have you not been troubled with the wolves?" "They have troubled me at nights, but not seriously. I have had to break camp several times to get rid of them. So far all right. In the future I shall know more about them. How is the road from here to Carlin?" "There are two roads thereto; one way is to follow the railroad, the other is to take the old emigrant road over the mountain, through the canyon, over the divide, down into Carlin. The emigrant trail is much the nearest, and a good road except the canyon, that you will find rough, as all canyons are. I thing you can get through all right, however." "I make a practice of starting early in the mornings, so that I can camp early in the evening; how much shall I pay you for the hay for my cattle?" "Hay, for your cattle, I would not be guilty of charging you for hay or anything else. A man that has set out on such a journey; why, I feel that all on your road ought to feed you and your cattle; such an undertaking. I will go down with you and look at your cattle; come, wife, go with us. You have a fine looking cow, and so is your horse. I hope you will be able to get home all safe and sound; as yet you have but just started. Do you ever take anything strong?" "Yes, I like good strong coffee." "Yes, so do I, but I mean something else." "So do I." "Go back to the house with me." I went with him. "Here, stranger, take this; it is good bourbon, there will be times when it will do you good, at any rate you will think of us." "Yes, I shall often think of you." On leaving me he said, "The freight train from the east is due soon, and often tramps are put off the train who are stealing a ride. If they trouble you, call out and we will come to your help. Good-night, stranger." "Good-night, landlord."

I left Beowawe on the morning of the 9th. I was

awakened by a passing train from the west, and on getting up I found it was a little past three o'clock. I fed my cattle and got ready for an onward move; it was four when I started for Carlin. The first part of the road was on the river side, which soon I had to ford, a good gravelly bottom. After journeying about a mile I came to a fine Eastern built house. A half mile beyond there were many horses feeding by the road. After passing them, they fell in my rear and continued to follow me; I attempted to drive them back, but they took no notice either of me or my dog, whom I set on them. They kept following close behind the cow, which annoyed her. I thought it best to turn back to the house, this being the best way to get rid of them. I returned, they following me, and drove up to the house, but could not see any one around, so I called out loud and strong. This brought a man to the door. I told the man I was travelling East and in passing nearly two hours ago, those horses fell in my rear, I tried to drive them back but could not, so I had returned with them as I did not know how far they would go with me, thinking best to get rid of them. "Well, stranger, I am sorry they have given you this trouble. How far are you travelling?" "I belong East, in Massachusetts." "That is my home also." "What part of Massachusetts is your home?" I asked. "Fall River was my home; where are you from with this outfit?" "I am from California, more than three hundred miles north of San Francisco." "You have come a long distance, and led that cow all that way?" "Yes, sir." "That beats the d—l all hollow." "How is the road from here to Carlin?" "Most of the way is good—you will find it rough through the canyon. I came through a few days ago on horseback, there is no trouble travelling that way. You have a wagon, it will be hard for you to get through with it. There are some washouts, but you will be able to get over them. Stop and get some breakfast with us, we are late this morning, but it will be ready soon. I will give your horse some oats." "I will stop for the grain for my cattle as they need it. I think a great deal of the cattle and have to take great care of them, or I shall not be able to get them through this tramp." "Go in and get a dish of coffee. By the way, will you take something that will help you along?" "Yes, I will, there is nothing better than a good cup of coffee, and I want nothing more. It is just what I need this morning, anything else would be out of place." I had breakfast with them, it was a good one, and with strangers from my own State of Massachusetts. It was seven o'clock as we bade each other good-bye, he hoping that I would get through my journey all right. It was not very long before I was at the top of the mountain; there was a fine landscape before me. To my right I could see a long distance, a vast plain, nothing to hinder or obstruct my view. Some smoke in the distance attracted my attention; it was from an engine and was travelling from me, as it gradually went out of sight. I pulled from my box a map of the Central Pacific Railroad, and found that it was the express train from Palisade to Eureka. I drove down the mountain to its base and came to a trail that led to my right. I concluded this trail took me to Palisade, while my left led to Carlin, which I took. I travelled up grade about a mile to the canyon; the first of the mile was good, but the latter hard and rough. I was obliged to stop on coming to a bad washout and said to the horse, "Fanny, what do you think of this, we can't get over this ditch, it is too big!" I left my team and went on to see in what condition was the remainder of the canyon. Should it prove as bad or worse, I would not attempt its passage, but return and go to Palisade. I did not find anything worse; on my left I found water that evidently came from the Emigrant Springs, which are situated at the head of the canyon, which was as far as I went. I turned back to were I had left my outfit, and found that they had got other company. They had been joined by a band of gypsies, with two large covered wagons, drawn by four horses each. They saluted me as I came up, saying "Stranger, you all alone?" "I am not all alone, I have just received company from the west; two teams of gypsies." I remember passing these teams at Reno, some two weeks ago. "Well, stranger, how does it look to you?" "To me, it looks rough and tough; when I came to this ditch I stopped and then made an inspection of the road to the springs, and find this the worst part." "Can we get through, or shall we have to go back and go by the way of Palisade?" "Here is the worst place to get over, especially with your wagons, as they are much larger than mine. We can get across, but it will take some engineering; there are five of us, beside the women and children." My plan was to take out the horses and lead them across the gulch, then slide the wagons into the gulch, running them up the opposite side of the bank as high as we could, then by putting all the power we could and lifting in the rear, drag the wagons out of the washout, which we did after considerable engineering, hard labor and patience. Having done this successfully, the remainder of the canyon was only rough and stony. The gypsies said, "I had done them a great kindness, and that I understood this kind of business and must be a Yankee, and where was I from?" I answered, "That I was a Yankee, from California and was going to Massachusetts." "We have heard often of the Yankees, but never saw one before; we are from California, but our home is in Salt Lake city." "Then you are Mormons, I have often heard of that people; what horrid people they are. If you are Mormons, I would risk myself with them at any time." "You need not be afraid of us, and we shall remember you as long as we remember this canyon. We have some good whisky in our wagon, which I think was made for this time and occasion, will you have a taste?" "Well, I seldom ever take any, but if you wish me, I will at this time and occasion. Should I ever make a record of this, which I think I shall at some future time, and you happen to see it, you will remember the whole story. It is getting late, we must be going on further." So we moved on, I leading the van; with my light team I could travel faster than they with their large, top-heavy wagons, which would rock to and fro like a ship at sea. It was about half-past ten o'clock when we got to the washout and it was three o'clock as we left. When we reached the springs just out of the canyon, we camped for dinner. After eating and resting we again moved on and gained the top of the mountain. We were delighted with the view, the surroundings were grand and imposing. We reached Carlin just as the sun was setting from our view. I at once made for the hotel and inquired for the proprietor. A person answered, "I am the man of the house." I requested him to go to the stable and see my outfit, and said "I am a traveller, just from California, with the outfit you see. The cow is a fresh cow and I milk her twice a day; she is a fine cow and gives good milk, and I think so much of her that I am taking her along with me. She supplies much more milk than I can use, so will you take the milk in exchange for something that I have not got. This is my way of introduction, will you excuse me, landlord?" "Yes, sir; with pleasure. I saw an account of you in the Reno papers, a few days ago. Then you are the man that is going to Massachusetts?" "I am, sir." "Come in and take supper with us, it shall not cost you anything. Milk your cow and bring the milk in, she looks as though she gave good milk, and we will try it." "Where can I camp, I sleep with my cattle?" "Take them into the yard where those stacks of hay are and let them eat all they can. If you prefer to sleep with your cattle, you can; it is a good place and you will be safe there." I drove into the yard, gave the cattle water and allowed them to eat as much hay as they would. I milked the cow and gave the milk to the landlord, he in return gave me a good supper. "You say that you are going East; you have a long journey before you, do you think you can make that journey as old as you are?" "Why not; I am not too old. It takes a man so old to accomplish it." "I see you are the man for it. A young man would back out before he got half the distance you have already made. What little I have learned of you, unless sickness or accident happens, you are the man to make it a success." I told him that I should leave him early in the morning and thanked him for his hospitality, and that should he ever come to Massachusetts, to remember me and my horse, carriage and cow and come to Webster, and we bade each other good-night, he wishing me success.

On the morning of the 10th I left Carlin for Elko, a distance of twenty-three miles. Leaving Carlin I crossed the railroad and travelled on its left for a distance of ten miles, when I recross the railroad to my right, down on to a flat plat of mowing land, which brings me to the river that I had to ford. It is now a fine trail. I came to a house, which was a poor, shanty and knocked at the door but no one answered. I then went to the barn, which was much better than the house, but could see no one around. I stopped and made a fire, fed the cattle, and got myself a breakfast of boiled eggs and coffee. After breakfast I travelled about a half mile but could not find a trail. I was on the right of the river, close to its bank, but could see no place to ford, on the right was a high bluff rising from the river. I was completely shut in. I returned to the house again but could find no one around, then I retraced my way back to the railroad. On crossing the railroad I saw some men at work a short distance away. I looked around for a place to hitch my horse, but could see no tree or shrub, so I took the horse from the carriage and fastened her to the wheel. I then left them and was just getting on the track to go to the men, when I saw a band of Indians coming down the bluff on horseback; there were eighteen of them, and were about twenty rods away from me. I called out to them to stop; two of them rode up to me and I saluted them, which they returned. I told them that I had come from Carlin and was going to Elko, but had lost my trail; I had been to that shanty but could not find the trail. "Here is the trail to Elko," said the Indian. I should not have crossed the railroad, but have followed it a short distance further and then crossed. I put the horse into the shafts again and went on, travelling on the left of both river and railroad. About a mile further I came to a dry canyon. In passing through, I counted twenty-two dead animals, no doubt frozen and starved to death. When in Elko I spoke of this fact, and was told that it was nothing; thousands of cattle were frozen every winter. Go into the canyons in the months of June and July, you could not bear the stench from these dead creatures. I am now journeying where it is necessary and we are commanded to open and shut gates in crossing the railroads. This command I always comply with. I am travelling on the river, running between Carlin and Elko. I have to open and shut gates as the trail runs from pasture to pasture. Many times I am tempted to cut the wires which fence them in, but I dare not, as I might be followed and made to smart for so doing. I am passing through fine fields of clover, of which I allow my cattle to eat as they go, it is such a change from the dry, barren canyons and roads I have just left. Those that journey on wheels have to make their own trail, which was bad for me as my carriage was light and was very trying to myself and horse. I arrived at Elko just as the freight train came in at half-past five o'clock. I went for the hotel at once and sought out the proprietor, whom I found and telling him my story, said, "My cow is a fine animal, gives good milk and a large quantity. I am short of money and obliged to make what little I have go a long way, will you take milk in exchange for food?" "I will, sir, with pleasure. You are the man for whom I have been looking for some days. I read in a Reno paper and also in a Battle Mountain paper, that a man from California with a horse, carriage, cow and dog was on his way east, and you are the man, I suppose?" "I am, sir." "You are a plucky man, you ought to be following a band of music, with all the people in your rear. Why, stranger, you do not look like a crazy man, you do not, surely. The world moves on, and we read that there is nothing new under the sun, but that is a mistake. They did not have such men as you in those days, you bet. Well, stranger, I am going to give your cattle a good supper, write that down." "I will, sir, with pleasure." Supper was soon ready and he conducted me to the table and told me to take a seat. "But, landlord, I do not care to take this seat, it is too conspicuous." "Not so, I propose to introduce you to my family and guests." The bell rang for supper and when all had come in and taken their seats, the landlord introduced me as follows: "Ladies and gentlemen, it is with pleasure I introduce you to a gentleman from California, travelling with a horse, carriage, cow and dog East, to Massachusetts." After enjoying a hearty supper I was questioned by his family and guests, asking what part of California I was from, which way did I come and how did I get along with the Indians and the wild animals and so on. The landlord commanded his man to take the cattle to the barn and feed them with all the hay and grain they could eat. By this time quite a crowd had gathered about me and many were the questions put to me. I made excuse to the man of sickness and would like to lay down. He told me to take some hay and make a bed for myself, which I did and laid down for a while. I then got up and milked and when about finishing milking the landlord came to me and I handed him the pail, saying, "Here is the milk that I have just taken from this California cow, that I think so much of." He told John, his man, to take it to his wife and put it on ice and when cool he would have a drink of it. "Stranger, won't you go in the house and stay to-night, it will cost you no more and give you a good rest?" "Landlord, I thank you kindly; but prefer to sleep with my cattle." "All right, suit yourself." "I want to leave about sunrise to-morrow morning." He turned to John, his man, and told him to get up early and feed the cattle and give them a heavy feed that night. I thanked him for his great hospitality, had received much on my journey, but his exceeded all others. He replied, "I was welcome, and if he was in my place he would like the same treatment. You had better stop and get a good breakfast before leaving, it will help you along wonderfully. Come in the house about four o'clock and we'll have something hot for you, a bit of steak and a dish of hot coffee, it will do you good."

Elko I left about five o'clock in the morning and journeyed to Halleck station, a distance of twenty-four miles. I arose early, as was my custom, and made all the preparations for the day before any one was up. I called John, the man, to feed my cattle and to get the cook to make breakfast while I was milking. This being done I carried the milk into the kitchen and then breakfast was ready. While I was eating, the landlord came in and bade me good morning and said, "You are about to leave us. I am glad you have made so much of your journey safely, but you have a long distance to make yet." "Yes, sir, I am aware of the fact." "Cook, put this man up something for dinner, and here is something that will help you along." "Landlord, please give me your name?" "My name is landlord, that is enough. I do not want to see my name in print, it will not look well. Stranger, success to you. Good morning." I made ready and started for the day's journey, feeling in excellent spirits; but learned the landlord's name before I left, as I thought I might want to write to him after getting home. It was a bright, lovely morning. About half-past eight o'clock the freight train for the west passed me, and at nine o'clock we came to Osino station. I made a short stop, giving the cattle water and grain; after feeding I continued on my journey, our road being heavy and sandy with sage bushes on either side. At noon I stopped for a short rest and rations for the cattle and then journeyed on until three, when I arrived at Peko station. Here I stopped, giving the cattle the remainder of the water in my cans and feeding them, and to make a dinner for myself made a fire to do my cooking. As I was leaving, the freight train from the east passed and at six o'clock I reached Hallocks station. The surroundings at this station I did not like. I gave my cattle water and went on, taking the trail that led to the right and followed it until I came to a house, which I found untenanted, so I journeyed on still further and came to another house where I found the people at home, and asked "If I could stop there for the night, I having come from Elko and myself and cattle were very tired?" "Yes, stranger, you can, I like the sound of your voice. It is Eastern, if I am not mistaken; you are or have been an Eastern man." "I am. Will my cattle do any harm to let them in to those stacks of hay and let them eat all they want?" "You can let them in there and they can have all they need." I led them into the yard and turned them loose; the horse took to rolling and the cow to the grass. The man of the house asked me in, saying he had a wife and two children and had many questions to ask me. So I went into the house and he said, "Wife, this stranger is going to stop with us to-night, get him some supper while I ask him some questions." "No Sam, wait till he has had his supper, then we all will listen," answered the wife. So as soon as the supper was ready we all gathered around the table and partook of a hearty meal. The man of the house asked for my story, where I was from and where going. I answered, saying, "Well friend, I have come from California, more than three hundred miles north of San Francisco, having left Eureka city, June 1st, following the railroad most of the way and have travelled more than a thousand miles already." "What, and brought that cow that distance?" "Yes, just as I am, horse, carriage, cow and dog." "And where are you going to, I would like to know?" "Well, friend, I belong in Massachusetts, and am going there; that is my intention." "Well, stranger, ain't you a little crazy?" "You are not the first that has thought me so, but as yet I am all right." "Well, well; what a long journey before you, and you think you can make this journey; how many miles will you have to travel to make it?" "About four thousand, perhaps a little more." "Why, that cow can't stand it; she will wear off her feet and legs." "But, friend, she has on her feet iron shoes, and so has the horse. So far, the cow has stood the journey the best." "I did not think she was shod, and should not wonder that the cow did stand it best; does she give milk?" "Yes, I milk her twice a day; I have milked her three, and once four times a day, and have sold milk all along for fifty cents a gallon to the station agents. When I have sold on the trains I have got twenty cents a quart. When I came through Reno, where I got the cow shod, I was obliged to stop four days, as she was lame from the shoeing. This was her first shoeing and as she had travelled more than seven hundred miles her feet were very much worn, and putting on the iron shoes contracted her feet, causing the lameness. The blacksmith told me not to take off her shoes, and the soreness would wear away; she could not have travelled much further without shoeing, so I stopped over. The four days I was at Reno I sold over seven dollars' worth of milk, so you can easily see that she is worth something on the road." "What part of Massachusetts are you going to?" "The town of Webster, Worcester county." "I am from the State of New York, so you see I also come from the East." "What brought you out here?" "Oh, I came out here to get rich by raising cattle." "You have got rich, I suppose?" "Well, I am not rich, but I can make more money by raising cattle than I could by raising corn in Nebraska. We can grow potatoes and small grain, but no corn; we can cut any quantity of hay. You see those four stacks, there are eighty tons of hay in them." "How many cattle have you?" "I have thirty-six head on my own ranche. There are three of us, each having a ranche, about one hundred head of cattle in all." "Do you feed your cattle in the winter?" "Oh, yes; we do not intend to have them freeze to death. We give them shelter and feed with hay. We do not have such barns as you have down East, as lumber is too costly. We have long sheds fronting to the south, boarded on the north side and ends, about twelve feet wide and seven feet high, covered with straw. This gives our cattle a good, comfortable shelter in a storm and breaks the cold wind. This mode is an improvement of our own, and there are but few in the State like ours." "Friend, it is now about time to milk my cow, can you let me have a pail and I will go and milk her and give them some water and grain." "I will go with you, we have plenty of good water." While I was milking my host came with two pails of grain for my cattle. This was wholly unexpected. I gave the grain to the cattle and then carried the milk into the house, giving it to the wife, when she remarked: "Sammy, what a lot of milk his cow gives, more than all ours put together. Well, stranger, I suppose you would like to go to bed soon?" "Yes, I feel as though I would like some rest." "Any time when you are ready I will show you your room." "But, friends, I always sleep with my cattle; I have had good beds offered me, but I always decline them. I dare not leave my cattle; should some one borrow them I fear they would not return them in season. I carry my bedding, make the cow fast to one wheel and the horse to the opposite and myself and dog lay between them. Many nights I have been awakened by the snorting of my horse. I always keep my lantern burning. Many times I have been awakened by the wolves around me, but as yet have come to no harm. To-morrow I would like to reach Wells, what is the distance?" "Wells is about thirty miles from here; you can not travel to Wells in one day, can you?" "I travel about two and a half miles an hour, day and night if I wish; sometimes I crowd three miles into an hour and some times only two, but I average the two and a half miles. I suppose I am not far from the river?" "The river is north of us, about a half mile, and a half mile from here you ford the river, then there is a good road to Wells." "I must reach Wells to-morrow. I can travel that distance in fifteen hours, with stops, and should like to start at six o'clock. If you make a good fire I will take advantage of it and make myself some coffee. I have some good, that I brought with me from San Francisco, so you see what I carry with me. Well, friends, I will go to bed with my cattle." "Stranger, you had better sleep in the house, it looks like a cold, frosty night; your cattle will be safe." "You do not know that. When coming through Hallecks I intended to have stopped there over night, but things did not suit me, so I came on here. Perhaps some of those I saw may follow me; I have been advised to look sharp after my cattle." So lighting my lantern I left them for the night and went to my quarters, securing the cattle for the night and laid down for sleep.

I left the ranche at Hallecks on the 12th and reached Wells on the 13th, a distance of about thirty miles. It was about break of day as I awoke from my sleep and got up and gave the cattle their liberty to eat hay or grass as they choose, and then went back to bed again. It was a cold and frosty morning. After a little while the owner of the ranche came out to me saying. "Well, stranger, did you sleep well, and could you keep warm during the night?" "I did, sir." 'It is a cold, frosty morning, come into the house, I have a good fire; your cattle are all right and doing well, go in." I took my lunch basket and went into the house; the lady was making the breakfast ready. While this was going on, I went out and greased my wagon, which I do every other day. As I was returning to the house I met my friend with two pails of grain which he gave me for my cattle. After breakfast I prepared to leave and turning to them, said "Friends, what can I say to you for your hospitality; I shall ever gratefully remember you; good morning." "Good morning; success to you, I trust you will get along all right. I should like to hear how you get along on your journey." It was just half-past five o'clock as I left the ranche. After travelling about a mile I came to the river which I successfully forded. My road now lies between the railroad and the river, the latter on my right. It is a fine morning, a fine trail and we are all feeling finely. Shortly we shall leave this long alkalie desert. About half-past six the express train we met and at eleven o'clock we came to a stop. It was where I could get down to the river to water my catttle. Here I made my dinner; while we were resting the emigrant train from the west passed by, the hands on the train saluting us, as they still remembered me and my outfit, and at one o'clock resumed the journey towards Wells, and at half-past two we came to the river once more, that had to be forded again and for the last time I had been informed. I have followed this river, right and left, for more than three hundred miles, crossing and recrossing many times, and only once on a bridge. This ford looked a nasty one, with only about thirty feet of water to cross, the rest appeared to be all mud. I got on to the carriage and spoke to the horse, saying, "Fanny, this is a nasty, muddy hole, but we have got to cross, so let us try it." We went down the bank into the mud, the horse sinking up to her knees at every step and on getting to the water there was good stepping, as we were then on a sunken bridge. Here I stopped to let the cattle drink all they needed, and having drank all they would, I spoke to the horse saying, "Fanny, go on." After stepping about eight or ten feet she left the bridge, got into the mud and floundered over, breaking both of her thugs, and bringing me and the dashboard face downwards into the mud and water, leaving the carriage, cow and dog in the creek. I was a muddy fellow, you bet. My thoughts quickly comprehended my situation; here I was, far from any help and nothing to get my carriage out of the creek with. What to do, was the question; I want two ropes about thirty feet long. First, I detached the cow and the dog from the carriage, then unloaded my goods and secured my horse to a alder tree, let the cow loose to graze for herself and then started for Wells for some means of extricating the wagon out of the creek. I knew that Wells was a large town for that part of the world. The railroad was about fifteen rods to my left. I took the railroad and went on travelling, I think about four miles an hour. About five o'clock I saw a man with two horses about a quarter of a mile from the railroad and went to him; he was travelling West, where he did not just know. He had made a fire and was cooking beans for his supper. I told him the fix I had got in, in crossing the river and was on my way to Wells for two ropes, so that I could hitch them on the forward axles and make them fast to the tug-buckles, then I thought my horse would drag the carriage out of the creek. He replied, "Stranger, if I had not these beans cooking, I would break camp and go back to help you. But I can let you have the ropes, they are on my horses, take them. I can hobble one of them, the other will not then go away and you need go no further." I took the ropes and went back, finding all right but the cow, she was no where to be seen. It was dark, so that I was not able to see any distance. For a few moments I had some peculiar feelings. Where can she be and where gone? On going for the ropes I remembered seeing a herd of cattle, so I thought that she might have strayed off with them. I called for her, "Bessie, Bessie," and the horse would call after me, for a time without success. I continued calling for the cow, when after a time she came scampering back into camp with a large herd of cattle after her. I had been feeling pretty blue, but her appearance cheered me up. I caught and made her fast, giving her some grain. My wagon was still in the creek and in the wagon was a box made to fit the body of the wagon. In this box I kept all needful articles, and now I wanted my lantern and some kerosene oil. I took off my boots, stockings, pants and drawers, put on my overcoat, fastening the skirt tight around my waist and went into the creek and got my lantern and oil, and made the ropes fast to the front axles of the carriage. With the oil I filled my lamp and the balance I poured on the ground and set it on fire. The water I used to wash me. After this I re-dressed and ate a cold supper, not being able to find wood for a fire. Then I fed the cattle and went to bed to rest as I was very tired. During the night I was awakened by the passing express train and the herd of cows that my cow had become acquainted with, kept around the camp all night and disturbed me some.

Early on the morning of the 13th I was up and connected the ropes with the tug-buckles, and then hitched my horse to the ropes and it was not much trouble to drag the carriage out of the creek. I put my things back in the carriage and got all ready for moving on. Just at six o'clock I left Humboldt river and have not seen it since. Reader, should you ever go west by the Central Pacific railroad, nine miles west of Wells, you pass within twenty rods of this ford; so do not forget to look into this ford. I started for Wells about half-past eight o'clock and met the man from whom I had borrowed the ropes. "Good morning, friend; I intended to have started sooner to help you, but my horses had hobbled off some distance and have made me late." "Stranger, all the same, I came out all right; have you any whisky?" "I have some, I got my flask filled when I came through Wells. Let us take a smile. I would rather take a drink with you than any one in this part of the world; how have you got along, I would like to know?" "Stranger, I have got along so far, about twelve hundred miles." "From where, what part of the world, I would like to know?" "Stranger, I am from California, three hundred miles north of San Francisco, and going to Massachusetts." "You never can make that much." "I don't know that, time will tell." "My friend, I hope you will go through all safe and sound, it will be a big feather in your cap, you bet. Well, good-bye to you and I hope you may get along all right." "Stranger, thank you for the loan of those ropes, good-bye." I left him and about nine o'clock entered the town of Wells; as I passed along Main street, a number of men stood in front of the Post Office and one of them sang out, "Here he comes." I was then in their midst and said, "Who comes?" "The man from

California with his horse, carriage, cow and dog and you must be the man, I read about it in the papers. The engineer of yesterday's noon train said he passed you and thought you would arrive here last night." "Gentlemen, here I am, but look at my wagon!" "I see it looks as if you had been in the mud, you must have crossed on the railroad trail on the sunken bridge?" "I did, sir." "You ought to have come by the old emigrant trail, your ford would have been good; how did you get across?" "I drove down the bank into the mud and I found that sometime there had been a bridge, which was now under water. I stopped on this sunken bridge and allowed my cattle to drink all they needed and then spoke to Fanny to go on, when down she went into the mud as quick as electricity; she gave one big flounder, breaking her tugs, I holding on to the lines was dragged over the dash-board into the creek; this accounts for the mud you see on us. I fastened my horse to an alder, went into the creek and detached my cow from the carriage and turned her loose to eat as she choose and then went back for my dog, then I unloaded the wagon and started for this place for something to draw my wagon from the creek; I came within a mile of this place when I saw to my right a man with two horses camping. I went to him telling him in what a fix I was, and wanted the use of two ropes about thirty feet long. He had the ropes and I could have them, he would hobble his horses and I need go no further. I took the ropes and turned back; this morning I made them fast to the wagon and the hame tugs, then the horse dragged the wagon from the creek, then I reloaded my things and here I am." "Stranger, we are glad to see you, come in and have a lunch, you must be faint by this time." "I am, and so are my cattle." "Come in and get some refreshments, and when dinner-time comes around you will not be so hungry." I went in and had a lunch with the stranger and soon became acquainted with many of them.

"Take your cattle down to the stable and give them a good dinner, I will go down with you. John, take this horse and cow, give them all they will eat, hay and grain. This man will give you directions how to feed them. They have come from California and have got still a longer road before them." I went into the hotel and asked for a pail in which to milk, the cow not having been milked since the previous morning; her bag is full and it must be painful. I returned to the barn, milked and took the milk to the hotel; the pail was full, but the cow had not been fully milked. I returned and finished milking and took the remainder to the hotel, saying to the landlord, "What do you think of a cow that gives such a quantity of milk, travelling more then twelve hundred miles?" "I think she is a fine cow and I would like to buy her, but suppose you would not sell. I would not if I was in your place. I would do the best to get her through. When the train arrives from the west, take this milk to the depot and sell it, you can, at ten cents a pint." "Landlord, I would like you to have it for your trouble." "Never mind that, there must be fourteen quarts, it will make you two dollars and seventy-five cents. I will find you a dish that holds just a pint, fill it for ten cents, no one will object paying that price for milk." When the train arrived they ran past the depot and backed on a siding opposite the barn where my cattle were. My wagon was in sight of the train. I went down with the milk and the conductor of the train said, "Well, friend traveller, you are here, I thought you would be along about this time. I have passed you many times, we all know you now, when did you arrive?" "This morning, I intended to have been here last evening, but did not. I have just milked the cow, perhaps some of your passengers would like some, call out to them." He did so, saying "Here is a man from California, going East to Massachusetts, with horse, carriage, cow and dog. There is the carriage and his cattle are in the barn; he has just milked, who wants milk?" The passengers flocked around, also many citizens. I commenced pouring out the milk and was asked, "How much for the dish-full?" "Ten cents," I answered. It was quickly sold. Having disposed of the milk, the passengers asked me a thousand and one questions, which I cheerfully answered. The conductor called all aboard, and after the train had gone I found two dollars and sixty-five cents, the result of the sale of the milk. At this time the gong sounded for dinner and the landlord bade me go in, I saying that the lunch had taken away my appetite. He said, "I am glad of that, you will not eat as much." After dinner I inquired for a harness shop, and was told there was one down street, two doors this side the barn. I went to the shop taking my harness with me and said that I wanted my harness repaired; yesterday my horse broke these tugs in two. "You must have been in a tight place to break such good tugs," said the proprietor. "Sir, I will tell you a part of the story. It is lengthy." I then told him of my mishap and said, "How much are you going to charge me to splice them?" "I will splice them for one dollar, as it is you; if it were any of my customers I should charge them one dollar and fifty cents, but under the circumstances I will charge you but one dollar." "Can you do them this afternoon, as I wish to leave early to-morrow morning?" He agreed to do so, and late in the afternoon I called for the tugs, asking "Have you spliced those tugs?" "I have, they are much stronger than before." "If I mistake not, your charge is one dollar?" "That was the price, but I have concluded to do better than that, I will not charge you anything; you have come a long distance and have a much longer one before you. I do not think you can accomplish the undertaking." "Friend, I thank you for this favor, I appreciate it; my funds are almost exhausted and I can have no more until reaching Ogden. **My cow** is doing finely, her milk helps me much. I sell it when I can for money and when I cannot I exchange it for something to eat. When I left Sacramento she was fresh in milk, she is milked twice a day. I would use what I can and carry the remainder, but it would go sour and I should have to throw it away. I have done this many times, so I have changed my milking time. For instance, if I were at some ranche or station and could part with it, I milked; when away from a ranche or station I did not milk, but let the cow carry it, as it does not sour in the bag. I have taken milk from the cow as many as five times a day and have met tramps who have asked me "If I had anything to eat?" "Yes, my bread is crackers, you can have some." I would then take out from my wagon the lunch basket and hand out the crackers. "Have you any meat?" "No, not a bit." If the tramp was a fair sort of fellow I would milk the cow and give it him with the crackers. This I have done many times; some have offered money, but as yet I have never taken a cent.

Wells is situated on the Central Pacific Railroad, about two hundred and twenty miles from Ogden. It is a smart, lively, business town. Large amounts of freight are brought here, left and taken by teams to the mountains and mining camps. On entering the town from the west, you travel up Main street; on your left are the railroad and station house; on your right is a long block of buildings, mostly brick. These buildings are mostly occupied by stores, with many kinds of merchandise. Post Office, express offices and a hotel with a livery stable. On the side streets are blacksmith, carriage and harness shops.

On the morning of the 14th I left Wells. About eight o'clock I reached Cedar station. This is simply an accommodation station for the drawers of wood; on my right there is cedar timber in abundance. So far my trail has been good but hilly, the surrounding country rolling; no more alkalic deserts for the present. Two miles further I came to Moores station. This is a section station, and I made a stop here to feed and water the cattle. A lady from a house close by came out to me saying, "You are travelling?" "Yes," I replied. "You have a fine looking cow; do you milk her?" she asked. "I do; she has not been milked this morning, would you like some milk?" "Yes, indeed; milk is a luxury here," said the lady. "How much would you like?" "I will take a gallon; how much do you ask for a gallon?" "Fifty cents a gallon to the stations, when I sell to passengers on the trains I ask more." "Fifty cents a gallon is what I pay when I can get it; I will take a gallon," said the lady. I sat down and milked my can full, which holds just a gallon. She paid me for the milk and said, "If you come this way again, please call if you have your cow with you, I will take some more milk of you. Goodbye," she said as we parted. At Wells I was informed that at Independence I should find grass in abundance. On our arrival I found some grass, but more cattle than grass. There was a large meadow fenced with wire and when we came to this fence I stopped; the trail had been fenced in. I turned sharp to my right and crossed the railroad, going on until we came to a small creek; before crossing I looked around and saw a herd of cattle rushing after me and we were soon surrounded by them. I should think there were seventy-five of them. I was a little frightened, so was the cow, but the horse was not. I took the dog out of the wagon and set it at the cattle, which made them scamper away. Then I crossed the creek over a plank bridge and followed the trail, in fact, the road, as money had evidently been expended on it. I went on leaving the railroad on my left, and in front a high bluff or mountain range. I saw that I was leaving the railroad to my left, and supposed the track was obliged to go round the other side of this mountain and my trail would come on it again, so continued onward. The sun was fast going down. I crowded along as the day was getting darker and I could see no houses, but to my right there was a light. I think the horse saw this, for as soon as the horse came to the trail she took it, and after travelling about forty rods we came to a log-cabin. Two men were standing in front, to whom I said, "Good evening, gentlemen." "Good evening, stranger." "I am travelling East; am I on my right road to Ferrice?" "You are not; you are from the west, I suppose, as you answer to the description of the man that is travelling from California to Massachusetts. When you were at the creek near the railroad you should have taken the trail to the depot, this side of the bridge." "Must I turn back?" "Yes, you will have to return to the depot." "Can I stay here to-night; I see you have hay and I would like some for my cattle?" "Yes, you can have all the hay you wish and I will not charge you a cent." "I carry grain, and when not able to find grass or hay, I fall back on grain." "There is the hay, help yourself to what you want; down there a few rods, you will find water, and good at that." Taking my basket to the cabin I asked permission to make some coffee. "Yes, if you like, but, stranger, you can take some supper with me." "Thank you, I have plenty to eat, as I carry tea, coffee, sugar and milk." I see you have a fine looking cow, does she give milk?" "She does, I will milk her and you can have the milk, it may be a luxury to you."

At five o'clock on the morning of the 15th I left Cabin Ranche for a return to Independence station. My taking the wrong trail had made fourteen miles of extra travel. About half-past seven I reached the station and rested a short time, giving water to the cattle and then went on.

At half-past ten I made Otego station, giving grain and water to the cattle and preparing a lunch for myself, and after resting one hour went on. My trail was not as good as usual, hilly and rough. At two in the afternoon we passed Pequoy station, but did not stop until I reached Toano station. Here I stopped for a feed, making a fire I made some coffee, it tasted good and was refreshing. I spread my blankets and laid down for a while. There was a good moon, so I concluded to travel a while longer, and broke camp at eight o'clock and went on. My trail had improved, it was not so hilly, but sandy. About half-past ten o'clock p. m., we reached Loray station and passed through without stopping. A little after midnight the express train from the west passed and at two o'clock the express from the east. I had almost reached Monticello station. On making this place a little later I stopped, all of us being very tired. I hitched the horse to a telegraph pole, spread my blankets and laid down on them, being very tired I was soon slumbering.

On the morning of the 16th I was awakened about five o'clock by a passing train and got up, the sun had not yet risen, but I thought it was late. I am a great talker to my cattle, having no one else to speak to, and said, "Well, Fanny, how are you this morning; you must want some water about this time?" I fed them with grain and gave them water, greased the wagon and went onwards. At nine o'clock we reached Tecoma station; this is a telegraph station. On entering the town, on my right I saw a stack of hay and I drove along side of it giving the cattle a chance to eat, which they did right smart. After a little while a Chinaman came along, saying nothing and passed on. Soon he returned with another Chinaman and on coming up to me said, "Your cattle eat my hay." I took from my pocket a dime and gave it to him; he took it seeming much pleased. I then told them I was from

California. "Yah, you from California?" "Yes, I am from California and going to Massachusetts." "Yah, here take dis money, you go to Massachusetts." "Keep it," I said. "No, no-keepee, you go to Massachusetts," said the Chinaman. When the morning freight train from the East arrived, about half-past four o'clock, three tramps were ejected from the train, having stolen a ride from Kelton; they were about twenty years of age and rough appearing fellows. They had been prowling around some four or five hours, came where I was camping and began asking questions quite familiarly. They said they were from the east, and I asked them what part of the East? "From St. Louis," they answered. "Where are you going?" "To California." "How long have you been on the road?" "About a month; will you give us something to eat, we are hungry?" "Have you no money?" "Not a cent." "And going to California without any money. You will be hungry all the way." "We have had no money since we left Ogden." "Where did you get on the cars last night?" "We got on at Kelton and rode to this place, when we were put off." I got my lunch basket and a four quart measure that I use to measure out the feed for my cattle, I filled the measure with crackers and got a can of salmon, having two, milked the cow until I had about four quarts and gave them to them saying, "Here, boys, is your milk, salmon and crackers, it is the best I can do for you." "This is more than we asked and hope we shall do as well to-morrow." While they were eating I got ready and started, leaving them eating their breakfast. I went to the depot for a sack of grain, but having forgot to take my milk can, I went back for it, saying, "Well, boys, how do you make out?" "First rate, you are every inch a man; we wish we could meet you every day." "Have you drank all the milk?" "Yes, long ago." I got the can from them and started for Terrace, it was just half-past ten o'clock.

It has been my custom to follow the railroad as close as I could, so that should I become sick or disabled I could have ready access to the railroad, This custom I have generally adhered to. I have often been told that the old emigrant trail was always the best, and now I am advised to keep the old trail to Terrace, and on leaving this station there is but one trail for some distance. I took this trail, travelling with the railroad to my right, until about one o'clock in the afternoon when I came to some grass, known as bunch grass. This grass grows in bunches, some as large as a bog. The small bunches look beautiful, on the alkalic plains and among the sage bushes. I stopped here, taking the horse from the carriage, removed her harness and turned her loose, and the cow also. This they enjoyed for about an hour and at two o'clock we resumed our journey. In front of us was a mountain, a noble looking fellow. It appeared to be about five miles away, yet it might be twenty-five. We went on, the railroad was out of sight, I could not see a telegraph pole and began to feel uneasy, and wished I had taken the other trail. The more I thought, the more foolish I felt and concluded to change my course. All around me was a flat surface; the sage bushes were quite thin and scattering, and I was bound to find the railroad that I had left to my right. I had been travelling east by the sun. I then struck out on a south-east line and continued on that course for two hours; the sun almost down and no railroad in sight. I changed my course to the right and just as the sun was dropping out of sight I came to the railroad. I then changed my course to the left and came on the railroad trail near to Bovine station, which I soon reached. It had got dark and cloudy, no moon to be seen. My lantern was minus oil, I having neglected to fill it. I poured some oil on the ground and set it on fire, then I filled the lantern by its light. Having a light, I then saw a house close by and went to it, to ascertain if I could get water. I knocked at the door and a voice asked, "Who is there?" "Madam, I am a stranger and have come a long distance; I have a horse and cow and would like some water for them, they have not tasted since morning. I want some good, I dare not give them alkalic water. All the way from Wadsworth I filled my cans from the cisterns at the stations." "Where have you come from?" asked the lady. "I have come from California, am going East to Massachusetts, which is my home." "I dare not let you in, my husband has not yet come home, he will be here soon." "I do not care to come in, all I want is water for the cattle." I had to wait. I went back to the camp and gave the cattle some grain and got ready to go to bed; as I was about to retire the freight train from the west passed by. I made my cattle fast to their post, went to bed and soon fell asleep. About one a. m., I was awakened by a passing train, which came to a dead stop. Two men got off the train and went to the house. Soon after these men came to where I lay; my lantern was hanging on the hub of the wheel, burning. I called out, "Halt! advance and give the counter-sign." They stopped, right short. "We have just got off the train and went into the house where we belong. I am boss of repairs. My wife said there was a man on the other side of the railroad, with a horse, carriage, cow and dog from California, going East, to Massachusetts; is that so?" "It is, I told her every word of it." "Is that true?" "It is true; I have come from California and it is my intention to go East, to Massachusetts." "Stranger, come into the house and take a bed, you shall be welcome." "Friend, I thank you; I never have left my cattle alone over night. All times, day and night, I am with them. I do not intend to have any one take my horse or cow without my knowledge." "Your cattle will be safe here." "Perhaps they would, but I do not intend to take any chances. Friend, my cow ought to be milked, she has not been milked since yesterday morning, she will be more comfortable; you get me something to milk in and you can have it." He went for a pail and I filled it, about four quarts. He took the milk into the house and gave it to the lady. "Stranger, there will be a train from the west soon, is your horse afraid of the cars?" "No, not the least, but the cow is." "Well, stranger, if you will not come in and sleep, we shall have to leave you for the night. Good night."

Bovine station I left early on the morning of the 17th, for Terrace. It was a dark, cloudy morning, looking as though it would rain at any moment, and should it rain there was no place for shelter. I said to myself, the next station is eleven miles; I must make it, rain or no rain. At half-past five I moved on, and at half-past six I heard thunder; it was dark, too dark for that time in the morning, so I crowded along as fast as possible; remember it is all walk. Again I heard thunder and kept talking to my horse, saying "Go on, Fanny." I was sure we were going to have something terrible; it was something new to have rain, I had seen nothing like it. To my right I could see a long distance, many miles; so flat was the surface. After having made about five miles, I saw to my right a very dark cloud, a black cloud. Thunder and lightning were more frequent and such streaks of lightning and thunder I never before witnessed. I stopped and made things on my wagon as fast as I could, put on my rubber coat and went as fast as I could. Every streak of lightning went to the ground, the thunder was terrible. It seemed to me, as if it had got out of patience with the lightning and was bound to smash things generally. The rain came but it was of short duration; then followed hail, as large as hen's eggs and it fell with great force, striking on the head of the horse. I stepped back to the wagon, pulled out a sack and threw it over the horse's head. Here I stopped for the storm to pass over. The cloud passed on and left behind it hailstones to the depth of four or six inches. This made it fine travelling on alkalic soil. I had about six miles to go so we went on. It took me three hours to travel that distance, less than two miles to the hour. On my arrival in Terrace I was informed that it was the severest storm ever known there.

Terrace is situated on the Central Pacific Railroad, about one hundred and twenty-five miles from Ogden. It is a station of the first-class; here the railroad has a machine shop for the repairs of the rolling stock, which gives employment to many hands; this makes it a stirring town. You enter the town from the west on its Main street; on the right are the machine shops and a little further is the station; on your left, there is a long block of buildings in which all kinds of business is carried on; a post office, several stores, saloons and many boarding-houses.

On the morning of the 19th I left Terrace for Kelton. It was six o'clock when I started; the morning was cold and cloudy and I hesitated about starting, but being anxious to reach Ogden, I went on. I was told after travelling a mile to cross the railroad, as the trail on the south side was the best for travelling. My trail was anything but good. Having made the first mile and could see no crossing I stopped and looked for it, but found none. I carry four pieces of wood, two by four feet long. This timber I put on the side of the rails so that my carriage wheels would run over the rails without straining my wagon. At first-class stations there is timber laid for the crossings. I looked around for a suitable place to cross and found a good one; I laid my timbers and crossed the track and struck a good road and went on with good cheer. About noon I made Matlin station and stopped, gave my cattle a feed and went to the station. Here I found a man sitting reading a newspaper beside a stove; I passed the compliments of the day with him, and said "I am travelling East to Ogden, will you give me the privilege of making some coffee on your stove?" "Oh, yes; with pleasure." I made some coffee, boiled some eggs and ate my dinner. "You say you are travelling, how far have you come?" "I have come a long distance; from California." "What part of California?" "The north-western part, three hundred miles north of San Francisco, Eureka city, Humboldt Bay." "I know where that is. It is a large lumbering place, and you have come all that distance, with that horse and cow?" "Yes, sir; I have." "Which way did you come?" "There is only one way to come with a team; the overland road to the city of San Francisco, through Humboldt and Mendocino counties, through Ukiah to Cloverdale; which is the terminus of the North Pacific Railroad." "When I went there it was by the steamer Humboldt, and you have come all that distance. Well, well; you are a brick, well-burned; you say you are going to Ogden?" "Yes, sir; but I do not intend to stop there long; to be short, I am on my way to Massachusetts." "Is Massachusetts your native State?" "It is not, but it is my home. I went from Massachusetts to California and I am now on my way back." "Well, well; I am from Maine. I went from Maine to California to work on the lumber, but did not like California, so I concluded to return home, to Maine. I became acquainted with a man that was going to Terrace to work and I came with him, and here I am instead of Maine. Do you honestly think you can get your horse, carriage, cow and dog in this way to Massachusetts?" "Yes, I honestly think I can." "Well, I hope you can, but it is a big thing; you will find it so before you get there." "I am aware of it; by the time I get there I shall have travelled four thousand miles. But, friend, I must leave you." I returned to my cattle and found that the horse had not eaten her grain, so I gave it to the cow and she soon ate it up. It was now almost raining, there being a heavy, cold mist. No sheds being nigh in which to shelter, I go on to Ombey, which is ten miles further. Travelling on until about five o'clock, I came to some grass; here I stopped and allowed the horse and cow to have their fill of it, and they seemed to relish it well. "Well, Fanny; we must make the next station, Ombey." We moved on and reached there about half-past six. This is a section station, a house for the boss and a shanty for his Chinamen assistants. I went to the house and in answer to my call, a man came to the door asking, "What do you want, stranger?" I answered, "I am travelling with a horse and carriage and have come a long distance, as far as from California, and have led a cow that distance; to-day I have come from Terrace. It has been a hard day for my horse and she is not feeling well, having refused her dinner at Matlin. Now, friend, what can you do for my cattle and me?" "I have no shed or wood-house for your cattle, but I can find a place for you." "Friend, you have got what I want some distance back, that would suit me." "What is that?" "It is your hand-car shed." "I never thought of that, you can use it for your horse and cow." This hand-car house was but a short distance from the boss of repairs house. He went with me and ran out the hand-car and put in my carriage, horse and cow. "Friend, I am all right now; will you give me some- think to milk in, and I will give you the milk?" The lady of the house handed me a pail in which I milked and filled it full, and gave it to the lady. By this time the lady had made some coffee expressly for me. I carried in my lunch basket, but it was not needed, as she had provided plenty of eatables. After supper many questions were asked, such as where I was from, where going, how long had I been on the road, and whether or no I would ever make Massachusetts. "Friends, I am tired and would like to retire; if you will go with me to the shed you may lock me in, but must let me out in the morning." "You may stay in the house if you wish." "I prefer to sleep with my cattle; I have done so every night since I left California." We went to the shed, found all right and the cattle seemed satisfied with their quarters. I gave them water and grain, made up my bed and laid down for the night; the stranger saying as he left me, "I think it is best not to lock you in; should anything happen, you will be able to get out and let us know." "Very well, perhaps that would be the best; good night." My thoughts of accidents troubled me until the trains which meet at this station had passed, then I slept soundly the rest of the night.

On the morning of the 20th I was up as usual getting ready to move onward. I gave the animals their breakfast and was greasing the wheels of my wagon when my friend of the station came along. "Well, stranger, I see you are making ready to go on; how did you sleep last night?" "Well, the first part I slept with my eyes open, and the latter much better with them closed, the trains having passed." "Our breakfast is about ready, come in and have a dish of hot coffee. It takes milk to make good coffee, I find." "Yes, it improves it very much." I went and took breakfast with them, and as I was leaving said to them, "Friends, I feel very grateful to you for the kindness to me. I am sure, could my cattle speak, they would also; good morning." "Good morning," was answered. "Take the first right trail after crossing the railroad, it is the best and the nearest." It is just six o'clock as we move on another stage of our journey. After crossing the railroad I left the road to my left, my trail taking me down into the canyon, while the railroad went around, both coming together again before reaching Kelton, which place I reached at eleven o'clock. I drove down to the stock yards and asked the proprietor if he would sell me some hay to bait my horse and cow. "Lead your cattle into the yard and we will feed them on hay." "How much will you ask me?" "Fifty cents a head." "Will you sell me some to take outside of the yard?" "No, not a pound." I went down town, coming to a small barn. I stopped and went into the barn and heard some one say, "Whoa, Fanny, whoa." On looking around I saw a lady putting a saddle on a horse and I said to her, "Madam, I have just come into town and stopped back at the stock-yards to see if I could buy some hay for my cattle; I have a horse and cow. I am a traveller, I have come a long distance and still have a longer distance before me." "Where are your cattle?" "Outside the barn." She stepped out, saw them and said, "You have a fine looking cow; where have you come from?" "I have come from California." "Not with that horse and cow?" "Yes, I have." "Drive to the barn, take the horse out of the carriage and lead her into that stall, put the cow into the next and give them all the hay they wish; there is grain, help yourself," said the lady. I did as told. "How long do you intend to stay?" she asked. "I would like to stop over until to-morrow morning. The cow gives milk, but she has not been milked since last night." "I would like the milk, I keep an eating-house on Main street; I will get a pail for the milk," she said. She brought me the pail, I milked and gave it to her, when she said, "This is a fine mess and a large quantity of milk. I would like that cow; come in and have some dinner." I took dinner with the lady and as we were about to leave the table, a gentleman came in and sat down to dinner. The lady said, "This is my husband, stranger. This man says he has travelled from

California to this place with a horse, carriage, cow and dog, and is going East, to Massachusetts." "Then you are the man I read of in some Western papers?" he said. "I am, sir." "You are a gritty fellow to undertake such a journey. There is not a young man that dares do as much." "His cattle are in our barn, go and look at them after dinner." "I will, wife." He went to the barn and looked my cattle over, saying "He has got a fine looking cow and a good one." "John, look in this pail and see what a large mess of milk he has taken from her," said the lady. The husband left, but as he went out he told everybody that I had arrived, and the people came to see me. The landlord said to a friend, "Bill, the man from California has got along with his horse and cow; they are in my stable, come and look at them; my wife thinks everything of the cow." They came. "Well, stranger, you have a fine horse here." "Yes she is a Morgan mare." "I see she is. Where is the cow?" "Here she is." "She is a daisy; handsome and beautifully marked. Have you come from California with this horse and cow?" "I have, sir." "You are a brick, well burned. If you succeed in this enterprise we will run you for next president." "Over the left. Landlord, where shall I find a blacksmith to repair my carriage?" "I will go with you and introduce you to the blacksmith." We went to the blacksmith's shop, the landlord saying, "Jack, this man wants some work done on his carriage. He has come a long distance; in fact he is the man we read of in the papers who is travelling from California to Massachusetts. His horse and cow are now in my barn; what you do for him remember to do it well and cheap." "Yes, I will remember; where is your carriage?" "Over at the stable, let us go and look at it." We went back to the stable and the blacksmith examined the carriage and found that a bolt would make all right, so he went back and got a bolt and put it in its place; when the job was done I asked him

"How much shall I pay you?" The blacksmith answered, "I have done as John wished me. I have put in a good bolt, it is well done, and for cheapness I will charge you nothing. A man travelling as you are, should be kept in good running condition." "Thank you, sir; I will remember you in my last will and testament." "You have a good looking horse, and I think she is as good as she looks. The cow is a beauty; it is wonderful that she has stood the journey so well. I should suppose that she would have worn out her feet several times." "You see she travels on iron." "Oh, I see, she has on shoes made of iron. You are all right."

Kelton is a first-class station, about ninety miles from Ogden. It is the most northerly on the Central Pacific Railroad. Large amounts of freight are brought and left at this station, then carried by teams to the mountains around, Idaho city, Bois city, Albion, and other places.

On the morning of the 21st, I was up as usual, that is, early, getting ready to leave. I was strongly urged to stay and get breakfast before starting. Having been well cared for I could but stop; a good breakfast was at my disposal. While getting my breakfast I inquired for the lady of the house, when soon she came. I bade her good morning and said, "I am about to leave you and thought I would like to bid you good-bye." "Why need you start so early?" she said. "It is my custom; if I make an early start I can make a long or short day as I chose. I am informed that I shall have many sloughs to get through, some of them are deep and will be troublesome to get through." "Yes, I am afraid you will, and bad to get over, the rain we had a day or two ago made the marshes bad. I suppose it will be of no use to offer you any more than I have already done for your cow?" "Madam, you have already offered me more than she is worth. I have been told many times that I could not get her East. At all times I have thought to the contrary, and it is my desire to give it a fair trial. The cow has not been milked this morning, but I intend to, give me a pail and I will milk her. I milked and gave the lady the milking, saying, "My dear friend, this is all I can do. I have but one dollar; that is all the money I possess. I have as much grain as will last me to Corinne. Then I can get a sack and have as much as will pay for the same." "Stranger, your cow has paid your bill and more. Here is a lunch for the day," she answered. "Thank you, good morning." "Good morning, I hope you will get along all right."

It was just six o'clock as we left Kelton and on passing the blacksmith's shop he called out to me, "Here, friend traveller, is something you will need after crossing the sloughs. It's worth all I ask. You can not travel until you get rid of the mud; you will know more after you have crossed one." "What do you ask for it?" "Oh, I sell cheap. It will be nothing to you, that is cheap enough." After thanking him I moved on, soon coming to one of these sloughs. These sloughs are flat or level pieces of land, of from forty to one hundred rods in length, composed of sand, mixed with salt and alkali. When rain falls on this soil, it becomes soft like mortar, for plastering. It is not deep, from one to three inches, but its adhesion to the boots, wheels or feet of animals is very strong. I drove on to this slough, mud we will call it. As I walked through, my feet seemed to double in size; so did the horses and cows, and the rims of my wheels became very thick and clumsy. It does not fall off as ordinary mud will; it hangs like a load-stone until you scrape it off with some instrument; the blacksmith had given me the right kind of an instrument, it was nothing more of less than a shovel; the blade was two inches wide, three inches deep, and about one-eighth of an inch thick and about one foot long. After crossing one of these sloughs, I would have a half mile or more of good road before coming to another. After passing through one, I would clean off the mud from my boots, the horse's and cow's shoes and from the rims of my wheels, but with the latter I was not so particular. I found it best to remove the mud at once before it became dry, as it hardened as quick as cement. In travelling about seven miles I crossed five of these sloughs. At noon I stopped, giving my cattle water and grain and took a bite myself. About half-past one we passed Monument station, making no stop, and about four o'clock I made Lake station, or the salt works. Here I stopped and then went to the Lake. This lake is the most northern part of the big Salt Lake; from the railroad to the lake is not more than forty rods. At this point of the lake the water is very dark and blue and very strong of salt; seventy-five per cent. stronger than the Pacific Ocean. Here I was advised to leave the railroad and take the old emigrant trail, which would bring me out on the railroad near to Promontory; both Royal and Promontory will be left on the right. Should I continue on the railroad trail I would encounter many sloughs. I was told that two days ago, two teams attempted to come through on this trail, and one of the wagons had to be left in one of these sloughs. Crossing the railroad, I took the left trail as advised, and coming to a small creek I stopped. I took my pail and filled it with water, I tested it and found it of a salty taste and hesitated about giving it to my cattle, not knowing what its effects might be on them; both were thirsty, so I gave them a drink of it and moved on passing Salt Springs. It was not yet time to go into camp, so we continued further. In front of me there was a tall mountain. My trail had been good and still was excellent, could not desire better; but what would be next I could not tell. I went on and soon came to another trail leading to my right; this is the old emigrant trail from Ogden to Corinne, Kelton, Terrace, Wells and on to California. The mountain which was in front is now on my left, soon there will be one on my right, and then I shall be between two mountains; this is known as the divide. From the west to these mountains the ascent is sharp and heavy; from the east the ascension is not so sharp, but it is long. From the west to reach the summit is two miles, but from the east it is nine miles, showing plainly the difference in the grade from the East to the West. When I reached the summit it was quite dark, so we went into camp, making the horse fast to the right rear wheel and the cow opposite, I gave them some grain, made up my bed and laid down, but sleep there was none for me, it appeared the longest night on my whole journey.

On the morning of the 22nd I was up before there was any light in the east, and waited anxiously for its appearance so that I could move on. I got up and gave the cattle their grain, but they would not eat it as they were so thirsty; the salt water I had given them was the cause. Soon I saw a light in the sky, which I thought was in the south, but which I found came from the east. I was anxious to move on to get rid of the noise and the presence of the wolves, which had been around us all night. Not being able to get any wood for a fire I was obliged to keep my lantern burning; but that was not enough, they were so bold. My dog I kept tied up that he might not go for them; once I came very near losing him by setting him on a coyotte. This animal turned on him and I had to go to his rescue to save him; since then I have chained the dog at night. The lantern alone not being enough to keep the wolves away, I poured oil on the ground and set it on fire and used about three quarts; I have often done this before. It having now grown light I moved on, leaving my camp about five o'clock. My road was a down grade and about six o'clock, just as the sun was coming up, I saw to my left a herd of horses some distance away. Grass was in abundance on either side, so I thought I would stop and give the cattle a chance to eat it, but changed my mind and went on. They were so thirsty that I thought they would not eat enough to do them any good, as it was water they wanted and must have. I urged them on and travelled now at a gait of three miles an hour, and at eight o'clock we came in sight of the railroad. I was glad of it and I think my cattle were also; I have an idea that they knew some things as well as I did, "and don't you forget it." Soon I was on the railroad trail that I had left at Lake station. On my left is a mountain; the old trail goes over it, the railroad trail runs around it with the track. From this point over the mountain to Blue Creek, is three miles; from the same point by Blue Creek station, by railroad is fourteen miles; by crossing the mountain I save eleven miles. This is one of the instances where many miles might have been saved, if I had not determined to follow the railroad where possible, and which I have done most of the way.

I am now at Blue Creek station. Here I have access to water, taken and brought by rail from Bear river to this station. My first care was to water my cattle as they have had none since yesterday morning, except the little salt water I gave them. I gave each two pails at once and after a little while gave them two more and then their grain, but they wanted more water, so I again gave them two pails each; this appeared to satisfy them.

Blue Creek is a telegraph station, in charge of a Mrs. Nichols and son, formerly of Vermont. She is a lady in its true sense. After making myself known, she seemed quite anxious to do all possible for our convenience. She asked me many questions, which took up some time, then she said, "Stranger, I am going to get dinner ready. I am out of most everything that makes a good dinner, but will do the best I can." "Madam, I see you have some fine looking peaches, I have not tested them, but their looks I admire. Now, let me make a suggestion; I have a cow that has given me milk ever since I left Eureka and she has not been milked to-day. Have you ice? I will go and milk her. Now, what I want, is some of those peaches and milk, simple and good; madam, what have you to say?" "Well, stranger, your milk I think much of; it will be a luxury to me and my son, all the milk we get comes from the city. Now, can I not get something you would like better?" "I don't think you can; I really would like some of those peaches in milk. There is another point, I cannot stop long, I must make Corinne to-night; what is the distance?" "To Corinne is seventeen miles." "It will take me seven hours to make that distance; it is now half-past eleven o'clock. If we start from here at one, we shall get there about seven or half-past." "Well, bread and milk it shall be," said the lady. "I would rather call it peaches and milk it shall be." "It won't take long to get that dinner," she answered. "That will suit me better; the dish of peaches and milk takes the place of meat. If you have something that would be good to come after, bring it on, we will look at it quickly." While she was getting it ready, I gave my cattle some more grain, so that we all would be ready to move at one. The dinner was soon ready and we sat down to a dinner that I shall long remember. At one o'clock I bade the lady good-bye, thanking her for the hospitality I had received. I kept on the old trail, following it for some four miles. I found that this trail went to Corinne, but it was going to make twenty-five miles more of travel, so I at once left this trail and struck across to the railroad trail coming to Quarry station. From this place to Corinne was a good road all the way, and we reached Corinne about dark. A little distance off I saw a man with a lantern go into a barn, and I went for him as he was coming out and said, "Good evening. Friend, I have just arrived in town; I have a horse and cow and wish to stop for the night; I would like some hay for my cattle; can you accommodate me, sir?" "I have hay; stranger, which way are you travelling, sir?" "I am travelling East." "Travelling East, sir," he repeated and then stepped out to where my cattle was. "You say you have come from the west, sir. What part of the west?" "From California." "What, with that horse, carriage and cow; you must be the man I read about in a western paper, who is going East?" "Yes, sir; I think I am. The papers are ahead of me." "Lead your horse up to the barn, take her from the carriage, remove the harness and put her in that stall; the cow, what shall we do with her?" "She will stand beside the horse, she knows her very well." "Well, put the cow beside the horse and give them all the hay they will eat; grain, do they know what it is?" "Yes, sir; they have had grain every day since I left home." "Home! where is your home?" "My home is in Massachusetts; when I said home, I meant where I started from." "What part of California did you start from, sir?" "From the northern part, Eureka city, Humboldt Bay." "That is a long distance; more than a thousand miles." "Yes, sir; more than three hundred north of San Francisco." "Well, sir; you have done well, but you have not gone half the way yet." "No, sir; not more than a quarter." "Come into the house and get something to eat, your cattle are doing well." We went into the house, my host saying, "Wife, here is a man that has travelled more than thirteen hundred miles, with a horse and carriage, and leading a cow all that distance. This is the man we read of in the papers coming from California to Massachusetts. I have just put his cattle in the barn and they are feeding on hay, and I asked him in to get something to eat; what have you got that is good for him? I think he is worthy of something good." "I can give him such as we have had for supper." "Can't you do a little better? I do not think we shall ever put up another man that has travelled that distance with a single horse, carriage and leading a cow. No, I think this is the last man, I am sure he is the first. Go on, and what you omit to-night, make up in the morning." "You are right, sir; madam, do not trouble yourself in the least." "Stranger, sit up to the table and take a lunch; to-morrow morning we will have something to make up for this." After supper I went back to the barn and gave the cattle more hay and some grain. Then I did not recollect having loosened my dog, so I went and got him and returned back to the house. The wife then asked, "Has that dog too, come all that way?" "He has," I answered. "Oh, you little beauty, you shall have some supper." "Well, stranger, there are many questions I would like to ask you, but you must be weary; how far have you come to-day?" "I do not know the distance; yesterday I left Kelton, taking the railroad trail as far as Lake station. Then I left the railroad trail, following the left trail over the mountains, or divide, coming back into the old trail and on reaching the summit I camped there." "Have you come from there to-day?" "I have." "You have travelled thirty miles; wife, think of that! Thirty miles that cow has travelled in one day." "I travel two and a half miles to the hour, day or night. If I travel ten hours, I make twenty-five miles; I left Blue Creek at one o'clock and have come seventeen miles since that time. It is not a hard pull but a steady one; how far is it to Ogden?" "Thirty-five miles." "To-morrow I will make there, it is a good road

I suppose?" "Yes, it is a good road. We Mormons have good roads." "Are there many Mormons in Corinne?" "We are all Mormons, here." "Are you a Mormon?" "Yes, I am; are you a Mormon?" "I suppose not; I know but little about Mormonism, but I have heard much about them. If you are a Mormon you are the first one that I ever became acquainted with. Before leaving California, my folks said all they could to dissuade and discourage me, and endeavored to get the neighbors also to intercede with me, not to take this journey, but I was determined to go East on this plan. They told me I could not travel with a one-horse team; that it was not safe to travel alone; that the wild beasts would devour me; that the Indians would take my scalp; that the Mormons would surely kill me; that I could not travel in Utah, and I ought not to make the attempt. All this was said before I left, but on the first of June I left Eureka city, and have travelled about fourteen hundred miles, and not an injury, or as yet, an insult has come to me. You say that you are Mormons; if you are, I shall never be afraid of the Mormons in the least. Well, friend Mormon, if you will go with me to the barn, you may lock me in if you wish?" "We have no locks on our barns; we are not afraid of any one." "Do you not have tramps come around?" "Yes, there are some on the railroad, but they don't trouble us. You can sleep in the house; we will give you a bed." "I prefer to sleep with my cattle and have done so all the time on this journey." "Very well, suit yourself." I went to the barn, gave the animals some more hay, made me a bed and was soon asleep.

The morning of the 23rd found me up early. There was no one up in the house, I fed my cattle and made ready to move on. While they were eating I took a tramp around the town; on my return I found my friend at the barn, to whom I bade good morning. "Good morning, sir; how did you rest last night?" "I had a good rest." "I am glad of it for your sake. We are up early this morning, as we thought you would like an early start; I suppose you will make Ogden to-day?" "Yes, sir; I would like to do so." "You will have a good road, no better, east or west; you will find it as I say. Our breakfast must be ready, we will go in and see." We went into the house and as I entered I bade the lady good morning. "Good morning, sir; did you rest well last night?" she asked. "Very well, thank you." Breakfast is ready, take a seat at the table. Stranger, will you give thanks?" "Please excuse me." Then my host said, "Our Father in Heaven, we thank Thee this morning, that we are again permitted to come round this table. Bless this food, may it strengthen us in body; and our faith in Thee we will ever proclaim. This stranger, O God, Thou hast protected him on his long road so far, please continue on, watch over him both day and night; see him through this long journey, if it be Thy will, Amen." The foregoing is the prayer and utterance of a Mormon.

Corinne is situated on the Central Pacific Railroad, about twenty-five miles from Ogden. It was laid out for a large city. Large quantities of freight were brought and taken north by teams to Montana and Idaho. But since the building of the Utah Northern Railroad, it has been on the decline, and doubtful if it ever will come up again, at least for the present. But should the contemplated railroad between Dakota and Wyoming ever be built, its junction will probably be at Corinne. The Central desires a line of their own to the East.

On leaving Corinne I left the railroad to my right, my direction being south to Brigham city, crossing Bear river, distance about four miles; on entering the town I travelled but one street to the main road to Ogden. Beautiful was the water running down the gutters of the street; it seemed delightful. But being late and also anxious to reach Ogden I did not stop. A short distance to my left is Wahshat range of mountains. On my right is Salt Lake and Valley. The foot-hills of this mountain range is of the best soil and under good cultivation by the Mormons. What a contrast, from what I have passed through, on coming to such beautiful farms as the Mormons have made on the west of this long range of mountains. Some are so close to the mountain's base, that the morning's sun is hidden for some time. About twelve at noon, I came to a farm house, where I stopped. There was plenty of hay here, and a man was husking corn to whom I bade good morning, and then said, "I would like some hay for my cattle, but I have no money, not a dime. I paid the last dime in Corinne for a sack of grain; when I reach Ogden I hope to be replenished." "Your cattle can have all the hay they can eat in two hours; I will not charge you anything." I gave the cattle some water and hay; splendid hay it was, known as alfalfa. "You are travelling, it seems?" "Yes, sir." "How far have you come, sir?" "I have come from California, and have travelled more than fourteen hundred miles since I left my home, or where I have been staying in California the past two years; I am on my way home." "Home, where is your home?" "Massachusetts is my home." "Do you ever expect to reach Massachusetts in this way, with that outfit?" "Yes, sir." "That is a long distance; come in and take dinner with us; your cattle are doing well, let them eat all they will." I went in and took dinner with the stranger. There were four of us sat at dinner, two men and two women. One of the women asked, "Are you a Mormon?" "I am not, that is, I suppose I am not; I have but one wife. I suppose the Mormons have as many as they desire?" "They are allowed to have as many as they can support, but they are getting sick of that; they do not care to support but one, and not half support that one; they would rather do as you do down East, one wife or none. It is coming to that here, polygamy is playing out." "Are you Mormons?" "We are, but we don't go for polygamy. We belong to the Josephites." "Are there many of that order?" "There are many of them, and it will not be long before we are in the majority." "Well, strangers, I must be moving on; how far is it to Ogden?" "To the post-office it is fourteen miles; how long will it take you to travel that distance?" About five hours, on a good road." "It is a good road." "Thank you, for your hospitality." "You are welcome, and I hope you will make your long journey." "Thank you, good day." "Good day, call again." We went on and about half-past three p. m., I passed through Hot Springs. Here there are two roads to Ogden; the one to the right is the nearest, but there are a number of sloughs to pass over; the one to the left is the best, but it is the longest. I took the left road and soon I came to a peach orchard; how beautiful it looked. I stopped and accosted a lady in the yard, saying "Madam, can I take some of the peaches that are on the ground?" "Yes, sir; all you wish." I had a four quart measure which I filled and put them in my wagon. "You may fill it again if you wish," said the lady. I did so and then went on. Coming to a broad road and turning sharp to my right we travelled this road. The road here was about one hundred feet wide. Here I was told it was four miles to the post-office in Ogden; we went on and came to a more thickly settled district; passed some splendid farms with fine orchards of all kinds of fruit, and on either side many new houses built of brick. They are small, but neat and pretty. The sun is now going down and I asked a stranger how far it was to Ogden.

He answered. "Two miles." "Where can I stop to-night?" "Yonder, you see that large barn, a man by the name of Miller lives there; he has plenty of room and hay. He is a fine man and will keep you, no doubt, over night. I went there and turned into the yard and inquired if Mr. Miller was at home. "He is not, but soon will be; he has gone down town with the milk," said the lady. Soon after a man drove into the yard and I asked him, "Is this Mr. Miller?" "Yes, sir; that is my name." "Would you allow me to camp in this yard, and I would like some hay for my cattle." "Yes, you can camp here, and have hay for your cattle also." I led Fannie into the yard, took her from the carriage and fastened her to the wheel as usual, the cow opposite and gave them alfalfa hay; it is the best hay for a cow that is grown. "You are travelling; are you?" "Yes, sir." "Have you been buying a cow?" "No, sir; not of late." "How far have you led that cow?" "A long distance." "How long a distance?" "About fourteen hundred miles." "The d—l you have; where from? Tell me that, so that I can judge the distance?" "You say your name is Miller?" "Yes, sir; my name is Miller." "Mr. Miller, I have come all the way from California to this place." "I can't believe you." "Mr. Miller, I want to stop over a day or two, and will satisfy you that I am not a fraud. How far is it to the post-office from here?" "It is less than two miles." "I suppose there is some mail there, which I ordered to be sent and held until called for." "Where were you when you gave that order?" "In San Francisco. I mean what I say, every time, don't you forget it." "You look like a man that speaks the truth, but you are getting off some yarn; what is your name, sir?" "I have but one name; Johnson is my name, at all times and places." "Well, Mr. Johnson, come into the house, we will get some supper, I have not had any yet, and presume you have not." "I have not, and would like some." I went into the house, sat down to supper and the man said to his wife, "This man tells me some big stories. He says he has travelled over fourteen hundred miles, with that horse and carriage, leading the cow; what do you think of it, wife?" "Where did you come from?" she asked. "From California, direct." "But it is not fourteen hundred miles to San Francisco; only about a thousand, your story does not agree with that distance." "Very well, I now have to tell you more than I had intended; I have but one story to tell. When telling the whole it is a long one; when I can get rid of telling it, it gives me rest, but I will tell you the long story, no doubt you will pay me something for it." "Go on, we will see." "But I want to be excused at this time, as I wish to go down town to the post-office for my mail. I have had no mail since leaving San Francisco. I sent my pension papers to Boston, giving my post-office address at Ogden. I except there is a check there waiting for me." "The post-office is already closed for the night,' you can not have access to it, and to-morrow is Sunday; it will be open at six to-morrow evening." "Then I must wait patiently until to-morrow." "Yes, sir; you must." "Why did I not start sooner this morning from Corinne, so that I could have arrived sooner? Oh, I see; I stopped too long at dinner talking with the Mormons; that is what is the matter." "Yes, Mormon women, I suppose." "Are you Mormons?" "No, sir; we are not Mormons here." "I supposed you were all Mormons here?" "No, sir; not a bit of it. My wife was a Mormon before she was married, but since her marriage she is strongly anti-Mormon." "I know nothing about Mormonism, only what I have heard." After supper I remarked, "By the way, my cow is good for milk." "Does she give milk?" asked the lady. "She does, I milk her every day, and sometimes four times a day, but not often. Mr. Miller, I would like to stop here a day or two, or a short time before I go on further." "Go on; where are you going to?" "Oh, I have not got to my journey's end yet. Mr. Miller, I do not see that I can avoid telling you the whole story. Sometimes, I endeavor to get rid of telling it, I prefer a short story to a long one, and should I ever put it in a book it would be the same story over and over. Mr. Miller, I will give you the facts as briefly as I can. On the first of June last, I was three hundred miles north of San Francisco; on that day I left Eureka city, Humboldt county, with that horse, carriage, cow and dog, for Massachusetts. Travelled from Eureka to San Francisco and remained in that city some ten days; then I went to San Jose expressly to see the place, having heard so much about it. This was directly out of my way, fifty-seven miles. I did not return to San Francisco, but struck off to the right through Livermore Valley, Livermore Pass into the San Joaquin Valley to Stockton. From there to Sacramento and on to Gold Run; returning back by Colfax to Grass Valley. There taking the old turnpike, known as the Virginia and Marysville turnpike to Reno, or Verdi, twelve miles west from Reno. This turnpike was built on the Henness Pass, on the north side of the Sierra Mountains. From Reno I followed the Central Pacific Railroad most of the way to here. From Eureka to Ogden, the way I have come, it is 1427 miles. I do not intend to stop here any length of time but to pass on. Mr. Miller, so far, this is true; now you can ask me any questions you choose, such as, how could I make this or that; whether or not I was troubled with the wild beasts, or the Indians or the Mormons. Mr. Miller, I can say that I have not been insulted by man or woman, since leaving Eureka. I can relate many instances of travel, that no doubt would be of much interest, and will do so should I remain a short time with you, but I do not intend to stop long, if I do, I may get snow-bound in travelling over the Rocky Mountains.

CHAPTER V.

THE CITY OF OGDEN.

On the morning of the 24th, Sunday, after breakfast, I went down into the city looking around. My attention was called to a gathering of the people at a given place. On inquiring the cause, I learned that there was a mass meeting at the Tabernacle by the Mormons, in regard to the "Edmunds bill," then passed by Congress. "What is this bill," I asked. "The bill disfranchises those Mormons that have more than one wife, Mr. Stranger." "I have heard nothing about it," I answered. "It is going to make hot work here." I went up to the Tabernacle; it was full and hundreds were standing outside. I stepped up to a well dressed gentleman, bidding him good morning, and I remarked that this was a large gathering. "What is it for?" "The cause is this: Those Mormons who believe in Polygamy are not to be allowed to vote at the coming election by the new law of Mr. Edmunds, and it will make hot work here, stranger." "I am a stranger here, and have but just arrived from the West. It is my intention to remain but a day or two; I am in camp about two miles north of this place, on Mr. Miller's ranche, he is a milk merchant; perhaps you know him?" I remarked. About noon I returned to my camp and gave my cattle their dinner, took a lunch myself and then returned to the city to wait for the opening of the Post Office. I was the first at the office to call for mail, asking if there were any for Warren B. Johnson, and was told there was nothing. I then told the Postmaster there should be, as before leaving San

Francisco, California, I sent my pension papers to Boston for collection, ordering them to be sent to Ogden, Utah, and there held until called for. When giving him this information he ordered me to pass on, but I stood there until the crowd of people in my rear pushed me away from the window, then I said, "Gentlemen, this is not fair, I am a traveller from the far West. On the 15th of July, at San Francisco, California, I sent my pension papers to Boston, Mass., for collection, to be returned to Ogden, Utah Territory, there to be held until my arrival. Now I am here and there seems to be no mail for me. I have been ejected from that window on account of trying to explain and learn particulars about my mail." "Stranger, you shall have a hearing," said a voice from the crowd. "Post master, hear what the stranger has to say about his mail." "Stranger, come to the window, I will hear what you have to say." I then told him the particulars and asked if there had been any mail for Warren B. Johnson at his office and returned to Boston, Massachusetts. "No, sir; not to my recollection," answered the Post master. I turned to the crowd and said, "Gentlemen, I am a stranger in a strange land and have come all the way from San Francisco with a horse, carriage, cow and little dog; I am without money—not a dime. When I left Kelton I had one dollar, that was all. On my arrival in Corinne I spent that dollar for a sack of grain for my cattle and am here without a dime. I was sure that on my arrival I should find in the mail a letter containing a check for me, but there is no mail—no check." "Stranger, where is your horse, carriage, cow and dog?" "Gentlemen, here is the dog beside me." (Holding him up.) "The horse, carriage and cow are at Mr. Miller's ranche, about two miles from here. Mr. Miller is a milk merchant, I am informed." "You are all right with Mr. Miller," said a voice in the crowd. Here I am, what shall I do next? I went to the telegraph office and asked the operator if he would send a second-class despatch to Boston, Mass., for me, and how much it would cost. He answered, "One dollar, sir."

"Please ask H. W. Gooch, Pension Agent, Boston, Mass., where my pension papers are, that I ordered to be sent to Ogden, Utah Territory. They are not here, answer,

WARREN B. JOHNSON.

Ogden, Sept. 24th, 1882.

I waited four days, but got no answer and on the 28th I sent a note giving full particulars. On the 2d of October I sent another telegram, and on the 7th I received a despatch, saying, "No voucher received; will send blank by mail." On the 13th I received a blank to be filled and on the 14th I filled the blank and sent it back to Boston. On the 30th of October I received my mail which I ought to have had by the 24th; this made a delay of thirty-six days. Having received my money, on the first of November I was ready to move forward, and should have done so but I was advised not to do so by my many friends, Mormon and Gentile, I had made on being obliged to stop here. They told me I could not cross the Rocky Mountains so late in the season. I should perish in the snow storms and would be neither able to retreat or advance, so I concluded to winter in Ogden. Before relating my journey any further, I will state that my mail, which is my present text, was sent from Boston to Ogden, and returned to Boston. It showed that it had travelled the road three times. After deciding to remain through the winter, my first thoughts were to procure a stable for my cattle. I could get one, but the rent was more than I could pay. I was recommended by a Mormon friend, to another Mormon, to allow me to put up a small stable, 10x16, on some of her land, which she granted. I then went to a lumber dealer, he a Mormon, and selected such lumber as I needed, and put up the stable myself; cost of lumber, nails, bolts, screws, thirty-two dollars, all told.

This stable contained 160 square feet; I gave 90 feet to my cattle, leaving 70 feet for myself, hay and grain. This was my home for nearly eight months. While here I became acquainted with the leading men of the city, most of whom were Mormons; about four-fifths of the population were Mormons. I could not tell one from a Gentile, only when talking on the Edmunds bill, then you would readily know, as they spoke strongly against it every time, and don't you forget it. I never had any trouble whatever with the people. On my arrival in Ogden I stayed with Mr. Miller some two weeks or more and all this time I was in and out of the city, trying to learn the whereabouts of my mail. On the 9th of October we had a very severe thunder storm, which left its mark behind, consisting of rain, hail and snow. So severe was it that the fall of snow was so deep, the people were obliged to drive the cattle into the barns; this storm was an experience for me. I was obliged to look for better quarters for myself and cattle. On returning from the city after the storm I was overtaken by a fine looking young man. After talking with him I related my circumstances, how I was situated at that time. Said he, "I think that my father would give you barn room for your cattle; I am not sure, but think he will." "Where is your home?" I asked. "Only a few steps above the first house on the left, you had better call and see my father," said the young man. I went with him to his home. He said, "Father, please step to the door; this stranger is travelling from the West and is going East. He has been stopping with Mr. Miller and is obliged to leave on account of barn room. I told him that I thought you would give him barn room for a short time." About how long would you like to stop, sir?" "Not longer than time enough for me to get my mail from Boston, Mass.," I answered. "Yes, stranger; I will accommodate you." I went home and returned with my outfit. Here I remained until my stable was ready for dedication. After the dedication I gave my cattle possession "with right of way."

Ogden is situated on the west of the Wahsatch mountain, close to its base, fronting Ogden canyon and river. When the Mormons took possession of these lands, they laid out a road one hundred and thirty-two feet wide, six miles long, and commenced the building of their cabins on this road, equal distances apart. When the Atlantic and Pacific Railroad passed through the town, they established their depot near the river, on account of the water. This was south of its centre of population. The Mormons built their Tabernacle south of its centre. The two railroads establishing their depot where they have, soon made Ogden a fine city, with a population of about eight thousand. The Mormons having by far the greatest population, they have several places of worship, but the Tabernacle is their chief place. There are several other churches, Episcopal, Baptist and Catholic. There are three banks; two are National. The cashier of the First National, Mr. Young, told me that the directors of this bank represented three million dollars. There are several hotels, one of these is a very fine one, the Brown Hotel; it surpasses any hotel east of San Francisco, for thousands of miles; that takes you east to Cleveland, Ohio. There are many first-class stores for the sale of all kinds of merchandise and the proprietors are mostly Mormons. In fact, it is difficult at any time to tell a Mormon from a Gentile, except during the heat of discussion on politics. Having made many acquaintances with the people, I got quite familiar with their politics, always pretending ignorance or scepticism. There was one man that I became well acquainted with, whom I much admired, he was a thorough Mormon. I passed his house almost every day when going into town. One day as I was passing I said to him, "What is it that makes your fruit trees look so healthy and the bark so smooth and green; what gives them that healthy color?" "Mr. Johnson, I give them nothing, it is the soil they live on; alkali and salt are its compound. It is as good for grain as for fruit, and for potatoes still better. Mr. Johnson, I would like to have a long half day's talk with you. I am from the State of Illinois, and was one of the early pioneers over the Rocky Mountains. I was probably the first one who saw the Salt Lake and was one of five that left Salt Lake prospecting between Weber's river and canyon, and from there to what is now Ogden. Here we stopped and have remained here ever since. This is a wonderful place; we are between two rivers, Ogden and Weber. They are about eight miles apart. For irrigation we take water from the Ogden river. Our people are now engaged in an enterprise, which when completed will cost many thousands of dollars, and will be worth to us, many millions when finished. We are constructing a canal to carry the waters of Weber river a long distance on the plains, between Ogden and Salt Lake city. This canal will take the water from the river before it leaves the canyon, as the fall to the water is much greater. As I have said, Ogden is wonderfully situated. Look at yonder mountain, only one mile from its base, over there is Ogden river and canyon. Look at those lands beyond the court house, what a vast plain to the right and left of us; these are the foot hills of the mountain; see those lands on high ground, some eighty feet above the city's level; we call them shelves. These lands are easily irrigated. Mr. Johnson, I have said and still say, it is wonderful. Coming from the best State in the Union to this place, the Lord God Almighty was with us from the beginning and has been ever since. We have been severely tried since the railroad came amongst us. We had been here twenty years before the railroad. We have cultivated these lands and have brought them to what they now are, with their fine fruit trees and those beautiful fields of grain that you see yonder; all this we have done with our own hands. How was it before the railroad arrived in town? We were a happy, peaceful people. Not a saloon in town; no drinking or gambling places to be found. How is it to-day? Go down Fifth street; look in those drinking hells. The proprietors are not Mormons. No, they are Gentiles, formerly Missouri rebels during the Rebellion; they are the ones that make the most noise. Mr. Johnson, you know, no doubt, that when the government contracted with the railroad, it was to give and take equally. The government take a section and the railroad take a section of a mile each; with this understanding, that all citizens who had taken land as settlers and under cultivation, shall receive a patent for the same on payment of one dollar and twenty-five cents per acre. When the Pacific Railroad arrived in town their division comprised the most part of Ogden. Ogden was a large agricultural town, with many inhabitants. The railroad had passed through nothing like unto it, and in due time the people living on these lands were called upon to show their patents, or to purchase one. The leading Mormons were shrewd; they were citizens of the States. As the citizens came up to pay for their lands and take their patents according to contract, one dollar and twenty-five cents was not enough, much more was exacted; they refused to pay the advanced figures. A meeting was called of the land owners, the decision was to pay the figures of the railroad and take out their patents. This was hard on many of the citizens; most of them were living in their old log cabins, that they had built at first settling. But they came up and now most of these lands are ours. For instance, a Mormon dies, leaving a good farm, a widow and two daughters; the widow marries an anti-Mormon. He is satisfied with one wife, and don't care for a second one; and so is the wife. When the daughters commence to think of a husband, they are pretty sure to take an anti-Mormon. There are many cases of this kind." "Friend J., then Mormonism is going to die out in time?" I said. "I think polygamy will in time," said Mr. J. "I understand that the young women will not consent to their husbands taking a second wife on their marriage day; how is that, Mr. J?" I asked. "I don't blame them; I would not if I were they. I never had but one wife and never saw the day I wanted the second. We are thinking of doing as you do down East; one wife and as many concubines as you can bargain for. This, congress will consent, no doubt. Mr. Johnson, I have omitted one essential part, and it should have been first. While we were at Council Bluff, and about to leave for parts unknown, President Polk sent a squad of troops to Council Bluff and took five hundred of our best young men and sent them to Mexico to fight for these same lands that we are now living on. If we have no right to these lands, who are the people that have? Mr. Johnson, this was a severe blow to us; many of the men taken had families, they were marched away from their wives and children to see them no more. Some of them found their way back to us. When we arrived here, we were told by the Indians that corn would not grow, but we tried it and found that it would and did. The same God of ancient times was with us continually; we called on him daily and he answered our call. They believed in a God in those days and we Mormons do to-day. On our arrival here, we were destitute of those fine, young men taken to go to war; oh, how cruel it was, their wives, and children here, but they were not. Time moved on. We found by experience, that not only corn could be grown, but all kinds of grain; wheat especially was very productive, more so than any other kind of grain. Mr. Johnson, you have been with us about how long?" "More than seven months," I replied. "You have been with us seven months or more, with the worst people on earth, so say the people down East. Mr. Johnson, have we harmed you in any way since you have been with us? You can say when you get back to old Massachusetts, that you have been stopping more than seven months with Mormons; when do you intend to leave us?" he asked. "About the middle of the month; I shall leave as soon as you say it will be safe to cross the mountains," I replied. "The middle of the month will be early enough. I am afraid you will find snow on the mountains. Mr. Johnson, I hope you will tell your people the truth about the Mormons, the whole truth and shame the devil. Mr. Johnson, we have some bad Mormons and they are growing worse every day. Before the railroad came into town, we were a better people, but since, we have grown worse. They are not Mormons, but men from the East to work at the mines. Here they spend the winter and try to rob each other by gambling and carousing through the winter. Mr. Johnson, we have had a long talk, when do you think of leaving us?" "I think of leaving you on the 14th, next Monday." "What a long road you have before you; over the Rocky Mountains all alone; that is the worst part of it. All the rivers to ford, you must be something more than a man to stand it. Well, Mr. Johnson, I hope you will go through safe and sound; my daily prayer for you will be that you may reach your home in safety. The Lord our God protect thee. Good-bye, friend Johnson, I hope to hear from you," said this Josephite. "Thank you. Good-bye, friend J. Further, give my regards to your people, those that I have had the pleasure of being acquainted with while here. Tell them all to become Josephites; give up polygamy and come into the Union with a clean constitution; do it voluntarily and not be drawn to it is the wish of a traveller across the country."

CHAPTER VI.

FROM OGDEN CITY, UTAH, TO LARAMIE, WYOMING.

I left Ogden May 14th, 1883, for the East, and made Weber the same day, a distance of twenty-five miles. I followed the Union Pacific Railroad most of the way to Omaha. Leaving the city, I left the railroad to my right. My direction was south to Uintah, about eight miles. There I crossed the railroad and the Weber river also. Following the river and railroad to the canyon, I am on the right of both, the three running parallel for many miles. Crossing the river on the railroad bridge, I now follow on the left and enter the Weber Valley. This canyon that I have just passed through is most wonderful. There are places that are not sixty feet wide, from rock to rock, and the road is very narrow in places, not more than eight feet. On my right is a wall of solid rock, hundreds of feet perpendicular; on my left is the river, down to its waters are many feet. There are many rocks in the river that would weigh thousands of tons. Waters are dashing and roaring against these rocks that make one feel awful. As I was about to cross the river, I heard the sound of an engine's whistle. I stopped, looking up and down the railroad, but could see no cars; I was sure that I heard a whistle and soon came the train. The roar of the water was so great among the rocks that I could not hear the train as it passed. Soon after entering this canyon, I came to a company of men, who were building a flume to carry the waters of the river into a canal, which had been made for miles on the plains, south and west of Ogden; between the Wahsatch

Mountains, Salt Lake and Salt Lake city. I was informed by the superintendent of these works, Mr. Brown, that this enterprise would cost over one hundred and thirty thousand dollars, and can be made to cost any amount. The bridge on which I crossed is one of the best I have seen on my way, thus far. My road is now on the east side of the valley, winding around its foot hills; this valley is thickly populated by the Mormons. I have passed through a place called Enterprise; it looks as if there were some around. On the west side of this valley is a place called Peterson, a telegraph station. Before leaving Ogden I got my cattle shod; the horse was well done, but the cow was not, and she was troubled to travel. On arriving at Weber, I called on a blacksmith to ascertain if I could get the cow shod and learned that I could. The blacksmith said he could shoe her and would do so at five o'clock next morning.

On the morning of the 15th I was up early; fed my cattle, got breakfast and made everything ready for a start, and waited for the blacksmith till five a. m., the time set for shoeing the cow. He was on time, saying, "It was going to be a hard job." "I think you are going to be mistaken, she will behave like a lady; won't you, Bessie?" I said. "We will soon know," said the blacksmith. I led Bessie into the brake, and the blacksmith was about to sling her up, but I told him not to do so, but put the slings under her and let her stand on her feet. I will show you how when she is in the brake. The sling was then drawn tight under her, but not so tight as to lift her from her feet; a rope was then passed around both legs, below the fetlocks, and drawn tight so that it would not slip, and made fast to the brakes. The front right foot was taken up and the nail clinches cut, the pincers were put to the shoe for its removal, and after a strong pull it was quickly off all right. The other shoes were removed in a like manner. The shoes were then cut and made one half inch less in length and re-placed; this made a good job. In travelling there was no friction of the shoes and they were evidently easy to the feet of the cow.

I left Weber at 7 a. m., and reached Emory the same day, a distance of twenty-five miles. In making this place, we passed two stations, Corydon and Echo; the latter is a first-class station. It is a junction, a railroad from Park city comes in. On leaving this station, on the left you pass around a number of high bluffs; they are handsome and grand. Here, nature is to be seen at her best. Bluff after bluff arise one after another, hundreds of feet high—a short distance from the road. Between the bluffs, at their bases, are spaces wide enough to pass through with a team, and on emerging come out on beautiful plains. Reader, should you ever travel this way, stay and look at nature's works around Echo. On leaving this town I made the acquaintance of a gentleman, while sitting in his carriage, who said, "Stranger, you will just reach my place to-night; it is about a mile beyond the station; if you will call I will entertain you the best I can. I have plenty of hay and grain for your cattle; for yourself I will say nothing; my wife shall look after you." "What are you, Mormons?" I asked. "No, no Mormons at our house. I suppose you know all about them. You have been staying in Ogden?" "Friend, I do know something about them; I have had a good opportunity to learn. When I get East, should I succeed in getting there, you will hear what I have to say about them. It is now about twelve o'clock." "It is about eleven miles to my home; how long will you be in travelling there?" "I travel about two and a half miles to the hour, day or night, just as it happens; so it will take four and a half hours to make that distance." "I will overtake you before you get to the station; if I don't, it is the first house beyond the station, on the right of the road on the hillside." "All right, I will be going on." There was a large number of people around me, and as I was leaving, one of their number called out, "Three cheers and success to the man from California, on his way to Massachusetts." They were given with a will, you bet. "Good-bye yourself, and success on your journey." About four miles from the station I was overtaken by a cavalcade of Indians, eighteen in number, mounted on fine horses. They were civil and courteous and spoke fair English. I travelled in their company several miles. Before reaching the station, the gentleman who had invited me to stop over night overtook me and kept me company as far as his house. On our arrival he introduced me to his wife, saying, "Wife, this stranger is from California, just as he is, and is going East, to Massachusetts, where he belongs; make him as comfortable as you can; I think he is worthy of it." My cattle were put in the barn, fed with good hay and grain, and were made safe under a good lock; after this was done I went into the house to a good supper which was waiting. "Stranger, allow me to ask your name?" "Sir, my name is Johnson, W. B., of Webster, Mass." "Mr. Johnson, take a seat at the table and we will soon know what my wife has for supper." "Had I known that I was to have company to tea, I might have done better, however, excuse me," said the wife. Well, what did we have? It consisted of mutton chop, hot potatoes, biscuit, coffee and mince pies. That was all there was on the table; to me it tasted delicious. We sat at the table nearly two hours, asking and answering questions. When the time came for retiring, I told them that I had at all times and places slept with my cattle, having been advised to do so, so that should anybody attempt to take them, I should be there to see to them.

I left the ranche near **Emory** on the 16th, and **made** Evanston, a distance of twenty-six miles. I was up early as usual, feeding and getting ready to move forward. My friend of the ranche came to the barn and we bade each other good morning. "You find your cattle all here I suppose?" "Yes, sir; and doing well. I have fed them with hay." "You will find grain in that box, give them all you dare, you must keep them well, or fail in your undertaking." "I carry grain." "You do, then you are all right; put the grain into them. Our breakfast is ready. I told my wife that you would like to start early." We went into the house and partook of a good breakfast. As I was about to leave them I said, "We have all been well cared for, and are now ready to go on. Since leaving California, many times have we been well entertained, but your hospitality stands ahead of any. Yours was entirely voluntary; I have asked and received many times, but you did not give me a chance to ask; that is where there is a difference. I wish I could have an opportunity to do the same for you." After bidding each other good-bye I moved on my journey towards Evanston, leaving the railroad on my left. In reaching this town I pass but one station, Wahsatch, which is a telegraph station. Its location is desolate, being on a high elevation, cold and windy. The road to this 'station from the west is of a very heavy grade. Trains labor hard in making it; its elevation is six thousand eight hundred and seventy-nine feet above the level of the sea. The highway is good, and about five p. m. I reached Evanston, driving up to near the depot, I stopped at a livery stable and inquired for the proprietor, who came and asked what he could do for me. "I am travelling and would like to get my cattle out of the wind for the night. That shed would answer my purpose, if you will consent to it?' "Yes, sir; I will consent." "Will you sell me some hay for my cattle?" "Hay is very scarce with me. I ought to have gone for some to-day, but being so windy and cold I did not go. Your cattle must have some, I will go up and throw some down; when there is enough, call out." I did so when he had put down a liberal supply. I have now to feed strong on grain as I can not depend on hay or grass. "Which way are you travelling?" asked the livery man. "I am going East." "Where are you from?" "I left Ogden last Monday morning." "You come from Ogden since last Monday, with that cow?" "I have, sir." "That is a big story to tell; you look as though you ought to tell the truth. From Ogden to this place in three days; you have travelled more than eighty miles—yes, eighty-five. It is seventy-six by railroad, and your road around the foot-hills of the valley is more than that distance. Then you are from Ogden, where in the name of God are you going to?" "I am going to Green River city, and when I get there I am going to Laramie and so on to Omaha, and thus on to Massachusetts." "Are you the man that is on his way from California with a horse, carriage, cow and a little dog. I read about him in the papers a while ago?" "I think I must be the man; I am sure I am." "You are early to travel East, over the mountains; I do not think you can ford the rivers, they are already high and will be higher." "I am told there are two roads to Green River city, one to follow the railroad, the other to take the old Emigrant road." "If I were in your boots going to Green River city, I would take the old Emigrant trail every time. It is the best, travelled the most and the shortest." "How about fording the rivers?" "They are high at this time, but will be higher before you get through." "Are there more rivers one way than the other?" "No; either way you will have the same rivers and the same road a part of the way." "There is Bear river to begin with; how about that?" "It is the best river to ford on your whole route; a good hard bottom and no rocks." "Is it a broad river?" "Yes, it is; that makes it much better to ford. If it were narrow, the water would be much deeper and a much stronger current; when do you leave here?" "To-morrow morning." "On the morrow, I will harness up and drive my team to the river and across; you follow me closely, then you will be all right for the next river."

I was up early on the morning of the 17th. I had fed my cattle and was greasing my carriage as the proprietor came to feed his team. Coming up to where I was he said, "Come, go with me and get some breakfast; a dish of hot coffee will make you all right for fording the rivers." I went with him and got breakfast, came back and made ready to start on my journey. I drove along to the river and soon the man came with his team and said, "How does it look to you?" I answered back, "How does it look to you?" "This is all right; get on to your wagon and drive close up to mine; don't be a bit afraid." He drove down into the river, I close up to him; the water was much deeper than I supposed it to be, and I thought my horse would go under. I dared not look back to see how the cow was getting along. I felt as if I was swinging around, but when I looked on the wagon ahead I was all right. After crossing, the man said, "This is the largest river you will have to ford. Green river you will have to cross on a boat; it cannot be forded this time of the year. The next to ford is Muddy river, and muddy you will find it, and it is doubtful if you can ford it. Should it continue to be warm, it will cut the snow on the mountains and make the rivers much higher; that is the matter with the rivers at this time of the year. It is doubtful if you will be able to travel until the rivers fall." "How much shall I pay you for your kindness?" I asked. "Not a dime," he answered. "But this has been a great favor to me, and I feel as though you ought to be rewarded." "It is all right now. If we were on the other side of the river, perhaps, I would take something with you, but as we are it is all right. I hope you will get along all right; good morning." "Thank you, good morning."

Evanston is a thorough business town; one of more than ordinary enterprise. There are churches and schoolhouses, which are something new, I have not seen them with but one exception for a great many miles; yes, for hundreds of miles. There is more of New England in this place, than in any other town I have passed through, with one exception, since leaving California. All trains stop here and time is allowed for dinner. The express from the East arrives at 1:50 p. m.; from the West at 3:50 p. m. On leaving here, after crossing Bear river, my direction was eastward, the railroad on my right. After travelling about eight miles I came to another trail, but did not know whether I should take it or not. Having passed but one house since leaving in the morning, there was not much chance to get information. Looking around I could see but one way, and that was to my right. On my left were mountains and on the right the railroad. I thought it safest to take the right-hand trail, and did so. I am now on a good trail, travelling at the rate of three miles an hour. About eleven o'clock I came in sight of a covered wagon; before reaching the wagon I saw two men with a herd of sheep and made for them. On reaching them I made known my business, relating my long story and said I had come from Evanston this morning, and on coming to two trails I took this one," Am I on the right trail to Green River city?" "You are not; you should have taken the other trail," said the strangers. "I suppose I shall have to go back and take the other trail?" "I think you had better go back and take the other trail. If you were acquainted with the surroundings you might get through, but as you are a stranger it is doubtful if you could find the trail." "What is the time of day?" I asked. "It is about 12 m. Stranger, stop and get some dinner with us; we will give you some mutton and your cattle some grain, that is the best we can do." "That is good enough; I will stop; such an invitation should not be passed by." My cattle were fed with grain, myself with mutton chop, and at one o'clock I counter-marched back to the trail I should have taken, which if taken at first would have saved me five hours' travel, and lost me a good dinner. This new trail is a good road. After travelling about the same length of time, I came to a ranche, on approaching which I found two men present. After introducing myself to the gentlemen, I inquired of them "If I was on the right trail to the creek called the Muddy?" "You are," they answered. "How far is it?" "About two miles," they said. "Have you any objection to my company here?" "Oh, no; not in the least," they answered. It was then 6 p. m., so I told them I would camp with them. I took the horse from the carriage and turned her loose; the cow I staked out. After supper I secured my cattle to their several posts, spread my blankets on the ground and went to bed. About midnight I was awakened by the howling of dogs; they do duty at night, and are good shepherds and no mistake. There are two animals that are very troublesome to sheep owners, the wolf and the coyotte; they can smell sheep a very long way off, I am told. I will give you a description of a sheep ranche; there are two within two miles of where I am camped. This ranche is a long wagon, about eighteen feet long, by six and a half wide; covered with heavy canvas. In the front part is a stove suitable for cooking, with all the necessary utensils. In the centre there is a table four feet long, and in the rear part there is a bed, with the necessary bedding. Here you have a house with three apartments; kitchen, dining and lodging rooms. A man with two good horses will take this house to some secluded place suitable for sheep to graze and there stop. In his rear, follow from one to five thousand sheep. During the day sheep roam at large, grazing, and at night they are all gathered around this wagon, or ranche. Corn is fed to them which keeps them well content. They understand that outside there is danger; four dogs do guard duty every day and night. This grazing belongs to Uncle Sam; he has thousands of them. The best part of this ranche is the house; it is on wheels, and it can be taken where you please, one, five or twenty miles, if you don't step on the Indian's toes, that is all.

On the morning of the 18th I was up and around early, getting ready to go on and about six o'clock broke camp for Muddy creek, which I reached about ten o'clock. This creek is about four rods across; had it been six, it would have been much better to cross. A large body of water flows past and its banks are full and overflowing. A short distance below the ford, there is a bend in the river which sets the water back, making the ford deep, with a strong current. It was discouraging; I felt blue and being all alone I was disheartened. In order to ascertain the depth of the water, I took out my horse, got on to her back and made an attempt to cross, but she would not go into the water; I made several attempts, but with no further success. It was a warm day and I remembered what the man said at Evanston, "The warmer the day, the higher the river." I went back to my wagon, removed the harness and turned the horse loose, the cow also. I returned to the river and made a mark, so that I could tell whether the water was rising or falling. I then returned to my carriage, gathered some wood and made a fire; made some coffee, boiled some eggs and ate my dinner. Having some oil, I concluded to give my harness a good limbering up. Several times I went to the river to see whether the water was higher or lower. Before night the river had fallen about four inches, and I thought that by morning I should be able to cross.

On the morning of the 19th, instead of the river being lower, it had risen two feet. Just across the river, not more than four rods, was the railroad. As the water was higher, I concluded to turn back to a road that led to a railroad station, which I had noticed the day before. I had just got ready to return when I noticed a hand-car coming up the railroad track, with several men on it. I signaled them to stop, which they did, and inquired the distance to the station? They answered, "About four miles." "I came here yesterday and finding the river high, I dared not cross it." "It is very high; never saw it so high before; you had better go back to the station and take the road to Fort Bridges; you there cross the same river over a bridge, about a mile from the station," one of the men answered. I went back to the station, and on my way I came to a small village. The first building I came to was a store and Post Office. I introduced myself to a woman who proved to be the Postmistress, relating my travels from California to this place, and telling her that "Yesterday I came to a river about four miles below, but finding it very high, dared not cross and remained over night, hoping that the waters would be lower in the morning, but instead they were higher, and so I was advised to take this road to Fort Bridges." "Well, but I don't know but the bridge on this road has been carried away. I will take my horse and carriage and will go and see," said the Postmistress. We went to the river and found the bridge all right, but the road had been washed away and the river had made a new bed. Just above the bridge there is a bend in the river which was full and overflowing, so that the waters washed out a new passage. We turned back and reported the condition of the road, and that it looked as if several days would pass before travel could be renewed. When we got back, the Postmistress told me to take my horse from my carriage and put her and the cow in the barn and give them some hay, as I might have to stop several days. I did as bidden, staying with her through the night.

On the morning of the 20th, I was up in due season and made ready to move on. I went down to the river to see how it looked and found it about the same as yesterday; I turned back rather blue, and went to the Post Office where I found the proprietor, to whom I remarked, "I have been to the river; but saw no change in its condition. What can I do? my only chance is to go back and ford the river." "The river can be forded, but it will be a hard job. It is a deep and powerful current; you may be able to ford it, but you should not be alone," she answered. As we were talking, three teams came up to where we were and the drivers asked the road to Green River city. The Postmistress said to me, "Now is your time." The teamsters were answered, "There are two roads, one you can't go and the other you can if you dare ford the river." "Which road is that?" asked the teamsters. "The left road." "What is the matter with the other way?" they asked. "A heavy wash-out; a bridge to be built before it can be travelled. Rivers and creeks are very high, it seems." "They are high; we are on our way to Green River city, and still further East across the plains," said the teamsters. "I came to the river yesterday, but found it so high I dared not cross, and came here to take this road, but find it impassable, so here I am as you see," I said. "Get ready and go with them and cross as they do," said the Postmistress. We all went back to the river, and as we got there saw on the opposite side a herd of horses with three men in charge of them. They rode up to the creek, looked at it a moment and then rode down the bank and over the opposite—in no time. "That was quickly done," I said. "How shall I get across with my carriage?" I asked. "Drive down into the river, that is the way to cross; you can't do it while on that bank," said one of the horsemen. "If you will ride across, I will follow you," I said. He rode down into the river and I followed close after him and got across all right, but my wagon was full of water, but it soon ran out. I went on and did not stop to see how the three teams got across. In crossing my feed got wet, but it did no other damage. About twelve o'clock I came to a road that ran at angles. To the right is Fort Bridges, nine miles, and to my left is Bridges station, one mile. Here I stopped, fed my cattle on grain, no hay or grass, myself on bread, milk, butter, cheese and salmon, a very good dinner. I had just finished my dinner when the three teams I had left at the river came up. I asked, "What luck crossing the river?" "We came across as you did, but got badly wet. It was much deeper than we supposed; our wagon was under water. It has made work for us, we will not cross another creek as we did that. It is taking too many chances and won't pay. We shall have to overhaul our trunks and dry our clothing." Leaving them at dinner, I went on, and about six o'clock these teams overtook me; they passed me but soon after went into camp, and I camped with them; no grass or hay, feeding our cattle wholly on grain. I gathered some sage brush for fuel, made a fire, got some coffee and ate my supper. If you asked what it consisted of, I would say, hot coffee, cold salmon, boiled eggs, butter, cheese, milk, and crackers for bread. My neighbors having gone through the same routine, they overhauled their trunks, taking out their clothing, and got ready for a dry-out. I have a box which is water-tight that contains my clothing, sugar, tea, coffee and other things that water affects. On the top of this box are my blankets, covered with a rubber blanket. At half-past eight it was time to make up my bed, so I made fast my cattle to their several posts, made up my bed and laid down for a good night's rest.

The morning of the 21st found me up early, as usual, making ready to move onward. I fed my cattle on grain, no grass, nothing but sage bushes around. I made a fire, got some coffee and sat down to breakfast. The box from which my horse eats her grain serves me as a seat when not otherwise in use. After breakfast I moved on. My road is not as good as usual, it is rough and stony. About ten o'clock I came to a small creek and gave the cattle water; they were thirsty, drinking as though they had not seen water since crossing the ford, and there they did not stop to drink. "Come Fanny, we must go on," I said. About one o'clock I saw two teams approaching. As we met, of course we stopped, we do not have to stop more than once a day. "Good morning, gentlemen," I said. "Where are you from, excuse me asking?" "Oh, yes; that is all right; we are from Green River city." "Where did you camp last night?" "About ten miles from here." "Did your cattle get grass?" "Oh, yes; where we stopped the grass was good." "About ten miles. How is the road that distance?" "Very rough." We then went on and at three o'clock, stopped and gave my cattle grain; after eating we again went on until coming to the grass of which I had been told, and went into camp. It was not yet time to go into camp, but there being grass we must stop, as going on we might not come to any more for many miles. I turned the cattle loose, allowing them to have their fill, then I made them fast for the night. While they were eating, I gathered some wood for a fire, got my supper ready, ate it and went to bed. In the night I was awakened by the horse. I knew then there was something around. I got up and saw the horse looking in a given direction, and on turning that way I saw a herd of deer feeding. I went back to bed and did not awake until dawn.

On the morning of the 22nd I did not awaken as early as usual, my rest of the night having been broken. While I was making my breakfast I gave the cattle another chance at the grass and then gave grain, after which we moved on. It was six o'clock when we left the camp; my road was very rough. Can my carriage stand it? it is doubtful. I led the horse over every stone that I thought would strain the carriage, but as I progressed the road improved. I travelled as fast as I dared and soon came to a small creek; just what I wanted, as the cattle were very thirsty; here I gave them some grain and then moved on and soon came to the railroad, which after crossing I came to a large river, but did not learn its name. There being plenty of grass I concluded to go no further and went into camp, turning the cattle loose to eat as they pleased. I went to the river prospecting and found a junction of two rivers, and made marks to ascertain whether the river was rising or falling. As I went back to the camp I gathered some fuel and made a good large fire, and got me ready a good supper, that is, what I called good. I carry a variety of eatables, so that I had the stuff for a good meal. Well, here we are, the four of us; horse, cow, dog and self. It is just seven o'clock in the evening, on the banks of a river unknown. I secured my cattle, gave them grain, make up my bed and was about to lie down, when a train of cars came along from Ogden.

On the morning of the 23rd I was up and around looking to my cattle, doing this and that, not knowing what the next would be. I went to the river and looked at the marks made last night, and found the water four inches lower and went back to the camp and turned the cattle loose, that they might eat plenty of good grass, made a fire and got me another "poor" breakfast. Then I went back to the river, being anxious to see some team coming from the East crossing the river, to see if it was fordable. About one mile east of us is Grange station, which is a junction of the Union Pacific and the Oregon Short Line, running within twenty rods of my camp. About nine o'clock the express train from the East passed by. After the passing of this train I saw four teams coming from the East; three were heavy wagons and one a light Eastern wagon on springs, drawn by two horses each. On coming to the river they stopped; their trail from Granges was close to the railroad track, and not more than forty feet from the bridge. As they got to the bank, the men, women and children, to the number of twenty-three, got out and made for the river. I was some distance from them and went to the junction of the two rivers, opposite to them; we tried to talk across, but the roar of the waters prevented us from hearing one another. They went back to their wagons; two horses were then taken from one of the wagons, unharnessed and two men mounted them and rode down into the river and out on its opposite banks, then they rode on about eight rods and down into the larger river and across to where I was. The first river was about four rods across, the second about eight rods. As soon as they got to me, they commenced asking me, where I was from, where going and how long had I been at the river? I told them where I was from and where I intended to haul up, and so on. I told them that I reached this river yesterday, and had been waiting there since that time, and now I will cross with them. They recrossed the river, I following close after and got over all right. The teamsters now got ready to cross with their wagons and I watched them at a distance of twelve rods. They drove their largest wagon first down into the river, the two men on horseback leading. As the big, heavy team went into the river, the wheels sunk deep into the mud, but the horses were game and pulled it across the two rivers all right. The second wagon got across with the same good fortune and returned for the third team, which was the covered light carriage, with springs, the horses were fine and spirited ones. In this carriage were four women and two children. As they were going down into the river, the bank being cut up by the other teams in crossing, the horses stepped deep into the mud and began to act meanly. The driver, however, was an excellent horseman and spoke to his horses sharply, and led them out safely. One of the women, however, was so badly frightened that she lay unconscious for over two hours. The fourth vehicle was got across all right; it was eleven o'clock when we all had forded the two rivers, and seeing them safely across I went on my way and about three o'clock I came to another river. I followed this river for several miles, until coming to a fine plat of grass where I went into camp for the night. turning my cattle loose to graze. I made a fire and got my supper, and after bringing the cattle and fastening them up for the night I went to bed.

On the 24th, on the banks of the Black Fork river, I was up making ready to move on. While getting my own breakfast I allowed my cattle free range of grass and then a feed of grain. I left camp about six o'clock; it was a fine morning as I left the Black Fork river, and having a good trail I went on my way with merry glee. About eleven o'clock we came to some good water where we stopped; I gave water and grain to my cattle and took a dish of cold coffee myself; this was all I cared for. I did not stop long and as my journey continued the road grew rougher. About three o'clock in the afternoon I met a train of six teams; I stopped and passed the compliments of the day, saying, "Gentlemen, where are you from and where going?" "We are from Kansas and have not decided finally where to locate. We started, however, for Oregon, but it is a long road, and a rough one at that. Stranger, where are you from and where are you bound to?" "I am from Ogden and going East." "How far East, we would like to know, stranger?" "I can't say for certainty, no more than you, but should I have luck, I may go as far as Massachusetts." "Massachusetts, the d—l you are, that is almost the jumping off place." "How far have you come to-day?" "We have come from Green River city, about twelve miles I think." "How far is it to water?" "About three miles, I should think." "How far have you come!" "I have come from the Black Fork river, about fifteen miles." "Have we got to ford the rivers?" "No, you follow the river, you do not have to ford it; your next will be Hams Fork, about forty miles from here." After bidding each other good-bye, we went on. On coming to water, I gave my cattle water and grain and concluded to camp here for the night. My surroundings look rough, and not a house in sight. I gathered some sage brush for fuel, made a good, rousing fire, got supper and made everything ready for the night. As I lay on my bed, to the right of me, I heard the whistle of an engine, 'then I knew that we were not far from the railroad. After a time I was lost in a sound sleep.

On the morning of the 25th I was up before the dawn of day, getting ready to break camp. As soon as it was light enough, I hauled out and went on. About eight o'clock I descended a steep bluff into a canyon and after travelling about a mile came to some grass; I stopped here, giving my cattle a chance at it. While they were feeding I gathered some fuel, made a fire and boiled some eggs for my breakfast. Having heard so much about

Green River I was anxious to see it; so I got ready and went on. I am still in the canyon and ascending a heavy bluff and expect soon to reach the river, which I did at half-past eleven, and at twelve o'clock we cross Green River by the Ferry boat. I went on down to the railroad bridge; this bridge spans the **Bitter** Creek. Here I went into camp, giving my cattle the last of 200lbs. of grain I had bought at Evanston, and at three o'clock I went into Green **River** city for grain and other things. I made inquiries if there were two roads to Laramie city, and was told there were; one following the railroad, the other the old Emigrant trail, and I would do the best to take the Emigrant trail; nine-tenths of the travel from Laramie coming by that trail. The railroad trail is not travelled enough to make it good, if travelled more it would be better and not as far that way. When the emigrant is in Laramie they tell him to take the Emigrant trail to Green River city. "What is the distance to Laramie by the old Emigrant trail?" I asked. "By the railroad it is two hundred and seventy-two miles, and by the Emigrant trail it must be three hundred and twenty-five miles." "Can I get grain on my way?" "No, you will have to buy here all you need on the way." "How about grass?" "You will not find much grass, our Spring has been so late and cold. It will take you twelve days at least to get to Laramie. On the last two or three days you may get grass, and as you get nearer to Laramie you will find it much warmer." "How much will you charge me for 100lbs. each of corn, oats and barley?" "I shall charge you six dollars for 300lbs., that is the least." "Why didn't you say seven dollars; you could have got it as quickly as six; you have it all your own way and you know we must have it. In Evanston, I only paid three dollars for 200lbs. It came from Nebraska, right by your door, one hundred and twenty miles further. I suppose you only do business three months out of the twelve, which accounts for the high price." "You are right there, we do not have much trade after the emigrant season is over." I bought the grain and paid for it and my wagon had 300lbs. more weight on it. The wagon itself only weighs 325lbs.; pretty slender for the Rocky Mountains. In my wagon there is a box a half foot deep, a half foot wide, and three feet long, water-tight, in which are clothing, tea, coffee, sugar, several kinds of canned meats and some tools, such as a wrench, hammer, hatchet, saw, square and many smaller tools. The weight of the whole being about 175lbs.; making a total of goods of 500lbs. and 800lbs. for my horse to draw. When passing through creeks, rivers and sloughs I get on and ride, thus adding 180lbs. more, for the horse to draw through and up the rivers and creeks. About six o'clock I returned to my camping ground, inspected my wagon and made the weak places stronger and more perfect. After everything had been done as I thought could be, to make it safer, I prepared for the night; securing my cattle to their posts, made up my bed and went to rest.

On the morning of the 26th I left Green River city for Laramie, where I arrived on the 10th of June. Leaving the city I followed the railroad to Rock Springs, where I left it and did not see it again until arriving in Laramie. After leaving the city and having travelled about six miles, I came to Bitter Creek river. The waters are said to be poisonous and cattle are not allowed to drink its waters. In fording this river my cattle were not dry, so did not attempt to drink. About twelve I made Rock Springs, which is a telegraph station. Here I made a short stop, giving water and grain to the cattle and took a dish of cold coffee and crackers myself. Here I leave the railroad for a long time. About four miles or more from here I met an ox team, accompanied by two men, and inquired if "I was on the right trail for Laramie?" "You are not; you should have taken the other trail," they said. "Then I shall have to go back and take the other trail?" I said. "No, go on a little further and turn to your left, you will come into the trail." I went on and coming to the place turned to the left, as I had been told, coming back to the trail all right, and about five o'clock came to a slough; it was an awful looking hole. After looking at it I got upon my wagon and drove over it all right. After a little while I came to another of the same kind, which I passed all right. Went on, coming to some grass, which was fenced in and some cattle feeding, and going on a little further came to a house and barn. After passing the house we came to a good grass plat where I camped for the night. I turned my cattle loose to feed for themselves, while I gathered some fuel, made a fire, prepared some coffee and cooked some dried beef, partaking of an excellent supper. A good dish of coffee, well seasoned with milk and sugar, all alone, tastes good, you bet. After supper I brought in the cattle, gave them some grain and secured them for the night; spread out my blankets, laid down and allowed myself to go to sleep. Just think of it, in the dead of the night to wake up and find yourself alone and have a long talk with my cattle. My dog, Bertie, is at all times with me in my bed.

The morning of the 27th found me up before there was any light. I turned the cattle loose for grass, greased my wagon, made a fire, boiled coffee and eggs, and opened a can of salmon. My breakfast being ready I brought in the cattle and gave them some grain, then I sat down to my breakfast to be ready to move onwards together. After breakfast started onward and having travelled about a mile came to a house. Here was a man, his wife and two children. I inquired the name of this canyon. "It is called Miller's canyon, stranger." "How far is it to Green River city?" "Twenty-five miles, stranger."

"How far to the next house?" "I do not know the distance, but it is a long way; in fact I never was east of here more than fifty miles, stranger." "How long have you been here?" "Six years or more, stranger." I left them and ascended the mountain, attaining its summit—travelling three-fourths of a circle in the distance of eight miles. About ten o'clock I passed a trail to my left and on a board nailed to a post I read, "To Soda Springs, crossing Green River without Ferry." Went down the mountain and at its base I crossed a deep gulch on snow. A short distance from this gulch I came to a creek of good water. Here we stopped, my cattle took water and grain, myself and dog, bread, cheese and cold coffee. We go on our road to-day, so far good, no rivers, creeks or sloughs. The day is fast closing; it is time we should have come to grass. I have travelled all day and seen none; we must go into camp without water or grass. I spoke to my horse, "Fanny, we will go no further to-day; we have no grass or water; you will be obliged to eat your grain without." It is hard, plenty of grass and water one day and none the next. I drove into the sage bush, just out of the trail and stopped. Fed my cattle with grain, spread my blankets on the ground and laid down for the night, but could not go to sleep. I would lay awhile and then get up and talk to my cattle and then lay down again, but could not drop off to sleep. Several times I got up and laid down again, and after a while I dropped off to sleep, not knowing it at the time.

On the morning of the 28th I was up again before it was light enough to travel. I gave my cattle grain, but they would not touch it, they were so thirsty. As soon as light came I drove into the trail and moved on. I knew that my cattle must have water, so I drove on as fast as possible; after travelling about eight miles we came to water, which I tested and found it fair water, so I gave to the cattle as much as they would drink. After which I gave them their grain, and while they were eating had breakfast of crackers and milk. I did not stop long, but went on and about ten o'clock met a man on horseback, leading a pack-horse. "Good morning, stranger," I said. "Good morning, sir." "How far have you come this morning?" I asked. "About ten or twelve miles," he said. "Did your horses have grass last night?" I asked. "No, not any; I should have stopped at the creek, there was grass there," he said. "How is the trail on ahead?" I asked. "First best for me; I can go anywhere as I am, you can't with your wagon." "Where are you going to?" I asked. "I am going to California," he said. "California, I am just from there." "You from California; what, you have not come from California with that outfit?" he asked. "I have; just as I am, and I am going East, to Massachusetts," I answered. "The d—l you are. Well, I will give it up, if you have come so far, I think I ought to do as much; good-bye, stranger." "Good-bye, sir." We parted and went on, I saying, "Well, Fanny and Bessie, we must make that creek before night. There is grass, you did not get any last night; to-night you may get some." On we went, a good trail and down grade; we are travelling at the rate of three miles an hour, and about four p. m., I made a stop of about thirty minutes, giving the cattle some grain, after which we went on. Talking to my horse I said, "Come, Fanny, do your best, it is a good road, you shall have grass to-night." I was crowding along as fast as I could, when looking off to my left, saw smoke, and soon I came to tracks of wagons and was sure there was a camp some where near. When the horse saw these tracks she stopped, looking around. I said, "Fanny, we will go in here and follow those tracks and see what we can find." Travelling around a bluff we came in sight of a camp—a tent and three wagons and eight horses; five men, a boy, two women and a girl. As I went into the camp I called out, "Don't be afraid, I have come to see who is here!" "Come in, stranger; you are welcome," was answered. "I am going East and you are going West, I suppose. Can I stop with you to-night, or in other words, can I go into camp here?" I asked. "Yes, sir; you can," was answered. I detached the horse from the wagon and unharnessed her, turning her loose, and she went rolling about for some time. I gave the cow the same chance, but she went for the grass. It is half-past six and I went to gather fuel for a fire. "Stranger, do your cooking by our fire; don't trouble yourself in making a fire." I got my supper, such as coffee, boiled eggs, crackers and milk. I brought in my cattle for the night, securing and giving them their grain, made up my bed and went to rest.

On the morning of the 29th, all hands around the camp were up early, making ready for a departure; it is a lively camp. Cattle were fed, wagons greased and breakfast prepared. I was invited to breakfast with the rest of the company, all making the ground our table. The breakfast comprised bacon, eggs, warm bread and coffee. Remember, I have a cow that has given milk every day since calving; she is now four years old and has had two calves. On this occasion I found milk for all. After breakfast we made ready and moved on our respective ways. It is six o'clock as I leave the camp. It is a fine morning and the road good. The wind is freshening up and clouds are gathering; it looks as if we are to have a change of weather; it is warm and sultry and begins to look like rain. I crowd on as fast as I can—remember it is all walk and nothing else—after a while it began to rain and the wind blew a gale. I stopped to make the things on the wagon more secure; as I could see no place for shelter or cover, we have to stand and take it. A flash of lightning and a peal of thunder startled us and set me thinking of my loneliness; sometimes this thought troubles me considerably. What if some serious accident happens to me? The storm did not last long, but it left the roads dangerous travelling; my horse could scarcely ascend a hill, but descending was even worse, on account of the slipperyness. I continued on, hoping to come to some place where we could stay, at least over night. I came to a cross-trail, leading to the right and left; not knowing which to take, I concluded to stop, as I have found such trails to my disadvantage. I had not been here more than an hour before a team came along the right trail and stopped when he got to me, saying, "Stranger, I have been trying to travel since the storm, but my horse slips so bad I am afraid she will injure herself." "I am in the same fix. It is dangerous travelling; I have been travelling an hour down the mountains, and my horse has been down twice. I am looking for water. Antelope Springs are not far from here; have you come past them, stranger?" "No, sir," I answered. "Then they must be on this trail." "Are you alone," I asked. "No, stranger; there is another team a little ways back." "Where are you from?" I asked. "I am from Laramie; where are you from?" asked the stranger. "I am from Ogden." "You from Ogden! I am going there and then to Salt Lake city," said the stranger. "What! are you a Mormon?" "No, I am not a Mormon; are you?" asked the stranger. "No, I am not, but I know something about them, as I have lived amongst them some eight months. I left Ogden on the 14th instant, and have come so far since that time." "Where are you going to?" asked the stranger. "I am going to Laramie," I replied. "How is the road to Ogden; what rivers have you forded?" "I forded Bear river, Muddy creek, Hams Fork and Bitter creek. These are all of any account; small creeks are the worst to cross," I answered. He went on up the left trail, I following in his rear. We had gone but a short distance when we came to a small creek, were we stopped and gave our cattle water. We then went on our way and came to a good valley where we found a herd of horses, ninety in number, in charge of two men, who were bound to Laramie. Here, we also found an Emigrant train, twelve in number, bound for Oregon. Entering this valley, on our left are the springs, known as Antelope Springs. It is three o'clock and all propose to stop until we can travel. There is not much grass but plenty of water. The herd of horses have eaten nearly all the grass. I secured the cow with her lariat, the horse I dared not turn loose, nor stake her out. This is a most wonderful place; not more than fifty acres in extent, almost surrounded by mountains. There is two entrances to the valley; one from the East and one from the West. A fine harbor it makes, only one thing is lacking, that is wood; not a particle of fuel can be found, it has been so closely gathered up. I was informed that here was the best water to be found between Ogden and Laramie. Here I will say, that if I ever travel in this manner again, I will carry an oil stove for cooking purposes, it will save much labor in gathering fuel; you can gather sage brush, but wood is almost out of the question across the plains. When I entered this valley, beside the herd of horses, I found twelve wagons, twenty-four horses and sixty-three persons, men, women and children, all for Ogden. The other two teams were for Salt Lake city. It is six o'clock in the evening and time to prepare for the night. Supper comes first, there is no wood of which to make a fire. I have kerosene oil, but I use it for my lantern and lighting a fire, and have found it very convenient many times for this purpose. Of these teams, there are two which have no men with them. They are conducted by two women and eight children, four boys and four girls—ten persons in all. These women are Germans, and they had brought with them the spare wood from last night's camp, and they were the only ones who had any wood. This wood made tea and coffee for the whole camp. After supper preparations for the night were made. The ground is quite wet. The camp for the night had eleven tents, all arranged in a circle. In the rear of each tent is a wagon, and the horses are made fast to the rear of each. I was invited to come into the circle, but declined, having no tent—preferring to sleep with my cattle. This camp is under good discipline, and has a watchman for each night. This is essential; should anything strange or serious occur in or around the camp it is made known to all. Having the camp arranged for the night and while sitting around, one of the company said, "Stranger from California, we would like to hear from you, about your travels. We are going to Oregon, now give us a route thereto." "Captain, what part of Oregon do you intend to settle in?" "We intend to settle on lands that have been cultivated to some extent, say in the vicinity of Portland," said the captain. "Portland is about one hundred and twenty-five miles from the Pacific Ocean. Now, I would go from here to Green River city, following the Union Pacific Railroad to Ogden, by way of Evanston. At Ogden take the Central Pacific Railroad to Corinne, Kelton, Terrace, Wells, Elko, Carlin. About five miles beyond Carlin, take the old Emigrant trail to Beowawe; there you are on the railroad again. Then to Battle Mountain, Golconda, Winnemucca, Humboldt, Wadsworth, Reno. Then take the Virginia city and Marysville turnpike to Webber's Lake, Jackson's Ranche, Graniteville, Nevada city, Grass Valley to Marysville. There you should take the California and Oregon road to Oregon. This is as far as I can tell you. You will not have to leave the Central Pacific Railroad for any length of time, with one exception. That will be from Carlin to Beowawe."

On the morning of the 30th, all hands were up before the sun. A detail was made and sent in search of wood, but nothing but sage brush could be found, and enough of this was found to boil all the water that was necessary to make coffee for breakfast for the whole camp. I milked the cow and contributed it to the general stock, and the company were much pleased to taste milk once more. At six o'clock all had finished breakfast and got ready to break camp. It was decided to do so on account of the scarcity of fuel and grass, but we had plenty of good water, such as we shall not find for many miles. As we were about to part, the captain of the camp, John H. Standly, said, "Stranger from California, bound East to Massachusetts, we sincerely hope that you will succeed in your great undertaking. Travelling alone as you are, not knowing what you may have to encounter, (perhaps, it is as well you do not) we know, and can't help but think of you daily. We would like to know whether you succeed in getting through your journey safely." I answered, "Strangers from Kansas, I thank you kindly for your sympathy in my behalf, hoping that you all may reach your destination in safety. I know what you will have to encounter. Moving as an army; if you get into a tight place you can get out of it; you are not alone as I am. Strangers, I bid you all good-bye." As I left them, they gave three cheers for the man from California, bound East to Massachusetts.

It was half-past eight o'clock when we broke camp, each going his seperate way. It was a delightfully warm morning, but hard travelling for my horse, as she kept slipping, but as the day advanced the travelling improved. About twelve at noon, I stopped and gave the cattle a feed of grain. No water for them as warm as it had been in the morning; it was rather hard on them. My stop was short as I wished to get to some water.

About two o'clock I met a train of four wagons and I asked them "How far is it to water?" "We have seen none since leaving camp this morning, stranger." "How far have you come, think you?" "About twelve miles I think. Stranger, how far have you come?" "About the same distance." "When did you cross any rivers or creeks last?" I asked. "We have seen none for many miles." "How far from the road were you camped last night?" I asked. "Oh, not far; about forty rods, not more. We turned in on our right and made a high bluff, around the bluff we found both water and grass; you will see our tracks, we have made some deep ones to-day, stranger." "Where are you from?" I asked. "We are from Colorado. Where are you from, stranger?" "I am from California." "What, you all the way from California?" "Yes, all the way." "That beats the d—l. Have you brought that cow all the way from California, stranger?" "No, I did not say that I brought that cow from California, but led her all the way. She has walked all that distance," I said. "Where are you going to, stranger?" "I am going to Massachusetts." "Oh, h—l! where are you going, honest?' said the stranger. "Honest, I am going East, to Massachusetts. Where are you going?" I asked. "We are bound to Washington Territory." After this conversation we bade good-bye and went on our several ways. About six o'clock I came to the tracks made by the teams I had met. I turned in and followed the tracks around the bluff and came to water. Here I stopped and made my camp for the night. I detached the horse from the wagon, removing her harness and let her loose, the cow also; the horse went in for rolling, the cow for grazing. I went gathering sage brush for fuel and having gathered a large pile, I set it on fire, prepared a hot supper and ate it. After supper I brought in my cattle, securing them and gave them their evening meal of grain, made up my bed and lay down to rest. As I lay down on my bed my attention was drawn towards my horse. She was looking steadily towards the bluff, and continued to for some time. I looked in that direction but could see nothing; still she kept looking all the same. All at once I saw what had attracted the attention of my horse. It was a herd of deer coming down the bluffs for grass and water. They were not more than twenty rods from us. I did not trouble them, and told them to remain as long as they wished, and they did remain. I did not let my fire go out as I thought there might be something more than deer around. It has been my custom at nights to tie my dog to the wagon, since I was so near losing him when I was travelling among the sheep ranches and was annoyed by coyottes. They were around me continually; I did not know what to do to stop their infernal noise. One morning I was up early and saw one a short distance from me. I set the dog on him and the coyotte turned on the dog. I tried to call the dog off, but the little boobee was only the more courageous, and since that time I have been more particular about setting him on to the wild animals.

The last day of May, 31st, I was up early, as usual, getting ready to strike out. At six o'clock I left the camp and at eight I made the mountain's base on the left, travelling east, I came to a stop. I left my cattle and ascended the mountain, when about half-way up I stopped hesitating, but walked to the summit. Beyond I could see a great distance. Here my imagination carried me home. Well, here I am; my cattle are yonder at the base. I went back to them saying to the horse, "Fanny, can you make this mountain? I think you can, but you will have to work smart to do it." My weight is about 600lbs. in all. "Fanny," I said, "you can't take it all at once; we must make two loads of it." I took the grain from the carriage and left it at the foot of the hill. I did not leave the cow, knowing that she is good at going up hills, her halter being at all times slack. The horse succeeded in drawing up the load after a hard pull; then we returned for the grain, taking the cow back with us to act as a brake on going down the hill. I then re-loaded the grain and took up the second load; this is the worst hill I have travelled so far on my journey—if there are any mountains in Wyoming this must be one of them. In journeying from the East this hill is not near so hard as from the West. It was just twelve at noon as we made the summit the last time. I gave the cattle some grain and when they had finished eating went on further, and about two o'clock we came to a small creek at an opportune time, as the cattle were very thirsty and they drank freely. Going on we travelled a good down grade, with a tip-top trail, crowding along as fast as we could. In fact, to-day I am feeling well. As I travelled along I saw smoke in front of us and I am sure the horse saw it also, as she pricked her ears until we came to a camp, where I stopped and inquired if there was any water near by, how they had come and where they made camp last night and if there were any rivers to ford? I ask such questions whenever I meet such trains of travellers. This company consisted of five wagons, twelve horses, four tents and twenty-two persons, hailing from Kansas, on their way to Oregon. "Where are you from and where are you going?" asked the strangers. "I am from California, going East," I replied. "You from California, going East. What, don't you like California, stranger?" "Yes, but like the East much better," I answered. "That beats the d—l; ain't you just a little crazy?" "No, not much," I said. "You have not brought that cow from California, have you?" "No, I have not brought her a step, I have led her all the way as you now see," I remarked. "Ha, ha-ha!" laughed the stranger. "I'll bet you are a Yankee." "Yes, I am."

"Here, come with me." I went with him to his wagon, there he took out a small barrel that would hold about a gallon, took out the stopple and drank, I should think as much as a pint, and then handed it to me, saying, "Drink, Yankee, drink; it will do you good. I have plenty more." I took it and drank three small swallows, and handed it back to the man, he taking another drink and then handed it to me again, but I refused to drink any more. I then said, "I will stop here over night if you will allow me to do so?" "Yes, stranger, stop with us over-night. I will find the whisky." "I will milk the cow and we will have some good coffee, that will be better than whisky," I answered. It is now about six o'clock, rather early to go into camp, but we will make it up to-morrow. "Where is the water?" I asked. "You can have some of ours; we carry it in a barrel and don't intend to be without; we keep the barrels full. This we got at Platt River; we were in camp there last night and came from there to-day." About how many miles have you made to-day?" I asked. "About twenty miles." I gave my cattle water and grain, remarking that it was getting low, half gone, but it must last until I reach Laramie, as there is none to be bought this side of that place. The teamster said, "It was not so, I could get grain where I should cross the river, which I would reach to-morrow. Then you will follow the river to the bridge, just put up by Uncle Sam, and beyond the bridge you will come to a store. There you can get grain, flour, bacon, tea, coffee, sugar and all the whisky you want." When in Green River city I was told that I would have to take grain that would last me till I reached Laramie, and you say that I can get grain after crossing the river?" "Yes, all you want." "I bought enough to last me to Laramie. Had I known that I could buy, it would have saved me hauling it this distance. I will feed my cattle a little more. How many days have you been coming from

Laramie?" I asked. "Left Laramie on the 24th, eight days," answered the stranger. "About how many miles, think you?" "About one hundred and forty. We ought to travel about twenty miles a day, but our first day out, we only travelled to the river." "What river?" I asked. "I do not know the name." "I want some hot coffee and want to go to bed, as I desire to start early in the morning and make that store." "Oh, let your coffee go, take a drink of whisky, that will do you some good," said the stranger. "Friend, I am not in the habit of taking such strong stuff; it does us no good, you must excuse me." "Yes, I will, but stranger, I tell you that you had better get some whisky when you get to the store; it will help you along so much easier. You have got a hard road before you; you have got to cross what will make you quail." "Friend, I am alone and must keep my head clear; it will not do for me to meddle with that whisky much; it is good where it belongs, if you know where that is." "Well, we will go to bed and get up early in the morning for a good, early start." Securing my cattle I went to bed.

On the morning of June 1st, I was up at five o'clock making all preparations for moving on. My neighbors were not yet up, so I hollered out, "Strangers, I am all ready to leave you. If you have any message to send East, now is your time!" The old gentleman answered, "Hold on a minute! Stranger, you are going East and I West, we shall never meet again, so here is luck and prosperity to you, hoping you will have a good voyage." He drank and urged me to drink. I said, "Friend, I am not in the habit of doing this, but to please you, I do so. I really think it does more harm than good; good morning. I hope you will succeed on your long journey," I remarked. "Good morning, I hope you will get along all right, you have a hard road to Laramie." I left them soon after five o'clock; it was a very fine morning and a good trail, all were in harmony. About eight o'clock we came to a creek and I allowed my cattle to take as much water as they pleased, making but a short stop. Had I company, how pleasant it would be; my animals are my only company. I talk with them as though they were human and think they understand me; I have no doubt about this. This is my seventh day from Green River city, about half-way to Laramie. I am now in sight of Platte Valley. I have been descending since making the summit of the hill yesterday. A good road is cheering, such as I have had for the past two days; one hour more and I shall be on the banks of the river. I see smoke in that direction, also teams, any quantity of them. There appears a large camp close by the river; there is grass and horses feeding. "Come, Fanny, go on; we will soon be there," I said. At a distance she saw the horses and whinnied loudly. We made for the camp and as I made it was completely taken in; men, women and children surrounded me asking many questions. "Stranger, where in h—l have you come from, from the West, have you not?" "I have come from the West, but your first question I am not able to answer. I don't know that place; I never was there; I have heard of it, perhaps you can tell me where it is? Oh, I came through it my first day from Green River city; you will find it before you get there," I remarked. "You will, surely before you get to Laramie. I will bet you are a Yankee," was answered. "Well, you are a good guesser. I am. I would like to stop here to-night; you may ask me any questions you like. I am from California, just as you see me, with horse, carriage, cow and dog. I can make it interesting to you; I want my horse and cow to have some grass. I see there is plenty of it for all. I will let them both loose to feed, at the same time I will give you a history of my travels. Have you had your supper?" I asked. "No, we have not," said the stranger. "All right, I want some hot tea or coffee; I have plenty of it, and not only that, I have yonder cow; she has given me milk all my way from California to this place, just one year to day. The first of June, 1882, we left Eureka city, Humboldt county, three hundred and three miles north of San Francisco; following the Central Pacific Railroad from there to Ogden, arriving at the latter place on the 23rd of September. On the 14th of May last, we left Ogden and have travelled to this very place, North Platte River." "About how many miles have you travelled since you left California, stranger?" was asked. "On my arrival in Ogden I found that I had travelled fourteen hundred and twenty-seven miles." "Where are you going to, stranger?" "I am going to Massachusetts; when I get there I am at home." "About how far is it from here, stranger?" "About two thousand five hundred miles." "More than four thousand miles you will have travelled. How far has that cow come with you?" "She has come all the distance; I left with the same outfit I now have." "I saw last fall in some paper of a man coming from California and going to Massachusetts, and you are the man. Well, well, you are a brick; you will be well burned by the time you get to Massachusetts. We shall weary you all out asking questions. Our supper is ready, come with me and get some hot coffee, stranger." "Thank you, I will." After supper I asked, "How large a camp have you?" "We have twenty-one wagons, forty-eight horses and one hundred and one persons, all told, bound for Washington Territory. Now, how shall we go, to get there?" asked the captain. "What part of the territory are you intending to settle in?" I asked. "The western part, about one hundred miles from the Pacific Ocean." "Only a few days' ago I was asked about the same question, with one exception, that was Oregon; about the same distance from the ocean, only further north. Now, suppose I give you a route, due west, within one hundred and fifty miles of the Pacific Ocean; that would be to Sacramento, your road is a great thoroughfare. There is but one trail to central California, that is Fremont's; all other trails lead out of this. We will start from this very spot, North Platte River and go to Green River city, Evanston, Ogden. From Ogden follow the Central Pacific Railroad to Carlin; there leave the railroad and cross over the mountain to Beowawe, and on to Reno. At this place leave the railroad trail and take the Henness trail to Graniteville, Grass Valley to Marysville. At this last place you are on the great highway for Oregon; about one hundred and fifty miles from the Pacific Ocean. From here to Green River city it is a very disagreeable road, but had I had company it might have seemed different; travelling alone makes things look dreary. I have met many teams, most of them were from Kansas. Where are you from, captain?" "We are from Kansas." "I think you are making it a rough road for those in your rear." "We do cut it up badly." "It makes an awful road for me; how is it from Laramie to here?" "It is very good, but the rivers and creeks are awful to think of. The worst place was on our first day from Laramie, about fifteen miles out. It is a flat, wide plat of meadow, adjoining a river, which you have to ford three times in less than twelve rods. Before we came to this river, we came to a store and post-office. About a mile this side of the store is an awful muddy hole. It took us nearly all of the afternoon to get through. About half of our teams got through; the rest we had to double up to get them through. The fording of the river was not bad, a good bottom, but deep water; many things in our wagons got wet. Just this side the river was a hill, we stopped on this ascension to let the water drop out, which it did to some extent. We have forded but one river since, crossed three bridges and one creek. The creek not four rods across, was the worst of all, more mud than water. All of this you will have to encounter. Stranger, you do not know what you have to pass through before reaching Laramie; you should have some one with you at those places. Your next three days will be good. On leaving here you will follow the river to the bridge, and cross on a good, substantial bridge, built by the Government. After crossing, and going a short distance you will come to the store, where you can buy most anything you wish— grain, flour, bacon, pork, sugar, tea, coffee and a large variety of canned meats. It is a great accommodation store. While in Laramie this store was made known to us," said the captain. "When I was in Green River city, I was told that I could not get anything that I should need until getting to Laramie. They told me a big lie, you see. When you get there, tell the grain dealer that you met the man with the horse, cow and dog, and he sends his compliments, and says he could have got all the grain he wanted at the bridge over the Platte River, near Warm Springs." "It is about time to retire. We place a watchman over the camp at nights to look around while we are sleeping; should anything happen, it would be made known to us and we should be prepared for any emergency," said the captain.

On the morning of June 2nd, on the banks of the Platte River I broke camp, journeying on and following the river to a bridge, recently built by the Government, which I crossed. After travelling but a short distance I came to the store, before spoken about. This place is known as Hot Springs, and is about one hundred and thirty miles from Laramie. I travelled along the river until I came to some grass and stopped, it was difficult to get the cattle past, if I had desired; so I unharnessed the horse and gave the cattle a good chance to eat their fill, not knowing where the next would be found. We stayed just one hour and then went on, coming back to the old trail. This morning, when leaving camp, instead of fording the river, I chose to go over the bridge, as the river was very high. It is a good ford, but at this time of the year the water is deep and strong. Many in crossing, have been borne down by its force, so the Government has erected this bridge. As you make the river from the East or West the trail is good. Although from the East you have to descend a bluff, but not from the West. About one mile from the river I came to a junction of four roads. In my rear is the river; to my left is Fort Steal and the Union Pacific Railroad, about twenty miles; to my right is the bridge; to my left is the road to Laramie, a hundred and twenty miles away, more or less. It was four o'clock and moving in the right direction, hoping to make Laramie in five days, the road is good and all of us cheerful. About six o'clock, ahead of us I saw smoke; soon after we came up to three ugly-looking men who were putting up a tent; they had a wagon and three bulls. I passed the compliments of the day with them in a rough manner, asking some questions. I thought it best to go on as I did not like their movements, but I asked, "How far was it to water?" "Three miles to the creek," was answered. "How large a creek?" I asked. "A small one, but water enough for your cattle," was answered. "Where are you from?" "I am from Hot Springs." "Where in h—l is Hot Springs?" was asked. "About fifteen miles from here, near Platte River." It is about three miles to the creek, so I said, "Come, Fanny, we must reach the creek," which in due time we did. Giving my cattle a good drink I went on, not daring to make my camp there. I made up my mind to journey on as long as I could as my road was good. After a little while I saw a light ahead, which on our coming near, proved to be a camp. In approaching the camp the horse gave a tremendous neigh, startling all the camp, horses as well as men. I went right into the camp and said, "Don't be afraid, I am alone and will not harm you; I have come from the West and suppose you seldom meet persons from that direction. I wish to camp with you to-night, and would rather do so than stop with those I met two hours ago. I should have kept on if I had not struck your camp, until I was far out of their reach." "Who were those that you dislike so much?" I told him of the men with the bulls, whose looks and actions I did not like, and repeated the discussion I had with them, so I travelled out of their reach and here I am. I asked if they had any objections to my camping with them over night, and was told they had no objections. I lead my cattle into the camp and gave them grain, made my bed and laid down, saying that I was very weary and tired, having travelled a long distance that day. "Stranger, if you are not too tired, please tell us where you are from and where bound?" "Strangers, I have come from California. Three hundred and three miles north of San Francisco, from there following the Central Pacific Railroad through the States of California, Nevada, Utah to Ogden, Green River to this place." "Where are you going, stranger?" "I am bound East, to Massachusetts," I answered. "Going to Massachusetts! How far have you come with that cow, stranger?" "I have led her all that distance, about eighteen hundred miles. Where are you from?" I asked. "We are from Kansas and are going to Oregon." "I have met many from Kansas, all going to Oregon. What is the cause of so many leaving Kansas?" "We are from the western part of Kansas. The hot winds kill about everything there and the people are leaving, going West." "How many teams have you?" "We have four, also four men, four women, twelve children and two dogs, all for Oregon. Stranger, where has been your worst travelling on the whole route?" "My worst travelling, and also the most dangerous, was in California. From Green River to where we are, has been most disagreeable. All alone, as I am, it makes one think of home too much. I am continually thinking of breaking down, or anything serious happening to me; these thoughts trouble me continuously. Since leaving Green River city, there have been days that I have seen no person nor passed a house. I have yet about one hundred miles to travel, before I reach Laramie; how many houses do I pass in making that distance?" I asked. "You pass one, yes, two; both are at a river where you cross on a bridge, one on each side to take the toll. These are all until you get to New Laramie, where there is a post-office and a store. Now, friend, stranger, we will leave you until morning and hope you will have a good night's rest; good night." "Good night," I replied.

On the morning of June 3rd I was up before my neighbors, making ready to move on. I had fed my cattle and was greasing my carriage, when one of my neighbors came around and asked, "How often do you grease your wagon?" "I grease every other day; I travel about twenty-five miles a day, making about fifty miles between each greasing. Can I make some coffee by your fire?" I asked. "Oh, yes; you can make your breakfast by our fire." Soon all in the camp were up and around. I went to milk the cow and while doing so, one of the dogs came too near the cow; she made a plunge at the dog upsetting me and the milk. I cared but little for the milk, but the strangers seemed to feel bad about it. The poor dog had to take it on all sides. I told them I did not care for the milk, but felt sorry on their part. I finished milking and there was enough for the coffee of the whole camp. After breakfast, on leaving the camp I wished the company success on their long journey. They answered, "Friend, stranger, we all feel anxious for you, being alone; if you were in company with some one it would seem different, and when in a tight place would have some one to help you. Good-bye, success to you, stranger." We parted and I went on. It was a pleasant and grand morning; to my right are lofty mountains, covered with snow, which appear but a short distance away, but are many miles. High elevations give light and air, and the eye a long range of vision. About nine o'clock I met a long train, but made no stop, merely asking where they were from and where going? "We are from Kansas and going to Washington Territory. Where are you from and where going?" was answered. "I am from California, going East, to Massachusetts," I answered. "You are from there, and have you brought that cow from there, stranger?" "We have come from California just as you see us." I left them and at twelve o'clock met another train, who were at dinner. Having my feed ready for the cattle I stopped and fed them, and ate my own dinner. This company was also from Kansas, bound for Oregon. There were ten teams, twenty-four horses, twelve men, sixteen women and thirty-eight children, sixty-six persons in all. I left this company about half-past one o'clock; my road was not good, being badly cut up by the many teams. About three o'clock we met another train of six teams; they were also from Kansas, bound for Oregon, comprising eight men, eight women and nineteen children. Only a short distance further I came to another train of four teams, ten horses, four men, four women and thirteen children, from the same State. About five o'clock I met another band of emigrants of nine teams, eleven men, ten women and twenty-nine children, all for the State of Oregon. I asked the captain of the train the "Cause of so many leaving Kansas? It looked as though they were abandoning the State. I have met a good many teams to-day." "I will tell you the cause, stranger. Where we come from we have hot winds that cuts corn and many other things; we can't stand it, and it is very unhealthy. It is not so in other sections of the State. We made up our minds to leave the State and go to the West and see what we can do there." "Strangers, success to you," I said and went on. About half-past six o'clock I saw smoke in the distance and journeyed towards it, and came to a small creek and grass and gave my cattle water. Here, my first thoughts were to go into camp, then I thought I would go to where I saw the smoke. However, there being excellent water and grass at this creek, I concluded to camp here, so we left the trail to the right, went down the creek a short distance and pitched my camp, and turned the cattle loose so that they could have their fill of grass. I concluded to build no fire, but take my supper cold. After supper I spread my blankets, laid me down and went to sleep. I did not intend to sleep. When I awoke I went for my cattle and found the cow lying down, the horse I could not find. I called for the horse but no answer could I get. I then called the cow, while I was near that I might have her to help me call the horse. The second time of calling the cow the horse answered me and while taking the cow to the wagon the horse came into camp and I made them secure to their posts. A thought now came into my head to harness the horse and go where I had seen the smoke. It was not yet ten o'clock. I went on and came to the camp, which was but a short distance from the road. On approaching I saw two men sitting by the fire, whom I addressed, saying "Good evening, gentlemen. About half-past six I saw the smoke from your camp which I intended to reach, but coming to a creek where there was good grass and water, I stopped to let my cattle have a good nibble, so I remained there about three hours, and now I have come on here to see if I could remain with you the rest of the night?" While I was speaking the foregoing, the whole camp came around me. "Strangers, can I remain here? I have come a long distance, and perhaps can make a half hour of some interest to you." "Stranger, make yourself at home with us," was answered. "I have said that I have come a long way, which is true; I am all the way from the Pacific Ocean, alone." "You say that you are from California; where is your home?" "I am, and my home is in Massachusetts, and I am on my way home." "Do you think that you will be able to get that cow to that State, stranger?" "I do, she has already travelled eighteen hundred miles. You can see in what condition she is; she speaks for herself." "She is a fine looking cow. When did you leave California, stranger?" "The first day of June, 1882." "We are going somewhere, and have started for Oregon, but may change our direction. We have heard much about California, what a glorious State it is! You have had an opportunity to know something about it, stranger?" "Yes, I know something about the State. There are as many climates in the State, as there are counties; some parts are hot; some warm and some parts cold. You can get any temperature you desire; but that is not all. California gets her watering done in December and January; some parts in November, and some parts in February. Humboldt county I know more about than any other county. That county gets more rain than any other in the State, it is also one of the healthiest in the State. West of the coast-range of mountains the temperature is the most even, neither too hot nor too cold; on the east side of the range it is warm, in many places very warm. What I dislike, is the many months without rain. Say, the last rain was in February and there will be no more until December. The best months are February, March and April; they are fine months, but in May it begins to dry up; June and July are hot, and August is very dry. By the latter month you will have to start your sheep for the mountains, or they will starve on the way. A person from the East going to California will find the months of November, December, January and February much different from the East. They will forget our May's and June's, but when the sun gets high and the winds are blowing a gale, and the sands are drifting like snow, then, and not till then, will they think of home. We have better days in Massachusetts than they can have in California."

On the morning of the 4th I was up early, getting ready for another day's travel, and soon after my neighbors were stirring. Breakfast was made and disposed of and at six o'clock I am ready to break camp and move on. On leaving I said, "Strangers, I leave you; success to you." "Thank you, we hope you will get along all right, you have a dangerous road before you; I think you will accomplish your undertaking, you look just the man to do it. We would like to hear from you, good morning, stranger." I replied, "Good morning," and went on my way. About eight o'clock I came to water; it looked as if milk had been turned into it. I tasted and found it poor water, but not disagreeable, and gave my cattle a half pail each. Going on I ascend a high bluff and soon attain the summit of Medicine Bow Mountain. It is a high elevation, thousands of feet above the level of the sea. Here I stopped and gave my cattle grain, which they would not eat on account of their great thirst. In descending, on my right is a high ridge. After travelling about a half mile my road turns sharp to the right and then ascends this ridge. You descend from this into a valley and cross a small creek, turning sharp to the left. Travelling this valley about a mile, another ridge has to be ascended. This proceding had to be repeated until seven of these ridges had been ascended and descended, and came to a large creek. If this creek was in the East it would be called a river; in the West it is called a creek. Being in the habit of talking to my cattle, I think they understand me, I said, "Fanny, we have got to cross this creek, we can't go around it, we must go down into it, mud or no mud." I got on the wagon and drove down into the mud and water, about three feet deep, the wagon was full of water; we went on about two rods when my horse stepped on something that threw her down, completely covering her in the water. I leaped from the wagon into the mud and water, caught her by the head, and raised it out of the water that she might breathe. I was in full three feet of mud and water. "Come, Fanny, we must get out of this," I said, and at the moment she made a great exertion, and landed on her feet. She was frightened, she trembled and quivered. I thought she would die right there where she was. I **stood beside her**, petting and talking to her, and soon I saw she was coming all right again. We had about twenty feet more to cross before we reached the opposite bank. I spoke to her, saying, "Fanny, try it again." She pulled with a tremendous power, a little too much, as she tore the tugs in two, and landed herself on the bank; leaving the carriage, cow, dog and everything else in the creek. This is not the first time she has done this thing. On crossing the Humboldt river, there she left the wagon, cow, and all in the creek. Since that time I have carried two ropes about thirty-five feet long. I take these ropes and make them fast to the front axles, carry the other ends on hard ground where the horse can stand, make them fast to the harness; this being done the horse pulls the wagon out of the creek right sharply. Well, I am out of the water, but how do I look? Wet and muddy—more mud than water. I carry two pails for watering my cattle, these I take, plunge into the mud and fill the pails with water, come out on dry land and went gathering sage brush for a fire. Having made a fire, I took off my boots, stockings, pants and drawers, rinsing and wringing them as dry as possible, re-placing them and building more fire until I had made myself comfortable. I repaired my harness by the use of ropes and went on until coming where I could gather more sage brush to make a fire and there I stopped for the night. I did not get much rest, as I was both wet and cold. Could I have had what fuel I ought to have, then I should have been warm. I then said the first opportunity I have I will procure some of that fuel, so that when I get into another creek I should be prepared for the worst emergency. I have been in many tight places and every time came out all right.

On the morning of the 5th I was up as usual, making ready for the day's duty, but not feeling so well as common. Yesterday, I shall remember as long as time lasts with me. It was half-past five o'clock as I resumed my journey and a remarkably fine morning. About half-past seven we met a train of nine teams and stopped to ask and answer questions. My questions are so common; how far to water, are there rivers to ford, etc? I dread the rivers and creeks, they are a terror to me. "Are there any rivers to ford?" I asked. "Yes, one about ten miles from here; you can cross over a bridge or ford it. We crossed on the bridge. The next is the Medicine Bow river, which you will have to ford; it has a hard bottom; we have only forded two rivers since leaving Laramie. How is it where you come from?" In answer, I related my experience of yesterday; also on crossing the Humboldt river, early in my journey. After which I went on, coming to a river, I followed it to a house, just beyond which was the bridge. On passing the house I did not see a person about, so we made for the bridge and passed over, and after journeying a short distance came to another house, where there were two roads; I did not know which of the two I should take, so I went to the house to make inquiries and a lady came to the door, of whom I asked,

"Which of the two roads is for Laramie?" "The left road is the best to ford the river," she answered. "What river?" I asked. "The Medecine Bow river," she answered. I was about to leave her when she asked, "Did you pay toll on the other side of the bridge?" "No, I did not; is this a toll bridge?" I asked. "It is, you may pay me," she said. "How much is the toll?" "Twenty-five cents," she answered. "Twenty-five cents for a one horse team! That is as much as you charge for a two or a four horse team," I remarked. "Well, I don't remember ever seeing a one horse team before," and turning her conversation to some one in the house said, "How much shall I ask this man, with a horse and cow?" At this a man came to the door and asked, "Where is your horse, team and cow?" going up to my team and looking all around he said, "Where have you come from with that outfit?" "My dear sir, if you will not ask too many questions I will answer the first. I have come from California, just as you see me." "Oh, h——l! don't talk that stuff into me, you are a fraud. From California with that horse and cow; now tell me the truth, where are you from?" "Before I answer your question, allow me to ask, where is your native State? I think you are an Eastern man by your talk." "I was born in the State of New York; I left the State in 1861, at the time of the war. I was not going to help free them d——d niggers," he answered. "I don't know that I can convince you, but, sir, if you are from New York and have lived there many years, you know whether I am a Yankee or not. Were you ever in the State of Massachusetts?" "Yes, I have been in Massachusetts; are you from that State?" he answered. "I am, and now on my way to Massachusetts; when there I am at home. I left Massachusetts in April, 1880, for California, arriving there in May, I left California June the first, 1882, for the East. My stay in California was two years or more. I arrived in Ogden, September 23rd, and left there on the 14th of May last, and have travelled here since. What I have said is the truth and nothing but the truth. This is all I can say, I leave the rest for your consideration; how much for crossing the bridge?" I asked. "Stranger, go in the house with me," he said. "I have already made a longer stop than I intended. I am anxious to reach Laramie; when there my traveliing will be more pleasant. I shall have an opportunity to see some civilization; I have not seen much since leaving Ogden." I went with him to the house and the man said to the woman, "I am satisfied that this man has come from California; that he is not a fraud. He tells a big story, but it is bigger to perform it. If I were in the woman's place I would not charge you a cent. Now, stranger, take a little whisky with me." Handing me the whisky he said, "Here's luck and success to you on your long journey." "Thank you, when you meet another man from California like unto me, do thou likewise. Madam, how much shall I pay you for crossing the bridge?" "Nothing, sir; take the left road as that leads you to the best ford; be careful in going down the bank into the river, when you get into the water you are all right; good-bye, stranger." I went on; it was a fine morning, a good road and everything appeared fine. About eleven o'clock I came in sight of the river, and as I approached I met a train of teams; as they came up to me we all stopped. I said, "Good morning, strangers; how far to the river?" "Only a short distance." "What luck in crossing?" I asked. "Very good; getting up the bank is bad, as it is steep and muddy, and has been cut up by the many teams in crossing, but the river has a good, hard bottom," was answered. "Where are you from?" I asked. "We are from Kansas; we have started for Oregon, but may go to Washington Territory. If we like Oregon, we shall settle there, but can't tell till we get there. Where are you from?" said the strangers.

"I am from California," I answered. "From California! You don't say; what with that cow?" "Yes, sir; from California." By this time the whole camp, men, women and children, were around me, and were confounded. One of them asked, "What part of California are you from?" "The northern part; Humboldt county, three hundred miles north of San Francisco," I answered. "You are from California and brought that cow all the way?" asked the strangers. "Yes, all the way," I said. "Well, well, you are a hero, and no mistake; have you come alone?" "Yes, all alone," I answered. "How many miles, think you?" asked the strangers. "About two thousand," I answered. "Strangers, I would like to talk two hours with you, but I have not the time, I must reach Laramie this week; how long have you been in coming from Laramie?" I asked. "This is our fifth day, it is about one hundred miles to Laramie; how many miles do you travel a day?" asked the strangers. "I travel by the hour, two and a half miles per hour, all day. I left Green River city the 26th of May, and have made that distance, more than two hundred miles. One day I could not travel it was so wet and slippery; most of the time I have travelled on good time. I have met many teams, and it seemed to me I could scarcely leave them, which has caused me to lose much time; how is the road to Laramie?" "Well, most of the way it is good, still there are many bad places. The worst place we have found was our first day from Laramie. About the middle of the afternoon, we passed a store and a post-office and came to a flat meadow about a mile long; it was mud, nothing but mud. Our wagons were heavily ladened with grain and other materials, so that they sank deep in the mud. We were obliged to double up our teams to get them through. On coming to the river we found it deep and dared not cross at the main ford. We turned short to our right, crossing the river, then onwards about eight rods, turning sharp to the left, crossing it again; onward a little further, then crossing the river for the third time. We have forded but one river since, the one you now see." "Are there any more?" I asked. "Yes, there is another, but you cross it over a bridge. We dared not ford it, it was so rocky, we would rather pay the toll than run our chances." "What is the name of the river?" I asked. "Its name is Stony creek, and it is stony before and after crossing; we were in great danger of breaking our wagons. How is it on ahead?" asked the strangers. "All kinds of travel; I have had many miles of good roads. Then again, it would be rough and tough. You move like an army; I am alone. If anything happens to you, you have assistance at once, while I alone have to get out of a difficulty the best I can, if I get out at all. Well, strangers, I will go to the river; good-bye." We went on and soon came to the river and on my arrival I found another team of wagons ready to cross over. I stopped, fed the cattle with grain and watched the teams cross the ford; I sitting on the bank. A team came down into the river and across up on the bank all right. I watched this go on until three teams had been got over, I noticed that the bank was being cut up very badly and would be more before the twelve others were got over, so as the captain now doubled up his horses I said to him, "Will you allow me to cross; I see it is going to take you considerable time to get all your teams across." "Yes, sir; certainly. But, stranger, where are you from with that outfit and where are you going to?" "Captain, if I should answer that question, I should not get across the river to-day. Captain, I am from California and have come all this distance just as I am, horse, carriage, cow and dog." "Stranger, it will not take us more than an hour to cross, and perhaps not so long; I want to ask you a few questions. They may be worth something to us; we are going to Oregon and I think you are the man to tell us how to get there," said the captain. "Captain, I can tell you how I came here, I can do that much; as I shall stop long enough to get some hot coffee at least." "Boys, gather some fuel and make a fire, we will have some hot coffee; be smart about it," commanded the captain. Fires were soon made, coffee was cooking and there was a great stir around. Teams were being rapidly doubled up and brought over the river. I was thinking what I could do, so I took my pail and went to the cow and milked, taking about four quarts from her. The captain called us all to dinner and I gave the milk to the lady, whom I thought to be the captain's wife, saying, "Take this milk and do what you like with it." She took a bottle holding about a pint, filling it and laying it on one side; then asking her neighbors if they would like some milk for their coffee. After dinner the captain called the camp around, saying, "Stranger, from California, now please tell us where you have come from and the way you came." "Strangers, I am from California; from the northern part, Humboldt county, city of Eureka. I left there the first of June, 1882, taking the overland road to San Francisco, distance, three hundred and three miles. Followed the Central Pacific Railroad to Ogden; arriving there September 23rd. On my arrival I did not intend to stop but four days, but circumstances were such that I was obliged to winter there. On the 14th of May last, I left Ogden and have travelled as far as this." "Stranger, if you were going to Oregon, which way would you go?" asked the captain. "I would go from here to Green River city, from there to Evanston, and on to Ogden. From Ogden I would follow the Central Pacific Railroad to Reno. From Reno I would take the old turnpike, called Virginia and Marysville Pike, through the Sardinian Valley, Webber's Lake, Jackson's Ranche, Graniteville, Nevada city, Grass Valley to Marysville. **At Marysville take the California and Oregon turnpike** direct to Oregon. Captain, I have given you the main outline and I know that the trail is good. After reaching Ogden you have no mountains to get over or under. When you get to Wells, you are sure of grass all the way to Humboldt Valley, nearly four hundred miles. Captain, what is the number of men, women and children in your company?" I asked. "Stranger, this camp has fifteen wagons, thirty-six horses, eighteen men, twenty-two women, fifty-two children and eight dogs,—one hundred and thirty-six in all," he answered. "Strangers from Kansas, I must leave you; I wish you success on your long journey and hope you will succeed to your satisfaction; good-bye all." "Stranger, from California, we sincerely hope you will succeed in reaching your destination. In three or four days more you will reach Laramie. Beyond there you will be all right; we will go to the river and see you across." I drove to the river and descended the bank, I got into the river, but came near being upset, so much so that my dog was precipitated into the water, but I did not know this at the time. I succeeded in getting across all right. As soon as the horse gained the shore she whinnied; on looking around I saw the dog going down the river. I took the horse from the wagon, got upon her back and rode for the dog. Before I had gone far the dog was taken out of the water by a stranger, about twelve rods down the river, where there was a bend, if he had not been rescued here I should have lost him. I returned with my dog, feeling thankful; then I re-harnessed my horse, put her in the wagon and got ready to go on. The river I had just forded was about six rods across. "Strangers and friends, I thank you for your kindness, I shall ever remember you; should I be permitted to arrive safely at home, this incident I may make a record of in some form and hope you may in some way see it. Good-bye, strangers." "Three cheers for the man from California, bound East to Massachusetts."

They were given with a will. I went on up the bluff; for about two miles it was rough and stony. I thought surely I should break my wagon. I led the horse around the rocks which no doubt saved my carriage. About half-past three o'clock I noticed that there was to be a change in the weather, clouds were gathering as if for rain. I crowded along as fast as possible with a rough trail. From the East, I am now continuously meeting teams; but from the West no one overtakes me. You see it is all one way. At five o'clock I had not yet come to grass, or water, but about this time I saw a train of four teams coming. I asked, "How far am I from water?" "Only about two miles." I continued on and soon came to water and grass also. I stopped and gave my cattle water, then went on a short distance further and camped for the night. I turned my cattle loose that they might eat what little grass they could find, it was not much, however. I looked around for fuel, but in vain, not enough to boil water for my coffee. Having some cold tea I took my lunch basket, sat down on my blankets and ate supper all alone. About eight o'clock I brought in my cattle and secured them, giving them their evening's meal of grain, then made up my bed and laid down. The clouds were thick and heavy, looking as though it would soon rain, which it did about ten o'clock. I got up, rolled up my blankets, put on my rubber coat and stood up, taking the rain as it fell, which however, was of short duration, and then it began to hail; this I could stand better than the rain, but it began to blow very cold with the wind increasing; the hailstones dwindled away into almost snow. Fanny was making a fine fuss about it. The ground had become quite white with the hail, the wind was blowing quite strong and getting round to the East and the storm was increasing, and at eleven o'clock there had fallen four inches of snow. Fanny was complaining bitterly and she made the snow fly, making more fuss then was essential; the cow was quietly chewing her cud as she lay down, seeming to care little about the storm. I noticed that the storm struck the horse in the face, so I turned the wagon about half round, changing her position, and then I took the blanket off the horse and put it on the cow, then I took one of my blankets and a buffalo robe and put them on the horse, which change made her more contented. All this time I was getting cold. The snow had continually fallen; by midnight five inches had fallen. Still the storm increased. I little thought I should be snow bound in June. No, nothing of the kind. I was getting very cold, especially my hands and feet, having no mittens or gloves. I thought of one thing, and that was my kerosene. I got the can, cleared away the snow and poured some on the ground and set it on fire. It made a big blaze, so big it scared my horse. I warmed my hands by the blaze until the stiffness came out. At two o'clock the snow was six inches deep; it looked as if there was a slight chance for a sleigh-ride in June. Well, here I am alone. Yes, all alone, except my cattle. Ah, there is some consolation in talking to them, especially on the Rocky Mountains in a snow-storm. I am getting very cold, especially my feet. I took the oil can again and poured more oil on the ground, set it on fire and warmed me the best I could, my feet felt as if they were freezing. Another thought came to my mind, that was, to take a sack which had contained grain and place it on the ground where I poured the oil, which I did. There was considerable warmth, so I took off my boots and standing on the sack my feet soon became quite warm. This was quite an invention and had I patented it I might have been a rich man by this time. Well, here I am, not quite morning, eight inches of snow on the ground, feet warm but fingers cold; a little more oil will make them all "hunkey-dorey." I gave the ground another wetting with oil and fired it off.

The horse had by this time got used to this kind of firing and did not upset the wagon as she did at the first. This was a very long night, one to be long remembered. It is getting close on to day-break and soon light will be upon us. There is one point, or pint, I had forgotten. When back at the bridge, where I could have bought grain or anything else, I got a pint of that "anything else," but which so far I have had no use for, a full pint, and which now seems to be the proper time for its use, so I go to my wagon and get the "something else," and took a big "smile," holding it up so as to know what I was about. Instead of putting it back in the wagon I put it in my pocket. Soon after I began to feel warm and cheerful. I could run, which I did; I could talk to my cattle, but never knew what they thought about it, nor did I care, I was alone on the Western plains, surrounded by high hills, and "something else" was in my pocket. I took another "smile" and looked at the bottle and found that I had drank more than half of it, so I put it away where I could find it when wanted, or where no one could get it; knowing that neither Fanny nor Bessie would interfere with it, and there were no Indians around to steal it, being so cold and stormy for them to be out. Well, it is morning; what a long night it has seemed to me, and a foot of snow on the level and still more coming. As soon as I could see I tried to find the trail, but could not, so deep was the snow. "Well, Fanny, what have you to say this morning? We shall have to remain here for a while; when the sun comes in sight, then we will know what direction to take. "About five o'clock, there being a faint glimmer of light, I thought sure that was East. When I went into camp my wagon was standing eastward and when I made the change, the position I must have made was to westward; this was the only compass I had. Should the sun come out, it would not give me the trail, but the point of compass. About six o'clock I saw smoke to my rear. "Fanny, yonder is smoke, do you see it; there is a camp!" I did not pass it last night, so I thought it was in my direction, and tried once more to find the trail, but the snow was too deep.

On the morning of the 6th I fed my cattle with grain and took "a smile of something else," and started in the direction of the smoke, which I found proceeded from a camp about a mile distant. When about mid-way I commenced hallooing with all my might, which brought out two men and two boys from a tent. As soon as I got near them I bade them "good morning. We are having a heavy snow-storm." "Yes, I do not know what we will have to do," answered the stranger. "I have a horse, cow, dog and a carriage, a little distance from here, but I can't travel, not being able to find the trail." "How far from here?" asked the strangers. "Less than a mile, I think," I answered. "Stranger, I think you can get down to our camp. Here you will not be alone, and we may have to stop several days before we can travel further. We will assist you." With this assurance I followed my trail back, and on my returning my cattle gave me a good reception. I got all ready and went back to the camp, which I reached all right. As the forenoon advanced, the snow began to disappear, and by noon the sun was out in all its glory, promising that by to-morrow we should be able to travel. Having got everything in good shape in the camp we began to gather sage brush for a fire, and soon had a good dinner in preparation. The campers being supplied with water, I furnished the milk for the tea and coffee. I did not get much milk from the cow, the wonder was, I got any. The strangers said, "Where in God's name have you come from, with that horse, cow, carriage and dog. If you came from the East we would not ask, but coming from the West all alone, is what we want to know?" "Well, I will tell you a long story after dinner, as there will be plenty of time before we can travel." Dinner being now ready, we retired to the tent where the table was spread. After dinner many questions were asked and answered, in which I related my travels. About four o'clock, two men on horseback came into our camp from the East, who said they had been travelling all day. When they left their camp in the morning their was no snow. After journeying about six miles they came to snow, and continued along until the snow was so deep they could not see the trail? About two miles from here they saw smoke and continued until coming to this camp. "We have had a tough storm. Strangers, can I make your camp with my outfit to-morrow morning, if I travel on your trail. When I get there, judging from what you say, I shall have no trouble in travelling East."

On the morning of the 7th I was around early, making ready to go on. It is a very cold morning for early June, but remember we are more than eight thousand feet above the level of the sea. On leaving, I thanked the friends for allowing me to share their quarters, as otherwise, I should have had a cold time of it. I moved on and followed the trail of the men of the previous day and soon reached their camp. I found it was a large company and I was soon surrounded by the campers. "Well, stranger, you have got along so far," said one. "Yes, sir; but you did not make me a very good trail, but I came through all right." "There is more snow west than east of us, you think?" I asked. "Oh, yes; you will not find snow six miles from here." I left them, and soon after I came to water, of which my cattle drank as if they liked it, although but surface water. Travelling on, the snow gradually dwindles away, and I pass through any quantity of surface water. On this day I am obliged to ride as my shoes are not water-proof. About noon I pass Stony creek, crossing it on a bridge. The ford is a rough, stony one, so I preferred to pay twenty-five cents, rather than run the risk of breaking my wagon. Just above the bridge, there is a saw-mill, the owner of which is also the proprietor of the bridge. As I stood talking with him a large train came in sight. "About how much toll does this bridge bring you in a year?" I asked. "About one hundred dollars," he answered. "I have passed many teams since leaving Green River city. Emigration must be great this season. Are there any that attempt to ford the creek?" I asked. "No, not many. Should they break down, it would prove a dear toll for them," he answered. While we were talking, the train came up and the captain said, "Is this a toll-bridge?" "Yes, sir; it is, stranger." "How much toll for a team?" "Twenty-five cents." "Can't this river be forded, or must we pay toll?" asked the captain. "There is the ford; you are not compelled to cross the bridge, stranger." "What is the matter with the ford?" asked the captain. "This is a rocky creek, the name is an old one. Before this bridge was made, all teams had to ford the creek, and many wagons were broken in crossing, which caused delay, expense and much anxiety. I built the bridge and it pays me something, but it pays those crossing more than me, every time," he answered. "We have twenty-two wagons and forty-eight horses; will you make any reduction on that number?" asked the captain. "No, sir; no difference. Your extra horses I will not charge you for." "Captain, how many persons have you in your company?" I asked. "There are twenty-eight men, twenty-six women and seventy-nine children; one hundred and thirty-three all told," he answered. "How is the travelling to Laramie?" I asked. 'Very good; there is but one bad place, and that is before you reach the river. This side of the river is good." "How many days from Laramie to this place?" I asked. "Three and a half.

It took us a half day to cross the river, and a mile beyond we had to double up our horses to get to the river; such deep mud, no teams ever passed through." I left them and went on, the water in many places being quite deep, and in other places the mud much deeper, and the train of teams has made the trail much worse. Late in the day I pitched my camp.

On the morning of the 8th I resumed my journey early, and without breakfast, and went on until I came to another camp of emigrants, who were eating their breakfast. I bade them good morning. "Good morning, stranger," answered one. "Where have you come from, so early?" "I have come from the West, and thought I would call and take a dish of coffee with you this morning," I answered. "Come along, stranger, we have plenty." "But, hold on. I have a cow which has not been milked this morning, I will milk her," I said. I did so and gave the milk to a lady, took my lunch basket and sat down at the table without ceremony, handing my cup to her for coffee; she filled it full and bade me help myself to milk which I did. "Stranger, where are you from?" "I am from California," I answered. "From California! do you mean that, stranger; with that outfit?" "Yes, sir," I answered. "Stranger, take another dish of coffee and help yourself to milk?" "Thank you, don't be too lavish with the milk; keep that yourself. I have milk every day, Sunday's not excepted," I answered. "Stranger, I wish you had reached this camp last night." "I wish so too, but it was not ordained. Excuse me, I must go on; I am anxious to see the promised land. Good morning all, and thank you." It is a fine, cheerful morning and I have a good trail. It was six o'clock when I left this company and at seven passed a train of six teams, and at half-past eight o'clock another of four teams, but did not stop as I was anxious to reach Laramie the next day. I knew I could not do so and stop on meeting each train, and answer all questions that would be asked. About eleven we came to a creek, there was grass as well as water; I never pass grass, so I stop, giving my cattle water and a biting at the grass. I stopped just one hour and then went on again; my road continuing good. About one o'clock I came to another camp where I was obliged to stop, and could not avoid it as a man called out, "Hello, stranger, what part of h—l are you from?" "Well, sir; you do not know much about h—l yet, but will before you get to Green River city; I am almost in the promised land, already in sight of it, and to-morrow I propose to enter it," I answered. "Stranger, to-morrow you will be in h—l, take my word for it. You will almost get there to-day, but to-morrow you will surely find it; we have come through it, man." "Sir, I must have taken the wrong trail, judging by what you say. Could you not have passed around? I will go and look at it for myself, and see if I can't avoid it." I went on and thought of Watts' old hymn on this occasion; "Broad is the road that leads to hell, and thousands travel on it." Now, I am travelling a narrow road and think that the man is an imposter, there is no h—l on this trail, it is too narrow. I went on as fast as I could crowd along until it was time to stop for the night, but could see no water or grass and have not done so since eleven o'clock. I made the cattle secure to their posts, gave them their grain, but they being so thirsty they did not eat it. I made up my bed, laid down and was quickly asleep.

On the morning of the 9th I arose early, being anxious to know what was ahead. After travelling about five miles I came to a camp. "Good morning, strangers," I said. "Good morning, sir; where have you come from this morning?" was asked. "About two miles back. I went into camp late last night, hoping to come to water, but did not. How far am I from water?" I asked. "About three miles." "My cattle have had none since eleven o'clock yesterday. Last night they would not eat their grain being so thirsty." "Stranger, I have water on my wagon, I keep a small barrel full all the time, you may give your cattle some of it." "Thank you, I would like too," I answered. I took my pail and filled it four times, giving two to each, which they drank but were not satisfied. I said to the man, "Shall I give them more?" "Yes, I can fill the barrel where you got your last, no doubt." I gave them two pails more, which seemed to satisfy them. I then gave them their grain and they ate it with a will. "Strangers, I left camp early this morning, as you are aware; I have had no breakfast, but I have plenty to eat, sugar, tea, coffee, bread and canned meats, and one thing no doubt, you have not got, that is, milk from that cow. Now, strangers, I will milk the cow and we will have it in our coffee; how will that suit?" I asked. "First, best, stranger; wife make your coffee strong, we are going to have milk once more. This stranger is going to milk his cow, and we will have a good dish of coffee." I milked the cow, getting about three and a half quarts. I gave it to the lady, telling her to do with it as she pleased. I then went and gave my cattle more grain and returned to breakfast, which consisted of boiled ham, hot potatoes, biscuits and coffee, with sugar and milk; a good breakfast. "Strangers, I have come from California, and am going to Massachusetts." "Have you come from California with that outfit, just as it is?" "Yes, sir," I answered. My God! wife, just think of it; about how many miles, stranger." "Two thousand." "If you should be the man to make the journey, about how many miles will you have travelled, stranger?" "More than four thousand," I answered. "You never can accomplish that journey!" "I have already made nearly half of it; and think of the country I have passed through. When I get to Laramie, I am almost home, that is, I am among civilization and shall have good roads, which will be more cheerful and delightful." "Yes, that is true, but can the cow do that much, stranger?" "Thus far she has, and held her own better than the horse. But, strangers, I must leave you and go on. I am told that I shall have a bad place to go through at the river, how is that?" "Well, stranger, you will find a bad place after crossing the river; you will find deep mud; yet, your carriage being light, you will go through it better than we, with our heavy wagons. For nearly a mile our horses were in mud from their hoofs to their bellies." We bade each other good-bye and success on our several journeys. I left them and about half-past seven o'clock came to the creek. I allowed my cattle to drink and then went on again. Just as I was leaving I saw a long train coming towards me. I started up the bluff and turned into the sage brush, giving them the trail. There were two men on horseback who were in advance, and as they came up I bade them good morning. "You have a long train, how many teams have you?" I asked. "Twenty-three wagons, forty-seven horses in all," was answered. "How far is it to the river?" I asked. "About two miles." "I learn it is a bad place to get over?" I said. "Stranger, I never saw the like in my life; horses in mud up to their bellies, and a long stretch at that." "Is there no way of getting round it, without going through it?" I asked. "No, not without taking down the fences which are on either side." I shall soon know all about it, and soon came to the river. At one time there was a bridge over this river, but now there was none. The water here is deep and can not be forded. You have to ford the river three times, as it winds in and out. I drove down into the river, went across and came out all right. Instead of turning to my right, I drove out in my front and landed in a large pasture, for the pasturing of horses. I travelled close to the fence for about a mile and came to a store, which was also the post-office. I drove out into the trail, stopped and went into the store and explained why I did so. "In coming from the West, I would have done the same," answered the postmaster. I am out of the wilderness and have just entered the promised land. Here I went into camp for the night.

I was up before daylight on the morning of the 10th, turned my cattle loose among the grass and allowed them to eat their fill. So anxious was I to make Laramie that day, that as daylight came I commenced my journey, leaving camp about four o'clock; everything around me was beautiful and grand. On my right are lofty mountains, painted white with snow; on the left, as far as the eye can see, was a vast plain, covered with fine grass. O how beautiful, surely this is the promised land. We move onward as fast as possible; Fanny understands it, no doubt. Last evening, about nine o'clock, I heard the whistle of an engine, and spoke to my horse, "Fanny, do you hear that?" She replied, "Hah, hah, hah," that is her way of replying. About nine o'clock we came to water, a small pond. It was surface water, of which my cattle drank freely. I was talking to my horse, telling her that we soon would be there, when I heard on my left the whistle of an engine, the horse heard it also. "Fanny," I said, "we are almost there." We entered the city of Laramie about ten o'clock, Sunday, June 10th, 1883. At once I made for a stable, so as to get hay for my cattle; saying to the proprietor, "I have just arrived in the city, having crossed the plains from Ogden." "Oh, indeed; what kind of times have you had?" he asked. "Most of the way, good; others, not so good; one part was very rough; that was the snow storm," I replied. "Have you had a snow-storm on the plains?" "Yes, sir; on the night of the 5th and 6th, snow fell to the depth of eight to twelve inches. On the morning I could not find the trail to travel, so deep was the snow. Could you accommodate me with some hay?" "Yes, sir; you shall have all the hay they can eat, and not a dime will I charge for it." "Thank you, I would like to stop in the city two days, to give my cattle rest; they have come a long distance and have still a longer distance before them." "Stranger, where did you start from?" "As you would not take pay for the hay, I will tell you and you can rely on what I say. I started from Eureka, California, three hundred and three miles north of San Francisco; came down to that city, then took the Central Pacific Railroad trail to Ogden, and from there hereto. I left Ogden on the 14th of May, and have been nearly a month coming the journey." "You have had a tough time, and have had all the rivers to ford, or nearly so; who came with you?" "I have come alone. No one travels from the West but many from the East. Can I stay here to-night? I lie with my cattle at nights; I have blankets, but no tents." "You can stay with your cattle and give them all the hay they will eat."

Laramie is the capital of Albany county, Wyoming. A fine little city, with a population of five thousand. It is situated on the east side of Laramie river, with a vast plain on the right and left. On the east, about six miles distant, is a range of mountains; on the south, about three miles off, is Fort Sanders; on the west are the fine grazing plains, known as the Laramie Plains. In reaching the city I crossed these plains. To the right, stretch those lofty mountains which extend into Colorado. On the north, running to and from the city, is the Union Pacific Railroad. Laramie has one of the finest hotels and depots combined, on this railroad. The town is finely laid out in squares and contains many elegant buildings. The county building is uncommonly fine, and the grounds are tastefully laid out, and very becoming to the city. What is going to support this fine little city I can not say. It is an enterprising city and I hope it will continue to prosper.

CHAPTER VII.

From Laramie, Cheyenne, to Omaha.

On the morning of the 13th I left Laramie, travelling over the mountain, through the Cheyenne Pass, by Fort Russell, to Cheyenne city. When I arrived in Laramie, it was my intention to have followed the Union Pacific Railroad, but I was advised to take the old trail to Cheyenne; a very fine trail with the exception of about eight miles. By taking this route I should save one day's travel. In starting from Laramie I left the railroad on my right. About three miles from the city I came to Fort Sanders, there I took the old trail over the mountain, and on coming to the base of the mountain we stopped. It looked as if it was to be a long and a hard pull for the horse. The ascent was for some distance on solid rock. About noon we had accomplished the ascent. I am now standing on the highest elevation in my journey,—eleven thousand feet above the level of the sea, and shall have to descend six thousand feet. My first four miles is very rough. About three o'clock I came to a creek of good spring water, the best I have found on my journey. I stopped and allowed the cattle all they would drink, and gave them their grain. After an hour's rest, we went on, following a heavy descent for about eight miles, until we came to a plat of fine grass; I had no desire to pass it. Here we again stopped; I took the horse from the carriage, removed her harness and let her loose; she went to rolling; the cow went busily eating at the grass. It was not long before the cow went to bed, but the horse continued to eat. I had gathered wood and made a fire, making some coffee, boiled eggs, which I ate with cold ham and bread; it made me a good supper. I brought my cattle in, made them fast to their places and gave them a small ration of grain, spread my blankets and laid myself down to rest, being very weary. In the night I was awakened by the horse, but I well knew what was up, my fire had gone out, but the lantern was still burning. I got up and went gathering wood to re-kindle the fire. This was essential to keep my camp free of the wild animals. Having got the fire going once more, I returned to bed. I lie in the rear of the wagon, between the cattle, and I build the fires close by me. I did not drop to sleep as readily as at the first part of the night. As I lie I had a fair view of the horse. Her ears were well pointed down into the canyon where the infernals were, as I could tell they were there by the noise. Bessie lay there chewing her cud, as if she cared but little whether school kept or not. I was up and down the rest of the night, anxious for the day to come.

On the morning of the 14th, I made an early start, yet disliked to leave the good grass. My trail is much better than it had been the previous day. After travelling about two miles, on my right I saw a house. I continued on, circling a high bluff for more than a half mile. This bluff was so constructed by nature, that in following its base it brought me to this house, a well-built modern house. I went up to the door and rang the bell; a lady came in answer to the summons, to whom I said, "Can I make a dish of coffee here; I am a traveller, going from the West to the East, and have come a long distance. Last evening I went into camp about two miles from here, where was good grass; I broke camp early and did not make breakfast." "Wife, ask the gentleman in," said a voice. I went into the house and said "Good morning." "Good morning, sir; take a seat. I think I heard you say that you was a traveller and had come a long distance from the West. When I heard the west mentioned, I was anxious to see your face. Wife, how much coffee have you in the pot? We are not quite through with our breakfast yet, so take a seat at the table and eat with us. I like the tone of your voice; it sounds as though you have been East, sometime." "I belong in old Massachusetts, and am now on my way there," I said. "What part of the west are you from?" said my host. "I am from California, the north-western part, more than three hundred miles from San Francisco, north, on the Pacific coast," I answered. "When did you leave California?" "I left Eureka city, the first of June, 1882, and arrived in Ogden on the 23rd of September. I left Ogden on the 14th of May last, and have come the distance from there in one month to a day; travelling nearly six hundred miles, over the Rocky Mountains and through the red sea to the promised land." "Well, have you come that distance by railroad, horseback, or on foot?" asked my host. "Sir, I am here for some coffee or something else. I have not asked for anything more, but I may soon, but I will take the coffee first." After eating breakfast I said, "Friend, go with me to the gate of the corral?" "What for, what is there?" asked the stranger. "Come and see for yourself," I replied. We went to the corral, to which was a high and strong gate, which is to hold wild cattle. "Ah, stranger, where did you find that cow; it must be the one I lost some time ago?" "Well, friend, she must be the same. I found her in California and have led her from that State, in the rear of the wagon. If the brand on her corresponds to your brand, I must give her up. I think you had better give them some breakfast; I have had mine and am greatly obliged." "Stranger, your horse looks as though she could eat some oats." "Yes, sir; she is fond of them, and the cow knows some kinds of grain. I carry grain and have done ever since starting on this journey. The day I left Green River city I bought 300lbs. and she hauled it to Laramie." "She is a fine horse, and the cow I do not know about taking from you; if she has travelled that long distance, she is good for the remainder. I would like to hear from you when you reach old Massachusetts." "How far is it to Cheyenne?" I asked. "Just twenty miles; you think you can make that distance to-day?" "Yes, good morning," and I went on. As I was moving steadily along I saw a herd of cattle, not many rods away, to my right. The cow saw them and bellowed several times. After passing them, on looking around I saw them coming on a sharp run. There must have been fifty to seventy-five of them. They overtook and surrounded us and were very troublesome to the cow, and I could not beat them off. I took the dog from the wagon and set him at them, and they left us right sharp. Going on, I soon saw a large fellow coming down the trail in front of us; he was bellowing loudly and coming dead on the horse. I called out with all my power; he stopped sharp and stood for a few seconds; neither stirred; the more I yelled, the less he seemed to care. I caught hold of my hay-fork and went for him, at the same time setting my dog on him, this made him leave quickly for the herd. Many times I have thought of this incident, and wondered how I got out of it so easily. While standing facing each other, I thought the bull would make a dash at the horse, but the dog did a big thing in driving him away. Travelling on we came to water, of which my cattle drank freely. A few rods further, I came up to a man who was sitting on the grass; his horse was feeding, and at a distance of about twenty rods, was a herd of sheep. I spoke to him saying, "Stranger, you have a fine herd of sheep; how many have you?" "Nearly four thousand, sir," he answered. "I see those dogs understand their business. Stranger, this is something new to me; I have traveled a long distance, but have never before seen such thorough discipline in man or dog." This herd of sheep were moving and feeding at the same time in a square, with eight dogs in care of the herd; two dogs on each side of the square. If any of the sheep fell in the rear, the dogs put them back in line; and if any advanced the dogs put them in line, they were constantly on duty, their manœuvres is difficult to describe on paper. "Stranger, you remarked that you had come a long distance; where are you from?" "I am from California." "The d—l you are; from California with that outfit?" "Yes, sir; with that outfit," I answered. "Where are you going?" "I am on my way to Massachusetts," I answered. "My God, is that so. If you make that journey, you will be the biggest man out of h—l. From California to Massachusetts; I hope you will succeed. Do you ever take anything stronger than coffee?" "No, sir; I like my coffee very strong." "So do I, and I have something in my satchel that will do you good. You are much older than I, here take a smile with me and put that in your box, you will need another before you get to Fort Russell and another before reaching Cheyenne. To-morrow there is going to be a big circus in Cheyenne; I expect to be there, and will find you and fill it again for you, I think you are worthy." "Friend, I hope to meet you again; good-bye." "Good-bye; success to you and give my love to the folks in old Massachusetts." I left him and about three o'clock heard the whistle of an engine, and passed Fort Russell and reached Cheyenne about five o'clock. On entering the city I stopped at a livery stable and inquired where I could camp. "You can drive into my corral there, if you like," said the livery-man. "Can you accommodate me with hay?"

"Yes, you can have all the hay you want for your cattle." "How much will you charge me?" I asked. "Oh, never mind that. John," said the livery man, "go and show this stranger the corral and take a bale of hay with you. I do not know that your cattle will eat our hay, but you can try them." "John," said I, "this is a fine place to camp, I fear I shall stay longer than I ought." "How long do you intend to stay?" asked John. "Well, this bale of hay will last me two days or more." "We have a big circus here to-morrow from New York; you will want to see it?" said John. "Yes, I would like to do so," I answered. This corral is about one hundred feet square, with sheds on two sides. About twenty feet outside the corral, is a cottage to get to which I have to pass around the corral. I went there to see if I could make a pot of coffee, and on ringing the bell a lady answered it, of whom I requested the privilege of cooking my coffee, to which she gave me permission. She called her husband, saying, "Charles, come here. This gentleman has come here to make some coffee, and says he is a traveller from the West. I see he wears a badge like you do, which is why I called you." The man answered, "Comrade, how do you do. My wife says you are travelling from the West and going East; where are you from?" "I am from Ogden. I left on the fourteenth of May." "What way are you travelling?" "I am travelling with horse and carriage, leading a cow." "That is a strange way of travelling over the Rocky Mountains; where is your outfit, Comrade?" "In yonder shed; you can see the horse through that window." "I would like to see what you have for a horse that has crossed the Rocky Mountains. Come, wife, let us go and see it. Ah, Comrade, I see it is a fine Morgan. How far East are you going?" "I am on my way home to Massachusetts." "You have come from Ogden and going to Massachusetts. Allow me to ask your name?" "My name is Johnson." "What town and county is your home?" "Town of Webster, county of Worcester." "Comrade Johnson, stop with us as long as you stay in the city, you will be welcome." "Thank you, I will take dinner with you to-morrow. At present I am here to make a pot of coffee, if you have no objection, I will get my lunch basket and eat with you. My cow is four years old and has given birth to two daughters, and is now in travail and about the second of July, I expect another. She is now giving four quarts of milk a day, and if you will give me a pail that will hold a gallon, I will milk her and give you the milk.' I milked the cow and gave the lady the milk. "Comrade, excuse me if I ask your name?" "My name is Brown." "Comrade Brown, I did not tell you the whole truth, when I said I had come from Ogden; I will say that I have come much further. More than a year ago I left Eureka city, California, for Massachusetts; passing through San Francisco, following the Central Pacific Railroad to Ogden, where I arrived September 23rd. There I remained all winter and left there May 14th, and arrived in Laramie on the 10th of the present month. Comrade Brown, the above is the truth and nothing but the truth." "I remember reading in the papers last Fall of this journey, so you are the man. Well, you are a gritty, old soldier. What were you in the army, what rank?" asked Mr. Brown. "I was only a private, a musician in the band of the First Brigade, First Division, Twentieth Army Corps." "Do you draw a pension?" "I do, a small one, for hernia; only eight dollars a month." "Comrade, how is it that you have come so far and not had your cattle stolen from you? I think you can't travel to North Platte without having your horse stolen, as she is a fine Morgan mare, which makes the chances against you. Your only and safe way is, to stay constantly with your cattle. I would like to have you take a bed in the house, but think it safer for you to sleep with your cattle.

"If you wish to go down town, let us know, and we will look to your cattle while away." "I intend to; I have travelled two thousand miles, and every night have slept with my cattle and shall do so until I get a considerable way further East." "After you cross the Missouri you will be safe, yet you will find men all along the road who would steal the horse if they had a chance. If you succeed in getting safe to Massachusetts, you are a lucky man." I left these people and went to my camp, giving the cattle their grain, made up a bed of hay and laid me down to sleep and had a good night's rest.

On the morning of the 15th I was awakened by the whistle of an engine bringing into town the cars of the circus from Denver. I got up and gave my cattle water and grain and went to the railroad. I did not think of the safety of my cattle, when I did so, I immediately returned to my camp and found all right. Soon the city was alive with people anxious to see the circus horses and carriages. I was this day a little anxious about the safety of my outfit, on account of so many of the cow-boys and strangers from abroad. Comrade Brown was around soon after my return, and bade me good morning, saying, "Did you get a good night's rest," and that the breakfast was ready, and invited me in to a dish of coffee, which I accepted. For a time I remained with the cattle until I regained confidence to leave them. This I did, as they were locked in the carrol and Mrs. Brown said that she would look after them, so I once more went into the streets of the city to see the parade. In passing along, intent on sight-seeing, and while standing in front of the circus tent, I was tapped on the shoulder by my friend of the day before, the herdsman, who said he was "Up to his word." I told him he did not look as he did yesterday. He answered, "No, I suppose not. I have drunk more good bourbon this morning, than I have for a week past. Come with me, traveller, and I will fill your flask, as I am bound to keep my word. I am not a cow-boy, but a sheep-boy." He introduced me to several other of his acquaintances, and having expressed my fears for the safety of the cattle, he took me to a friend of his who keeps a large saloon, and has great influence with the cow-boys. Here I found a large crowd, and it was some time before we could get audience with the proprietor, Mr. A——. After a time we gained an audience and I was introduced in due form. Mr. A——, having been told my story and of my fear, said, "Mr. Johnson, I understand that you have been informed that you are in danger travelling through our county, from fear of the cow-boys; is this true?" "Yes, sir; it is," I answered. "You have been travelling from the far west, have you not; have you been insulted by any one on your journey?" asked Mr. A——. "No, sir; I have not," I answered. "About how many miles have you travelled?" asked Mr. A——. "Two thousand miles from California to Cheyenne, through the wildest country on the globe. Just emerging into civilization and have now stopped for fear of the cow-boys." "Mr. Johnson, you must be a brave man to have come through what you have to reach Cheyenne. Now, sir; do not be timid. You can travel from here to Omaha, and not a cow-boy, or any other boy will harm or insult you, you can take my word for it, it is not worth much; when do you leave here?" asked Mr. A——. "I intend to leave you, the day after to-morrow, the 18th," I answered. "Come in to-morrow, to-day is a great day with us; seldom is it that we have such a gathering. Mr. Johnson, do you ever take anything stronger than three per cent.?" asked Mr. A——. "I take nothing stronger than first-class bourbon, that is as much as my head will carry," I replied. "Well, boys; we will all take something on this occasion," said Mr. A——. We went into the bar-room, which was filled to its utmost. As we stood at the bar, Mr. A——, said, "Gentlemen, here is a man, a stranger to us all, who has travelled from California to our city, with a horse and carriage, leading a fine Ayrshire cow, and a little dog, Bertie by name, and he is on his way to old Massachusetts. He has come the long distance of two thousand miles and says that he has not received an insult thus far on his journey, from any man, bear or d—l. On his arrival here, he has become timid, on account of you cowboys. I have told him that he can travel from here to Omaha and not a cow-boy, or any other boy will injure him, or take from him any of his outfit." A voice in the crowd asked, "What part of California did you start from; which way did you come, by steamer or overland road?" "I started from Eureka city, Humboldt bay, three hundred miles north of San Francisco, and I came the overland road to that city, then following the Central Pacific Railroad to Ogden, and from there to this place," I replied. "That is a big story to tell," said a voice from the crowd. "Yes, I am aware of it, but it is a bigger thing to do it," I replied. "You are right, stranger, and have you brought that cow all the way from California?" said one of the crowd. "I have not made any such statement. She has travelled every rod to Cheyenne," I answered. This created laughter and the boys gave three cheers with a will for the man from California. "Mr. Johnson, how do you feel, with this crowd of cowboys around you, do you think if you should meet them on the road they would take your horse from you?" Cries of no, no, came from all sides. We would do all we could to help you along. "Yes, boys; help the old gentleman on his long journey; he is not half-way yet, and it is doubtful if he succeeds. I hope he may, it is a great undertaking. I say, boys, help the old gentleman along; give him a sack of oats for his horse and cow, and for himself, something good to eat and drink." A voice from the crowd said, "A bottle of good bourbon is the kind of help-along, every time." "Mr. A—— and gentlemen, allow me to make a remark. Before leaving California, I was told by my friends and neighbors, that the enterprise I was contemplating could not be carried out. First, because a one-horse team could not travel the trails of two-horse teams; second, my wagon was too light and slender, with no brake attached; third, I should have the wild beasts to contend with; fourth, I should be scalped by the Indians; fifth, the Mormons would kill me. Nothing was said about you cow-boys. In California I suppose you were not known and have only heard of you more recently. Now, gentlemen; I have travelled more than two thousand miles and have received but one insult, and that was from a couple of black bears, who were more afraid of me than I of them. The Indians were kind and obliging to me; I have been in their company several times and travelled with them for several hours; I have drank from their canteens and they from mine. Twice having lost my trail, they have put me right again; that was while passing through Nevada." Just as I had finished my last word the band of the circus struck up and the whole crowd rushed to the street to see the parade. I took the chance and returned to my camp. On arriving I found Mrs. Brown was entertaining my animals and a large number of people that had congregated to see my outfit which had come from California, but all left as the circus parade passed along the street. After the parade, Mrs. Brown said, "Mr. Johnson, come in and get a lunch, my dinner will be late, as Mr. Brown will not return until three o'clock, so I will defer dinner until that time." I went in and had lunch with Mrs. Brown, and while eating I saw "Fanny" looking directly at me, as if she would like her lunch also. I told her to wait till I was through and then she should have one. Mrs. Brown said, "Mr. Johnson, you think much of your horse."

"Yes, but no more than she does of me. I think so much of my animals that I would reluctantly part with them, but I may get into a tight place and be obliged to." "Mr. Johnson, I hope not, and hope also that you will succeed and reach your destination safely. If you do, it will be a record in your history." "Mrs. Brown, I will go and give my cattle a lunch and then return and shave if you have no objections?" She gave a ready assent to this. On my return, Mr. Brown had come home, and to him I said that I had made the acquaintance of many of his citizens and related my experience with the herd-man and his friend Bill Jones, and my interview with Mr. A——. "Mr. Brown, I have given you the particulars of my introduction to the leading citizens. I have no doubt, however, but that it will work to my favor; its results are in the future." "Comrade Johnson, this interview is calculated to work in your favor. It will carry you a long distance, even to North Platte. Beyond there, you will be travelling where it is more thickly settled. I think, however, it will be best to make the railroad stations your camping places.

Cheyenne is an old town, of long standing. It existed long before the Union Pacific Railroad was built. It is now a city with a population of eight thousand. It is known as the herdsman's city of the West. It is situated in the southern part of Laramie county, and is its capital. It is beautifully laid out, streets running at right angles, with an elevation of more than six thousand feet above the level of the sea. Here there is a fine view of Pike's Peak in Colorado.

On the morning of the 18th I left Cheyenne for Omaha, a distance of five hundred and sixteen miles. I followed the Union Pacific Railroad to Archer station; there I left the railroad to my right. About twelve o'clock I came across a train of eight wagons, seventeen horses, ten men, eleven women and twenty-seven children, bound from Kansas to Oregon. I **stopped** and gave grain to the cattle, made a dish of coffee and ate my dinner, and then **went** on. About six o'clock I saw a camp in front of me, as I approached and stopped, I said to the campers, "Gentlemen, have you any objections **to my** camping here with you to-night?" "**No, sir, not any**; we would like to have you. You seem to be travelling East instead of **West**; we seldom meet any **from** the West. Where have you come from?" "Cheyenne, I left this morning. Where are you from?" I asked. We are from Kansas, stranger." "Where are you going to?" I asked. "We have started for Oregon, but may change our direction to California; **where are you bound to, stranger?**" "I am going to North Platte," I said. "Are you going to take that cow with you?" "Yes, sir; **how many teams have you?**" I asked. "We have four wagons and eight horses, four men, four women, thirteen children and two dogs.

On the morning of the 19th near Burns station, I broke camp and went on; the railroad being still on my right. I had travelled but a short distance when I came to a creek and gave my cattle a chance to drink; they were very thirsty and drank as though the water was good. Going still further, we came to a spot where there was grass; here I stopped, took the horse from her carriage, taking off her harness and turned her loose, also **the cow.** I gathered some **wood and** made a fire and some coffee, boiled some eggs **and ate my breakfast, making a stop of** one hour and then went further. About ten o'clock I heard the whistle of an engine to my right and soon saw the train, a western bound train; not long after I heard another whistle and a train from the East came along. This was cheering to us, especially to me. I am travelling in a beautiful valley; on my right are large herds of cattle. I am in sight of Pine Bluff station, a noted place for the transportation of cattle to the East; on my left is a high bluff. As I circled round this bluff I drove into a valley, crossing the creek, and had a fine view of the cattle awaiting shipment. About six o'clock I went into camp for the night, near Bushwell station.

On the morning of the 20th I was up early, making ready to move onward, and at five o'clock broke camp. About eight o'clock we passed the western bound freight train, salutations being given while passing, and about ten o'clock we passed the western bound express. I was within forty feet of the track and I threw up my hat as a signal on passing. Coming in sight of a train of wagons, I stopped with the common salutation, "Strangers, where are you from?" "We are from Kansas." "Where is your destination?" "We have started for Washington Territory; we may stop short of that, and scarcely know where we shall finally stop, we can't get to a worse place than that we have left." "What is the matter with the place you came from?" I asked. "We came from where those hot, blasting winds burn up everything but the d—l, they did not seem to cut him down. Where are you from with that cow?" "I am from Laramie," I answered. "Where are you going, stranger?" "I am going to Sidney. How many teams have you?" I asked. "We have four wagons, eight horses, four men, four women and eleven children." "Good-bye, strangers; success to you," I said and passed on. Travelling further I came to water, here I gave the cattle water and grain, ate a lunch myself and then went on. About five o'clock I made Dix station. Here I found grass and an abundance of water, so I concluded to stay for the night. I took the horse from the carriage, removed her harness and let her loose, the cow as well. I spread my blankets on the ground and laid down on them. I had not lain long when a man came up to me and said, "Stranger, what's ye doing there?" I raised myself from the ground and said, "What am I doing here, don't you see what I am doing?" "Yes, I see." "No you don't see, or you would not have asked so foolish a question. I am a traveller, I have come from Cheyenne and am going to stop here for a while, so that my cattle can cut this grass for you." "That is all right, stranger; you are going to camp here for the night?" "I don't know, do you?" I asked. "No I don't. If you want to make tea or coffee you can make it in my house and welcome," said the man. I thanked him and accepted.

The morning of the 21st found me up early, as usual. I turned the cattle loose for grass and then returned to my bed. I concluded to travel in the early morning and rest in the early evening. I called in my cattle, gave them their grain and went on. About six o'clock I passed the western bound train; I flung up my hat to signal the train and kept on my journey. About nine o'clock I made Potter station. As I was watering my cattle the western express train came in and stopped, and about twelve o'clock I saw in front of me, an emigrant train in camp. On coming to the camp, I drove up along-side and stopped, after passing compliments, I said, "Your coffee smelled so good, I could not but stop." "All right, stranger, walk in, we have plenty of it," was the answer. "I would like a dish of good, hot coffee. I will bring my basket along, if you have no objection?" I said. "Bring it along, we have no objections," was answered. I took my basket with me, gave my cup to the lady, who filled it with coffee. I said, "Strangers, there is one thing lacking, that is milk." "Stranger, we have no milk, I wish we had!" "I will furnish you the milk." I went to my wagon and took the pail I carry expressly for the purpose of milking, I milked the cow and carried it to the lady, saying, "Take this milk, and as often as you see or handle milk in any shape, remember the man who took dinner with you on the plains of Nebraska. That cow which gives us this milk is a native of California and has come thus far in the rear of that wagon. Strangers, how large a company have you?" "We have seven wagons, fourteen horses, seven men, seven women and twenty-two children." "Where are you from and where going?" I asked. "We are from Kansas and have started for Washington Territory, we may not get that distance, we are late." I then left them and went on and about five o'clock when about a mile west of Sidney, I stopped and gave the cattle grass. As I lay on the grass I saw a lady on horse-back coming towards me; when she came up to where I was lying, she said, "I want to buy a good, kind, gentle horse, about such an one as this I am on." I told her I was travelling East, and was a stranger in those parts and did not know of any horse." "I am travelling West and have a sister in the town of Sidney. We have come from Wisconsin, with this horse and a light buggy. I have traded the buggy and harness for a saddle," said the lady. "You say you are from Wisconsin, with a carriage, yourself and sister. Where are you going?" I asked. "We are going to California," answered the lady. "Ah, I am from California, with this horse, carriage and cow; yes, and that little dog. All of us have travelled from California thus far, and you have come here with a carriage; when you leave your carriage you have to leave your grain. Had I left my grain in Green River city, instead of carrying it over the Rocky Mountains, my cattle would have been starved, as there was no grass for days, that would keep them alive. With your carriage you can carry grain, bedding, grub and clothing; without it, you will have to carry everything on your horse's back. I advise you to continue with your carriage." The lady left me and went on and I saw no more of her. As the western-bound freight train was passing me it came to a dead stop. I was anxious to know the cause and went near to the train. I heard the conductor say in a loud voice, "You will leave this train, or I will blow your God-d—d brains out." "Blow and be d—d," said the tramp. There were three of them on the train who intended to steal a ride through the night, but the conductor said they should not ride. He was obliged to call up all hands to put them off; there were only six hands on the train. The tramps left the train and as it moved off shots were fired from both parties.

Sidney is a town grown up from a Military Post, which was established many years before the building of the Union Pacific Railroad; it took its name from the Post. Since the building of the railroad, it has become a place of considerable note, and it is the capital of Cheyenne county. It is handsomely laid out, and is situated on a high elevation, four thousand feet above the level of the sea. Many kinds of business have been established here, and the surrounding country is well calculated to support and build it up. One of the best eating-houses on the road is to be found here. Its population at the present is a little over a thousand.

On the morning of the 23rd I left Sidney, my trail now being a good road. After travelling about four miles I came to a house; I went to the door, rang the bell and a lady came in answer, of whom I asked, "Madam, can I cook some coffee here?" "Yes, or you can have some of ours already cooked, as you choose," she answered. "If you have hot water, or a fire, I will cook enough for my dinner, as I have a large coffee pot." I made the coffee, had breakfast and then moved on. About seven o'clock I met the western-bound express train; the engineer recognized me and gave a salute. I returned the same and continued on my way. On coming to water, I gave the cattle water and grain. I took a drink of coffee and a lunch myself. About two o'clock I made Lodge Pole station; here I stopped, giving water and grain to the cattle; my stop was one hour. About seven in the evening I came to good grass and concluded to camp. It was my intention to have made Chappell station, but this being an extra good quality of grass, I thought it best not to pass it. I turned the cattle loose, made my supper and ate it. After securing my cattle I gave them their grain, went to bed and slept till ten o'clock, when I was awakened by the eastern-bound express train, but I was soon asleep again.

On the morning of the 24th I awoke very early, I did not know the time as my watch had run down. I turned the horse and cow loose in the grass, I then laid me down again and rested until it was light enough to travel. About five a. m., I reached Chappell station; soon after my arrival the Eastern-bound express train came in, and I called on the engineer for the time and set my watch; now I have the time again. It was just six o'clock when I left the station and at ten o'clock I reached Julesburgh. In making here, my road has not been good, it was the heaviest travelling since leaving Cheyenne. My stop here was two hours and then I went on, and about three I made Denver Junction, my last six miles have been very heavy with sand. Here I found good grass, and any quantity of cattle to take care of it. I turned the horse loose and staked out the cow; I dared not let her loose, it might trouble me to find her. I gathered some fuel, made a fire and made myself some dinner; while eating dinner, two teams came along-side where I was and stopped. "Stranger, which way are you travelling?" they asked. "I am travelling East, sir; you seem to be travelling

West," I said. "Where are you from?" they asked. "I am from Cheyenne, I left there the 18th," I said. "How is the road there?" they asked. "Your first fifteen miles will be sandy, after you get over that, your road will be good to Cheyenne. Where are you from?" I asked. "We are from Kansas," they answered. "Where are you going?" I asked. "We don't know where we will haul up yet. We are bound for California, and we may go to Oregon, can't tell," they said. "Here is good grass and we had better stop for the night," they said. "Yes, here is the best grass I have found yet," I replied. My last six miles have been from south to east, on a circle to Denver Junction, coming out into the Platte Valley. On leaving this station, travelling East, I journey parallel with the Platte river.

The morning of the 25th I left Denver Junction about four o'clock, and about seven the eastern-bound freight train passed me; all the hands seemed to know me. On my right, is Platte river; large herds of cattle are feeding on its banks and about nine o'clock I reached Big Springs, here I stopped to give my cattle grain and water, occupying just one hour, and then again went on, the day being very warm and sultry. At half-past two o'clock I made Brule station. Hot and not a shade to get under. I am but a short distance from the river; cattle are in the mud and water more then stride deep, to get rid of the flies; the flies are very troublesome to the cattle and are large and vicious in their bite. At four o'clock I made Brule station and about six o'clock came to grass and camped for the night, turning the cattle loose for their evening meal. I gathered fuel, made a fire and got my supper all alone, no one around or in sight, think of it. About eight o'clock I secured the cattle, gave them their grain, made up my bed and laid down, but no sleep came around, being troubled with mosquitos.

On the morning of the 26th, between Brule and Ogalalla stations I broke camp. After travelling but a short distance I saw the western-bound freight coming towards me; as we passed signals were made. I made Ogalalla station and on my arrival found the station but little inferior to Sidney. I fed my cattle and went to the station. Here I found a store with a general assortment of goods of all kinds. I went in and bought some good butter and cheese, and filled my basket with bread. I also got a sack of oats and meal for my cattle. I went for my wagon and drove to the store, put aboard my grain and basket and went on. At twelve thirty I reached Roscoe station, here I stopped long enough to feed on water and grain. About half-past five o'clock I made Alkali station; I stopped and gave my cattle grain and water and then moved on a little further, and at seven o'clock stopped for the night, all of us being thoroughly exhausted, almost suffocating. I gave my cattle all the oats they would eat; I drank a dish of coffee, ate some bread and cheese, made up my bed and laid down for rest, being so weary.

On the morning of the 27th, as soon as it was light enough to travel I moved on, and at six o'clock I made Dexter station; here my cattle had water and grain and I cooked some coffee and dried beef in milk and butter, with eggs for my breakfast; a very good breakfast I thought. About seven o'clock I resumed my journey, my road now lies between two rivers, the north and south forks of the Platte river. About eleven o'clock I made O'Fallons station. Just as I had reached this place, the eastern-bound freight train came in. I stepped up to the engine and said to the engineer, "Good morning." "Good morning, friend traveller," he answered. "You have an opportunity to see me often; you know about how fast I move," I remarked. "Yes, I see you are getting along finely, you will make North Platte to-day." "To-morrow noon I hope to be there." The train moved on and here I stopped for dinner and fed my cattle. About five o'clock I reached Nichols station. Here was good grass and I gave my cattle a chance at it for the night.

On the morning of the 28th, I left Nichols station for North Platte, distance eight miles, which I reached about ten o'clock. In making this place I travelled between two rivers, the north and south forks of Platte river. There are two trails to this place; the railroad and river trails. I went in on the railroad trail and encountered several sloughs, the horse was in blue mud, knee deep. Had I taken the river trail, I should have had a good road into the town, this I was told when in town, and too late.

North Platte is situated on the banks of two rivers, the north and south forks of the Platte river. It is the capital of Lincoln county, Nebraska. It is a beautiful town and finely laid out. As you enter from the West, you pass down a broad avenue. On the left is the railroad and station house, a large, noble looking building; on the right is the town. There are six streets leading out from the avenue to the right. Entering the town by rail, it looks grand and imposing. It boasts a population of over two thousand.

On the morning of July 1st I left North Platte for Omaha. After travelling about two miles I came to the north fork of the Platte river. Here we cross the river over the railroad bridge. This bridge is about nine hundred and sixty feet long, and sixteen wide. The railroad track is laid in the centre. All teams have the right of way across. Should a team get on the bridge the train stops until it gets across, this is according to law, I was informed. About a mile below this bridge is the junction of the two rivers, the north and south forks, below is the

Platte river. After passing Gannet station I came to two roads, and took the best, by so doing I took the wrong road, going some eight miles out of my way. On coming to a cattle ranche I learned that I should have to return some four miles and take the left trail, which would lead me on to the railroad trail. I returned as directed and came to the railroad trail, a loss of some ten miles for that day's travel. I was anxious to reach Brady station, but did not make it until late in the evening, about eight o'clock; a heavy day's travel, too much for the cow, as she was heavy in calf. I made ready for the night; the cattle I take good care of, myself will care "for himself."

On the morning of the 2nd I left Brady station early; I did not stop to feed, going on in the hope of coming to grass that my cattle would eat readily. I will say here that grass is plentiful, but too stout and heavy to be sweet and nutritious. I am, and have been particular, in their feeding; I must be so, or they will never reach Massachusetts. About six o'clock I stopped, fed the cattle and myself and then went on until coming to a creek, with a broad, deep ford. I was not able to ascertain the depth of the water. I drove into the creek and when more than half across, my wagon was under water, the cow was under, all but her head, that she kept dry. Making the opposite bank, in ascending, my horse was not able to get up out of the water on account of slipping. I was obliged to back into the water and detach the horse from the wagon that she might get up the bank. I carry two ropes, thirty feet long, these I made fast to the front axles, then carry them on to good footing, make them fast to the hame tugs, then the horse pulls the wagon out of the creek. This done, I took the horse from the carriage and turned her loose, the cow also. I unloaded the wagon to have a dry-out, as most of my things were wet. While doing this, my attention was drawn to the cow. I was about twelve rods from the railroad. On the opposite side is Willow Island; the cow was making for this island across the railroad. I saw her intention and heading her, I staked her out. I thought no more of her for a time, as I was busy drying my outfit. Two men came up to me where I was and one said, "Do you want to sell that cow?" "No, sir; I do not," I answered. "She is a fine looking cow, I would like to buy her," he said. "I have led that cow in the rear of that wagon a long distance; more than two thousand three hundred miles, more than three hundred miles north of San Francisco, California. If she were nothing more than an ordinary cow it would be foolish to lead her that distance. She speaks for herself, however." "She has a calf. I went towards her and she shook her head at me, so I went no further. Would you sell the calf?" he asked. "Yes," I replied, "but I do not know that she has a calf. If she has one, I will sell you the calf, situated as I am. We will go to her and see how things look." I went up to the cow all right, but the stranger she looked daggers at. I found her with a calf, "Is it a male or female?" the man asked. "It is a male," I answered. "What will you sell him for?" he asked. "I will sell him for twenty-five dollars, situated as I am," I replied. "I will give you fifteen dollars for the calf," he said. "No, I will take him along with me; I do not care to take him from the cow yet. It would be much better for the cow to have the calf stay with her two days." "I am in the cattle raising business on a small scale, and would like that calf. I would not have made you an offer had it been a female, but as it is a male, I will give you twenty dollars for the calf, that is the best I can do," he said. "Situated as I am, you can take him in two days." "I would like to have him to-morrow, as I am going to move about ten miles down the road," answered the man. "You pay me for the calf and on the 4th I will deliver the calf at Cayote station." "Here is your money, twenty dollars for the calf. Now, you are a stranger to me; I wanted that calf, so I have bought and paid for it. Twenty dollars is a large price; now I want you to go to, and stay at the depot until you get ready to go on the 4th," he said.

On the morning of the 4th of July, as soon as it was light enough to travel, I left Willow Island station for Cayote station, with the calf for John Murray, Esq., where I arrived about seven o'clock. On my arrival I was made welcome to a good breakfast by Mrs. Murray. The children were delighted with the calf. The calf had its parting breakfast from its mother, after which the little fellow was put into the barn and the mother was turned loose with a herd of cattle. My stop here was two hours and then went on. About one o'clock I made Plain Creek station. Shortly after my arrival the western-bound freight came up. This day I have been travelling through a fine farming country.

Plain Creek is situated on a high, rolling prairie, and is destined to be one of the best towns on the railroad. It is beautifully laid out; its Main street runs north and south, with streets running at right angles; all kinds of business can be found here. As I was travelling up Main street to my right I noticed a fine school-house and church, not large, but neat and elaborate. Here my stay was three hours; I left this place at four o'clock and travelled until coming to Josselyn station, where I stopped for the night.

At four o'clock on the morning of the 5th I left Josselyn station. About five o'clock the eastern-bound freight passed us, and at six o'clock I made Overton station, travelling on until I came to grass where I stopped to feed my cattle, made a pot of coffee and ate my breakfast and then went forward. On my right and left are fields of grass close up to the road. My horse obliques to right and left, nibbling at the grain, then forward, halt, stopped five to fifteen minutes, then forward, march. My horse does not understand the last, so I sometimes have to remind her with my cane. This way of travelling has never been complained of. The horse is not in the grain, only two out of four wheels were slightly in the grain. Well, where am I? close on to Elm Creek station, where I soon arrived as did also the western-bound freight. I gave the cattle water and offered them grain, but they would not eat it. Going on we came to a field of clover. I drove into the field among a large number of hogs, giving my cattle a chance to eat a mess of it, which they greedily ate. My stop was short, perhaps an hour. It is warm, yes, more than warm, very hot; not a shade can I get under. About eight o'clock a breeze sprang up and it became more comfortable travelling. Coming to a small grove, the first shade I had seen to-day, we stopped here for one hour, it was a luxury. Resuming our journey we passed Stevenson station, and after going about a mile from there we camped for the night. We were surrounded with good grass; I made the cow fast with the lariat, the horse I turned loose.

At midnight of the morning of the 6th, I got ready and went on. About two o'clock I passed by Kearney station, and about four I made Buda station. Here I stopped and gave the cattle water and then went on to Gibbon station where I stopped one hour, feeding the cattle and myself. As I was leaving the station, the eastern-bound express passed me. I travelled this morning in merry glee, my road being good. No flies to bother us, nor sun to burn, like yesterday. About eleven o'clock we made Shelton station. Here I inquired if there were any shade that I could get myself and cattle under? I was told there was none around the station, but a short distance below I could get out of the sun. "About how far below?" I asked. "About half a mile; you can see it yonder." I went for the shade; we came to a pine grove, in the rear of which was a house and barn; approaching the grove I saw a man, whom I went up to and said, "Would you allow me to stop a while with my cattle in your grove. I have been travelling since midnight and my cattle have come from Stevenson station, five miles below Kearney Junction?" "Oh, yes; stop as long as you like. There is hay in the barn, but if your cattle prefer grass take the scythe and cut them some; give them all they can eat, it will cost you nothing," answered the stranger. I took my horse from the carriage, unharnessed her and let her loose so that she might roll. The cow I kept confined allowing her all the grass she would eat. "Stranger, where have you come from with that outfit?" "Friend, I have come all the way from California, with that horse, carriage, cow and dog." "Oh, you are the man that I have read about in the papers, coming from California and going to Massachusetts?" "Yes, sir; I am the man." "Go into the house, I want my wife to see you!" "Please have her step to the door; she, perhaps, would prefer to see the cattle, rather than me." He called his wife, saying, "Here is the man I read about on his way from California to Massachusetts, with his horse, carriage, cow and dog. Look at the cow, see what a mark she has on her rump, that is enough to show she has come a long distance. Well, stranger, don't you want some dinner? He is worthy of a better dinner than we can give him." "While she is preparing dinner I will milk the cow; she has not been milked since very early this morning." I milked and took it to the lady saying, "Madam, there is the milk that I have taken from a cow that has travelled more than two thousand four hundred miles. She was born and bred in California, and has been led in the rear of that wagon all that distance."

On the morning of the 7th, soon after midnight, I left Camp Grove, between Shelton and Wood River stations, reaching the latter about half past two o'clock. I made no stop, but continued on to Alder station, which I gained about six o'clock. Here we stopped and had breakfast, staying one hour and then went forward, reaching Grand Island at ten o'clock. Here I remained most of the day, making the park my camp. By permission, I turned my cattle loose that they might have grass where they choose. At four o'clock in the afternoon I made ready for another stage on my journey and at six o'clock made Lockwood station. Here I gave the cattle water and then went on a short distance and camped. My camp is close to the railroad; on my right is a large field of corn. A little further is a field of oats. I led my horse to the oat field that she might eat a few oats, thinking they would do her more good than grass. After a while I returned to camp, making the horse fast to a telegraph pole for the night, spread my blankets and went to bed.

Early on the morning of the 8th, about three o'clock, I made ready and went on. At six o'clock I made Chapmans station; here we took breakfast. My cattle had grain, myself and dog took bread and milk; my stop was only one hour. About twelve at noon, we made Central City station. On making this last station, it had been warm, the flies did their best to torment my cattle; the horse becoming frantic, I thought surely she would break away from me. I covered my cattle with fly-blankets continually. About three o'clock I left Central City and travelled to Clark's station, which I reached at seven o'clock. I stopped and gave my cattle water and went on until I came to a fine place to camp. I took the horse from the carriage, unharnessed her and let her loose, the cow I staked out, as I was anxious to know her whereabouts. I made a fire, cooked some coffee, boiled eggs and ate my supper. After this was done I brought in my cattle, gave them their grain and went to bed for the night. While lying in bed I concluded it was better to travel in the night instead of the day, as the flies were so troublesome by day.

At midnight of the 9th, I broke camp near Clark's station and travelled until six o'clock, at which time I reached Silver Creek station; here we all took breakfast. We rested till eight o'clock and then went on and about twelve o'clock we made Duncan station. It has been a very warm morning, the warmest of the season and no shade to get into or under. Meeting a person I said, "Stranger, is there any shade that I can get my cattle under?" "There is none very near; which way are you travelling?" he asked. "I am travelling East, sir," I said. "About a mile east, you will find a good shade, no better in the State," said the stranger. I concluded to go on, rather than stop in the sun. I soon reached the shade, a beautiful grove, which I drove into. In the rear of this grove was a mansion. I went for a permit to stop a while at least. Stepping to the door I rang the bell; a lady came in answer, to whom I said, "Madam, I am travelling East; I have come from the West a long distance; I have a horse, carriage and cow. It is very warm and I would like to have my cattle stand in the shade, while they cool off and rest; it is the warmest day I have travelled." "Where are your cattle, sir?" asked the lady. "Yonder, near the road," I replied. "Drive them in here, I would like to look at them," said the lady. I went for the cattle and drove them into the yard. "Let them stand there in the shade, it will do them good," she said.

At three o'clock on the morning of the 10th, I left

Camp Mansion and arrived at Columbus at half-past five o'clock and found the city in perfect slumber. I thought that I must be mistaken in the day, Sunday, as not a person could I see to gain information. Soon, however, I saw a man crossing the street. "I asked him, "Stranger, will you tell me where I will find a hotel?" "Yes, sir, right here; this is a hotel." "I am travelling and have just made the city. I have a cow that must be milked and would like to exchange it for something to eat that I do not carry. Are you the proprietor, sir?" "We will take the milk and give you a tip-top breakfast," said the stranger. "Please look at my cow. By the way, where is your barn?" I asked. "In the rear of the hotel; I will show you." I went for the cattle and took them to the barn, milked the cow and went into the hotel with the milk. "There, stranger, take this and give me some breakfast in return," I said. "But here is more milk than breakfast," he answered. "Never mind, remember my cattle," I said. The landlord turned to his man and said, "John, give this man some grain for his cattle; give them a good breakfast." We all had a good meal, after which we went on and about ten o'clock made Benton station, where I watered the cattle. Coming to a wheat-field, I could not get my cattle by it, they were bound to have wheat for dinner. I did not try much to keep them from it, but allowed them to eat for about an hour and then drove on. About half-past three o'clock I reached Schuyler station, and on my arrival I inquired for the best hotel and went there. I inquired for the proprietor, who asked, what he could do for me? "I have come a long distance and have not got to the end yet." "Are you the man that the papers talk about, who is on his way from California to Massachusetts, with a horse, carriage, cow and dog?" asked the proprietor. "I think I must be the man; I have heard of no one else. I have my doubts whether there is another man that would be so foolish as to attempt the job again." "Stranger, you are not a fool, because a fool could not have done what you have. As to its being foolish, that is another question; you have had an opportunity that no other man has had to know the country, and should you ever get to the end of your journey, it is for you to give us your experience on paper, in black and white. I sincerely hope you will succeed," said the proprietor. "Friend, I am obliged to you for your advice. Should I succeed in reaching my destination and put on paper the facts relative to my journey across the continent, I will send you the contents in book form. Friend proprietor, I am going to travel to-night; it is my intention to reach North Bend. If you have some hay, I suppose you have no grass, that my cattle will eat, I will milk the cow and you can have the milk in exchange." "You can have all the hay and grain you wish; about what time will you leave?" asked the proprietor. "How many miles is it to North Bend?" I asked. "It is fifteen miles by rail and the same by the road," was answered. "It will take me five hours to travel that distance. I will leave here about half-past six or seven o'clock," I answered. At that time I left Schuyler and at half-past nine passed Rogers station, and just at midnight we made North Bend station. I gave my cattle some oats, spread my blankets and laid me down for rest. Just as I lay down the western express train came in.

I arose early on the morning of the 11th, but not as early as usual. Travelling in the night is more agreeable to my cattle than the day; we are not troubled with the big flies, they are so tormenting to my cattle. As I was making ready to leave, the hotel proprietor came along and said, "Good morning, stranger. Travelling, are you?" "Yes, sir; I came in from Schuyler last evening, arriving about midnight. Landlord, I have a cow that is fresh in milk; I am obliged to milk her regularly, but she has not been milked this morning. Will you take the milk in exchange for something to eat that I do not carry." "Yes, milk your cow, bring it in and get your breakfast. Will that answer you?" asked the landlord. "Yes, sir; that is just what I was driving at." I milked the cow and took it to the hotel-keeper, when he said, "Come with me and get your breakfast. You have a good cow, judging by the quantity of milk she gives. Where did you find that cow?" asked the landlord. "That cow is a native of California; I am taking her down East," I answered. "How far East?" "To Massashusetts," I replied. To Massachusetts; that is a long distance. Are you the man that is travelling from California to Massachusetts?" asked the landlord. "John, bring out two pails of oats for this horse and cow," the landlord commanded. John brought out the oats and gave them to the horse and cow. After they had eaten the grain we went on, leaving North Bend for Fremont. Not long after starting on my way, I noticed a change was taking place in the atmosphere; clouds were rolling up, I disliked their deportment; they were continually rolling and tumbling, trying to smash each other. Then came a streak of lightning to the ground, and the thunder was rumbling in our rear. I crowded my cattle along as fast as possible, hoping to come to some place where we could get under cover. Soon, on my left, a stream of lightning came down, the thunder following close upon it. Here I am between two armies, I thought; one on my right and one on my left. Perpendicular, there was not a cloud. These two clouds, or armies, were advancing and retreating. Soon the one on the right charged the one on the left; then, there was such a canonading that I never heard down South at the time we crossed the Ogeechy river. All the time this battle was raging, I was trying to get under cover. On my left, about sixty rods, was a grove of young willows, from two to six inches in diameter; about three hundred feet long and about fifty feet wide, running down to the road. We had almost made the grove when the storm burst upon us. First, it was wind, then hail mingled with fire from nitrogen; it struck us on our left. I was unable to hold the horse, she started on a full run for the grove. As soon as we got under cover of the grove we were all right. This grove was wide enough to shelter us from the storm, the duration of which was only forty minutes. After the storm had passed over I looked around, but no house could I see. I went around to the end of the grove; what did I see? A house made with hands, not more than two hundred feet from where I had been standing during the storm. I backed my horse out of the grove and went to this house, standing in front about a minute when a man came to the door. I said to him, "Stranger, when this storm, just passed, struck me, I was about twenty rods from your grove. I have been there all this time; I am wet and cold and would like to stop here for a while. I am a traveller and have come a long distance, and am not half-way until I reach Omaha." The lady of the house made a fire and I had a good dry-out. "Stranger, this storm has delayed my travelling for several days. Can I stop here until I am able to travel again. I carry a lunch basket and grain for my cattle; I would like hay or grass as you prefer?" I said. "There is a grass cutter, help yourself," said my host. "Have you a cow?" I asked. "I have, but she has not come in yet," he answered. "All right, my cow is fresh in milk. I will find the milk, you the grass," I said. When the time for milking came, I milked the cow and took it to the lady of the house, who said, "You have a fine cow to give that quantity of milk. John, come here and see what a mess of milk that cow has given," said the lady. "Stranger, you have a rare cow to give so much milk; where are you from and where are you going?" said John.

"Friend, stranger, I would like to stop with you until I am able to travel. To-day is Friday; with your consent, I would like to stay here till Monday morning. If I stay I shall have plenty of time to answer your questions. If I answer one it will lead to many more, I will now answer your first. I am from California, with that horse, carriage, cow and dog, having left that state June 1st, 1882, and arrived in Ogden, September 23rd. I left Ogden May 14th, 1883, and have travelled thus far since that time, about two thousand five hundred miles. To your second question, I answer, I am on my way to Massachusetts." "But Massachusetts is a long distance from here," said the stranger. "Yes, I am aware of it, but it was much longer before I left California. I have been working steadily along; I have killed half the distance, and if nothing serious happens I will kill the remainder in time."

On the morning of the 16th, I left Shelter Grove for Fremont. This place I call Shelter Grove, as it gave me protection from the storm of Friday and also of the Sunday, the 13th following, of rain and hail. My stay was four days instead of two, as I had intended. The storm of Sunday was very severe; the rain poured down in torrents, mingled with hail and fire that ran along the ground; the telegraph wires and poles were very dangerous. Cloud after cloud, charged with electricity, would come up and then such lightning and thunder, as could not be seen or heard outside of Nebraska, would follow. After such storms it is with difficulty that people can travel as the roads are so cut up and muddy, and travelling on this mud, as it dries becomes like frozen earth, only worse, for frozen earth will yield to the sun, but this only becomes harder. At Julesburg, or as it is more recently called, Denver Junction, I made the Platte Valley. From here the lands are very flat; since coming to the flat land I have witnessed many storms, not of rain and hail alone, but storm of fire and electricity. These storms are a terror to me. The day previous to reaching Columbus there was one of these storms. I was travelling beside the telegraph poles, my trail being close up to them, sometimes the hubs of my wheels would strike the poles. The lightning had split down pole after pole, so I left the trail and drove into the high grass where I remained until the storm had consumed all its ammuniton, as I was afraid of the electricity. I am travelling parallel with the railroad, which is on my right. After journeying about three miles I was obliged to cross, then turning sharp to my left, I have the railroad to my left, my road at this time being good. Between the road and the railroad is the old trail, covered with heavy grass. The flies are very troublesome to the cattle, so much so, that the horse will rush into the tall grass to brush them off. Here she took to the grass and I was afraid that there might be a ditch that she would run into and upset the wagon. I called out to her to stop, but Fanny would not stop. I tried to get around her, but she struck into the old trail, turning round and back to the crossing; I thought that here she would surely stop, but no, she crossed and went on. I was close up to the wagon and made a great effort to clutch some part of the harness, but did not succeed. She then started on a smart run, but the cow kept up with her with little trouble. In this way we all went back to Shelter Grove. After taking a good, long breath, I concluded to try it again and did so. Coming to the crossing I concluded it would be best to lead her through the tall grass, as she might try again to run back. In this escapade we lost over seven miles. Our road was rough, but we made Fremont about two o'clock in the afternoon.

Fremont is a fine town; it is the county seat of Dodge county. It is young, as most of the towns are on this line of railroad; still it is growing fast and handsome. Enterprise is stamped strong and firm upon its appearance. I had occasion to call at the Post Office and was surprised at its excellent appearance and good arrangements. I could not but ask myself who was the designer of this beautiful office? If I am not misinformed, it was built in New Haven, Conn., and shipped hereto. As I intended to leave early in the morning I went down town to learn of my direction for to-morrow. On returning, I passed a flouring mill and stopped to purchase a sack of grain. After it had been put up and paid for, the miller asked, where I found my cow? This question opens the gate for more, which I was obliged to answer. "That cow is a native of California; I have led her in the rear of my wagon all that distance, and we are going to Massachusetts," I answered. "Here is your money, I will not be guilty of taking a cent from you. Do you have to pay for what you have to subsist on?" asked the miller. "Not often. When they learn my story it costs me nothing," I answered. "I will keep you a week, if you will stay," said the miller. "Thank you; good-bye, sir," I said. "Good-bye; success to you all along the road," he answered.

On the morning of the 17th, at midnight, I left Fremont, travelling the old military road. On leaving Fremont I leave the railroad to my right, and going down into the valley recross the railroad, turning short to left and following the railroad. Going on as far as my memory would carry me and coming to two roads, I did not know which one to take. I followed one of the roads until coming to a house. I called out which was the road to Omaha. A man came to the window of whom I asked, "Am I on the right road to Omaha?" "You are not, you should have taken the right-hand road." "If you had a shingle on a post, I should have taken the right road, without being obliged to wake you up from your slumbers. I think I shall not be able to travel to-night without waking up the whole neighborhood," I remarked. "You go back and take your left road, go on a little distance further, take your next left road, then there will be no more turnings for a long distance." I retraced my steps and followed the road as directed, and came to a large river, crossing it on a good, substantial bridge, made of iron. This river is the Elk-horn. Going on, we ascended a heavy bluff, and further onward came to a store and post-office. Here we stopped for breakfast; after eating we went on till one o'clock, when we stopped for water and luncheon. Our stop was short as I desired to make the celestial city. I could see the smoke from the furnaces, indicating the location of the city, and we now went on with good cheer. About six o'clock we came to a plat of grass where we stopped. It was just within city limits. Here I concluded to go into camp for the night and early in the morning would enter the city. I camped and turned my cattle loose, giving them a chance to ramble. I gathered some wood for a fire as there was plenty around; made a fine pot of coffee, with plenty of milk and sugar, boiled some eggs and dried beef in chips; seated on a box I ate this good supper. We were all hungry. I spread my blankets and laid down, being very weary. Bessie went to bed, but Fannie was not ready to retire; she seldom lays down till late in the evening, and I have never seen her laid down but once in the day-time. That was at Willow Island, where Bessie gave birth to her fine boy. There I found her lying down with Bessie. I brought in my cattle, gave them grain and retired for the night.

Early on the morning of the 18th, I was awakened by the passing teams of the city market-men. I got up and turned my cattle loose for grass, made a fire and cooked a pot of coffee, drinking of it freely. It was not yet dawn.

Between us and the city was a heavy plat of timber, hiding our view of the city and also the East. Soon I discerned that morning was breaking upon us, so I called in my cattle and made ready to go into the city. After passing the timber lot I had a fine view of the city; we were on a high elevation and could look down on the city. We went into the city and coming to a convenient place we stopped. My first duty was to milk the cow, as she had not been milked for twenty hours; her sack was full. In milking her I took eighteen quarts from her; this made her more comfortable. My second duty was to see about the shoeing of my cattle. I had been recommended to a given shop; I went to the street and number and inquired for the proprietor, to whom I said, "I am a stranger in the city, travelling with a horse and carriage, leading a cow, and I would like to get them both well shod." "I can shoe your horse, sir, but your cow I can't, as I have no brake to put her in. I have shod oxen, but cows I have never shod," said the blacksmith. "Is there any one you know of, who has a brake?" I asked. "I think there is not a brake in the city. Where are you from and where are you going, to require the shoeing of a cow?" the blacksmith asked. "My dear sir, I will go and get my cattle, and while you are shoeing my horse, I will answer your two questions, it will take some time to answer them," I said. So I went and fetched my outfit, and on my return I found several strangers in the shop. I took the horse from the carriage and led her into the shop. She went very reluctantly, and several times did she call for Bessie to follow, but she declined. "Mr. Blacksmith, I will begin and answer your questions. To commence with, I will say it is a long journey and will need something good on the road, if it is nothing more than three per cent." About this time a large number of persons had gathered about the wagon. My dog, Bertie, sat on the seat, he was feeling finely, but was being petted and teased alternately, and some were pulling his tail. "Boys, don't pull his tail, you would not like to have your tail pulled," I said. The blacksmith also told the boys to let the dog alone. "Mr. Blacksmith, you see what condition those shoes are in; they have done excellent service. Those shoes were put on her feet in Ogden. She has crossed the Rocky Mountains with them, drawing that carriage all the distance. That is not all, she has hauled three hundred pounds of grain over the mountains, from Green River city until it was all eaten." "Where did you start from with the horse and cow?" asked the blacksmith. "I started from Eureka, Humboldt county, California, with these animals." I answered. "When did you start from California?" he asked. "One year ago, the first day of last June," I answered. "And you have been all that time coming here to?" said the blacksmith. "I have been all this time coming, going and stopping," I answered. "Stranger, I do not understand you," said the blacksmith. "I will explain; coming is not going; going is when on the wrong trail and have to return to get into the right one; stopping is when you can't go or come, you understand?" "I do, go on," said the blacksmith. "On the 23rd of last September, I arrived in Ogden. I was obliged to stop there until the 14th of May; on that day I left Ogden and arrived in Omaha July 18th, the present month. I am just half-way on my journey, California is West; Massachusetts is East, and Omaha is the centre; you understand, Mr. Blacksmith?" "I do, and what is more, I will bet ten dollars you are a full-blooded Yankee," he answered. "I dare not bet, I have no money to lose as I surely should," I answered. "John," said the blacksmith, "take the pitcher, go and fill it with beer." "What kind of beer, I drink nothing but three per cent., remember!" I said. "John, hold on, we will go out and get our three per cent.," said the blacksmith. We went out and took a smile of old bourbon, came back and finished shoeing the horse. This done, I asked the blacksmith if he knew of a place where I could stay over night and feed my animals. I preferred to be outside than inside. He told me of a place and went with me to it, introducing me to the owner, who gave me permission to camp there for the night. The property was owned by a Mr. Adams, a Mr. Briggs and a Jew. The two former gave their ready permission, after having heard my story; the Jew was away from home, so I could not get his assent on going to see him about it. In the meantime, I went down town and recruited my lunch-basket; returning I made my dinner, and was eating it when the Jew returned home, and seeing me camped came directly to me saying, "Stranger, who gave you leave to come here, you are on my premises, get out of here d—d quick or I will smash you up." I told him that I was a stranger, I had come to the city that morning and had been to the blacksmith to have my cattle shod, I asked him where I could stay for a short time and had been brought there. I had consulted his neighbors, Mr. Adams and Mr. Briggs, and had called on him for his consent, but not being at home was told to camp there, it would be all right. The Jew said it would not be all right, and he told me to get out d—d quick. Many people hearing our controversy had gathered around. Mr. Adams and Mr. Briggs both were there. It appeared that one-half of my wagon was on the Jew's land, so they hauled it off on their land, saying to me, "Stranger, don't you move a thing; you are now, not on his grounds, but on ours." At this the Jew was much excited; he left and went into his store and in a little while returned with a policeman. The officer came directly up to me and said, "Take your cattle and traps off these grounds, and quick too, or I will take them and you too." "Policeman," said both Mr. Adams and Mr. Briggs, "this stranger is on our grounds by permission, not on the city's, or anybody else's. You have no right to eject him from these grounds." While this controversy was going on the people had collected in large numbers. "Gentlemen, strangers, I am a long distance from my home." A voice in the crowd asked, "Where is your home?" "My home is in the State of Massachusetts. I have no other and I am on my way there. I little thought when I entered your city that I should receive such an ovation; especially of this kind. On my journey I have met all kinds and grades of people, from a Chinaman to a Yankee." "Where are you from?" asked a voice in the crowd. "I am from California, direct," I answered. On this three cheers were called for the man from California, which were given with a will. "Strangers and friends, I think I am not mistaken when I say friends." (No, not a bit of it, you bet.) "I am simply passing through your city, and stopped to get my cattle shod and give them a feed and rest, being directed to this place, I am here by permission. This controversy was uncalled for; a little feeling has arisen, because this man is unwilling that I should stop here, and has brought this policeman to eject me from these grounds; while on the other hand, those that gave me permission to use these grounds, are here defending me. As it now stands, I am sorry I came here." At this, many voices were heard in protest from among the crowd, who said they would stand by me, one telling me "To stand my hand and not be put out by that snob of a Jew." "Friends, you very well know that one of the parties must yield. You know also, that the police are very courageous at times, and then where are they? Then this policeman commanded me to leave the grounds. Friends, it is foolish to kick against the hackle." On my left was a board fence, about sixty feet long and five feet high, on the opposite side was a fine grass lawn; the owner of this lot was present and had been an observer of the controversy. "Stranger," said he, "I have been a looker-on of this foolish controversy; I think that our policeman ought to have known beans from potatoes, but he did not. Lead your cattle through this gate, into these grounds, there is plenty of grass, they can have all they will eat, it will grow again; we will draw your wagon round," said the man. I did as directed. After getting around, my friend said, "We will wait a little while and see if they will order you from these grounds; they have the same right, no more, nor no less. I think you was shamefully used on the other side; we will endeavor to make it up. I would like to know your name, so that we can address each other courteously, and by our right name?" said the gentleman. "Yes, sir; that would seem more home-like. My name is Johnson, W. B., of Webster, Mass. Please give me your name?" I said. "My name is N. A. Jones, of Omaha, Nebraska. Make yourself at home Mr. Johnson; we welcome you," said Mr. Jones. Mrs. Jones also pressed a welcome, saying, "When I think how mean you have been treated this day, it is hard to stand. If I was a man, I should show fight." "Mrs. Jones, I have not been shaved since leaving North Platte; I would like a good wash, shave and change of clothing, and then I think they will not know me on the other side of the fence, and perhaps not know me on this side," I said. They pressed me to take dinner with them which they said was then ready. I excused myself, saying that I had a late breakfast and was not hungry, but they insisted on my having a dish of coffee. I reluctantly went in to dinner and took some coffee. I excused myself and then went and washed up, and going to my wagon got a change of clothing, returned to the house and rang the bell, to which the lady answered. I said to her, "How do you do, Mrs. Jones?" "I am very well, thank you; will you walk in, sir," said Mrs. Jones. "You don't seem to recognize me, Mrs. Jones?" I said. "No, I do not," she answered. "I remarked a little while ago, that they would not know me on the other side of the fence; it seems also they do not know me on this," I said. "Why, why, Mr. Johnson, is that you, it can't be!" said Mrs. Jones. "Yes, madam, it is me. Mrs. Jones, I would like to walk down into the city and see what it is like; my animals are doing well and are in the shade. I will not be long," I said. With this I started down town, looking at this and that. I made my way down to the river, expecting to find a broad, deep stream, but I did not find one, it was about dried up, and yet it was the Missouri river. I expected to find steamboats, but not a boat could I find. A ferry-boat, I certainly expected to see, but there is no ferry for crossing the river. I made inquiry how to cross with a team, and was informed that the railroad did the ferrying of teams across, in cars. After roaming about the city until I was nearly exhausted, I returned to my camp. On my return, I found many people, men, women and children, had assembled to see my animals, who asked hundreds of questions, embracing my journey from California to Omaha, and even in regard to the policeman. Mr. Adams said, "That he was surprised that they had a policeman on their force who would do as he had acted, after learning from the proprietors of the ground, themselves having given permission for you to remain on the ground, and even remonstrated against your removal. It was a shame that it should have been done. Why, sir, a man of your years to have accomplished what you have done, is wonderful. Then, on your arrival, with those beautiful animals, having travelled more than two thousand five hundred miles on foot, remember not by railroad, but on foot, should be ejected from so fine a place for rest, when permission was granted by the owners. Stranger, had this thing happened in some of the places you have passed through, we should have thought nothing about it, but coming into civilization and receiving such treatment, is what I can't under-

stand. Stranger, when do you resume your journey?"
"Next Friday, the 20th, I think; but having such a fine
place to camp I may stay over one day longer. It will
give the cattle more rest and that is what they need," I
replied. "Stranger, success to you, I hope you will accomplish your undertaking," and with that we bade each
other good-bye. "Mr. Johnson, you have had many callers
this afternoon," said Mrs. Jones. "Yes, ma'am; I am
aware of it," I replied. "Our supper is ready, come in,"
said Mrs. Jones. "Mrs. Jones, my cow will want the
milk taken from her soon," I said. "After tea is time
enough," said Mrs. Jones. I took supper with them
and when through went and milked Bessie, taking nine
quarts from her, which I took to Mrs. Jones, saying,
"Here is the milk from my California cow, you are welcome to it." "Mr. Johnson, you have a lovely cow, so
handsome, and such a good mess of milk she gives. I
hope you will succeed in getting her through to Massachusetts; should you, she will be worth her weight in gold,"
said Mrs. Jones. I repled, "That makes her a valuable
cow, much more so than any animal that Barnum has."

Omaha is situated on the west bank of the Missouri
river, high up, on a large flat bluff, running back to the
west and north on a high elevation. It is a young city,
with a population of thirty thousand. It has come to
stay for a while at least, until the western part of the
state becomes more settled, then Grand Island will come
in for the star of the state. This will be strongly opposed by the eastern part of the state, but it will surely
come, like unto Des Moines.

CHAPTER VIII.

From Omaha to Des Moines, Davenport and Chicago.

On the morning of the 21st, I left the city of Omaha crossing the Missouri river into Council Bluffs, where I remained three days, being invited to stop over by a G. A. R. comrade, and see the many delegations from the East leave for Denver city.

Council Bluffs is located in the Missouri Valley, and is an old town. It takes its name from the assembling of the Indians and Whites in council on the bluff overlooking the city, to arrange the treaties made between the government and the Indians. On leaving Council Bluffs, I resolved to follow the Rock Island Railroad, as closely as I possibly could, this being the shortest line to travel.

On the morning of the 24th I left Council Bluffs for Davenport city. I travelled along the west side of the bluff, making a gradual ascent for about two miles, then turning sharp to my right and went on down a heavy descent into the Mosquito Valley, crossing the Mosquito creek, and on up another steep bluff until about twelve o'clock, when I came to a fine farm house, where I stopped for dinner, and turned my cattle loose among an excellent quality of grass. The roads, thus far, are fenced with barb wire. My stay here was about two hours, moving onwards about two o'clock, and about six o'clock

I made Oakland; here I went into camp for the first night in the State of Iowa.

Oakland.—On the morning of the 25th I left Oakland, making Atlantic about eight in the evening of the same day. Oakland is situated on the Nishnebotene river, and is surrounded by a heavy forest of hard timber. A railroad passes through this place from Sidney to Harlan.

Atlantic.—On the morning of the 26th I left Atlantic and made Adair that day. Atlantic is the county seat of Cass county, and is a remarkably fine town for its age. Two railroads pass through; the Rock Island and Burlington and Quincy.

Adair.—On the morning of the 27th I left Adair and reached Dexter the same day. Adair is situated on the Rock Island Railroad, in the county of the same name. In travelling to this place the road has been very rough and exceedingly hilly.

Dexter.—The morning of the 28th we left Dexter and made Van Meter the same day. Dexter is a small town on the Rock Island Railroad, in the county of Dallas.

Van Meter.—On the morning of the 29th we left Van Meter and made Des Moines. Van Meter is a town on the Raccoon river. The Rock Island Railroad passes through; on leaving the town we crossed the river over a fine iron bridge.

On the morning of the 30th I went into the city of Des Moines to hunt up Mr. L. F. Andrews, 834 Fifth street, having a card of introduction to him, from Mr. James Dobson, of Atlantic. I did not have much trouble in finding the residence. I went to the door and rang the bell, a lady came to the door in answer. After passing compliments I handed her the card of introduction. She said, "This is Mr. Johnson, the great traveller, who is crossing the continent. We heard of you when passing through Atlantic, by our brother, Mr. Dobson; he wrote us, saying, that he had given you a card of introduction. Mr. Johnson, we are glad to meet you; Mr. Andrews is down town and will not be back until twelve o'clock. Please lead your cattle through the drive to the barn, only a few steps, there you will find room for your animals, and both hay and grain, feed them as you think best." I did as directed, taking good care of my animals. Soon the lady followed me to the barn and said, "Mr. Johnson, how do you find things?" "All right, ma'am," I replied. "I thought likely you would. Come in the house soon, I have so many questions to ask you; I don't know but that I shall weary you out. I suppose the same questions I ask, will be asked by my husband." While we were talking, Mr. Andrews came in, when she said, "Mr. Johnson, I will make you acquainted with my husband, Mr. Andrews." "Mr. Johnson, I am glad to meet you; I have been looking for you for several days, and how have you got along?" asked Mr. Andrews. "Since travelling in your state it has been hard and hilly; your roads are laid out by the compass, a mile apart. Yonder is a heavy hill; the road is directly over it, instead of around it, which makes it hard pulling," I answered. "Mr. Johnson, how was your road through Nebraska?" asked Mr. Andrews. "It was very good. The western part of the state has no roads, simply a trail, but was good travelling," I replied. "Mr. Johnson, how was your travelling over the Rocky Mountains?" asked Mr. Andrews. "All kinds, good, very good; bad, very bad." "Mr. Johnson," said Mr. Andrews, "I have many questions I wish to ask, if you have no objections. I will note them down for one of our leading papers in the city, and will begin with the question, "Where did you start from, with your outfit; horse, carriage, cow and dog?" "I started from Eureka city, Humboldt bay, California, with this same outfit; travelling the overland road to San Francisco, from there to San Jose, through the Livermore valley and Pass, into San Joaquin valley to Stockton, up the Sacramento valley to Sacramento city; following the Central Pacific Railroad to Gold Run; returning to Colfax, thence to Grass Valley, Nevada city, Webbers Lake; through the Sardinian valley to Verdi. Here I came to the Central Pacific road again; following it to Ogden, where I arrived September 23rd, 1882. On the 14th of May following, I resumed my journey, crossing the Rocky Mountains by the old Emigrant trail to Omaha, and from there to this city, Des Moines. This gives you my line of travel from California to this place." "And you, Mr. Johnson, have led that cow all the distance?" asked Mr. Andrews. "I have, sir." "How many miles have you travelled, think you, to reach this place?" asked Mr. Andrews. "Fourteen hundred and thirty-seven miles to Ogden; from Ogden to Omaha, one thousand and seventy-five miles; from Omaha to Des Moines, about one hundred and fifty miles; making a total of two thousand six hundred and sixty-two miles," I answered. "By the time you reach Massachusetts, you will have travelled four thousand four hundred miles; across the continent from the Pacific to the Atlantic. Wife, what do you think about it?" said Mr. Andrews. "I think the cow will not live to see Massachusetts," she answered. "Mrs. Andrews, if you will please give me a pail, I will go and milk her, as she has not been milked this morning. She is fresh in milk," I said. "Mr. Johnson, when was she milked last?" asked Mr. Andrews. "Last evening about seven o'clock, I have the milk in my wagon. I have two cans expressly for milking. It may not be good as I am obliged to carry it closed up; milk needs ventilation to be good." I went for the milk and it was pronounced good. After milking Bessie I took the milk to Mrs. Andrews, about ten quarts, saying that "I would warrant that to be good." Last night's and this morning's milking made seventeen quarts, from a good cow that has travelled twenty-seven hundred miles. "Mr. Johnson, travelling slowly through the country, you have had a chance to judge of the goodness of the country superior to those who see it by railroad, and who pretend to know all about it, and yet really know nothing. Your movements are slow; you can count the telegraph poles as you go along. When you get to your journey's end, and quietly seated or resting on your lounge, go back to California and travel it over again, (Don't forget to stop here on your way,) and put it all down on paper, you are the man to do it correctly and life-like, from a Chinaman to a jack-rabbit." "Mr. Johnson," said Mrs. Andrews, "Mr. Andrews has kept you busy answering his questions; I now want to ask you, perhaps two. How could you cross the plains without being devoured by the wild beasts?" "Many times I have been surrounded by the wild beasts, and then I have thought of home and my lonely position. On such occasions, my most effectual mode of keeping them away, was by building fires. Where wood could be found, I kept them burning through the night; there were times when wood could not be got, then I would burn kerosene oil. I always kept my lantern burning also. Kerosene was a luxury, I burnt it night and day, and always used it for kindling. The night of the fifth of June was the most remarkable of my journey. I was on the plains, coming over the Rocky Mountains, when I was overtaken by a severe snow storm. I was in camp and had retired for the night. About nine o'clock it began to rain, which very soon turned to hail, and from hail to snow, and continued through the night. The wind had changed and the snow fell direct in the horse's face. I changed the horse's position by turning round my wagon which made it a little more comfortable to the horse. I took from the horse her blanket and put it on the cow, and then took two of my blankets and put them on the horse, which added to her comfort. All this time Bessie, the cow, was lying down, quietly chewing her cud, not caring whether school kept or not. But the horse stood the storm as it came. All this time I was exposed to the storm, changing my position, but getting very cold. I had no gloves or mittens for my hands, which as well as my feet were cold. I happened to think of my kerosene oil and went to the wagon for it, I took the can and after scraping the snow away, which had fallen to the depth of about six inches, I poured oil on the ground and set fire to it, which blazed up finely, scaring the horse who turned the wagon to the rear, some ten feet, but doing no damage. I had kindled a good fire and warmed my hands. I did this several times, but it did not warm my feet, which had become very cold. I got a sack from my wagon, scraped the snow from where I had been standing and poured some oil on the place and burnt it. After the blaze had died out I spread the sack over the ground, took off my boots and stood upon the sack, which soon made my feet quite comfortable." "Mr. Johnson, how was it in regard to the Indians?" asked Mrs. Andrews. "At first the Indians were a terror to me, but that soon wore away. I came in contact with them many times, and on several occasions they rendered me good service. Twice I lost my trail, and both times they put me on it again." "Mr. Johnson, you were in Ogden several months, were you not?" asked Mrs. Andrews. "I was,' I replied. "You must be posted in regard to the Mormons; what do you think of them?" asked Mrs. Andrews. "What little I know about them, I can speak highly of them. At first I could not tell a Mormon from a Gentile, only by their conversation; their deportment was as good as the Gentiles. The Edmunds bill had just passed Congress and the Government had commenced the enforcement of the law. The troops of the Government were there, which caused much excitement among them. I became acquainted with some of the leading men of the city, who were Mormons. The First National Bank of Ogden is a Mormon bank. I was informed by its cashier, Mr. Young, that the directors of the bank represented three million dollars. Mr. Farr, formerly of Vermont, was a leading man of the city, a gentleman in its true sense and a Mormon. When I was about leaving Ogden he said to me, 'Mr. Johnson, when you are on the eve of leaving us, come to our store, we may have something you would like on your long journey.' When about to leave, I called upon him, reminding him of his word. He answered, 'I am glad you have come in; I think you are a fair man. Since my acquaintance with you, we have discoursed together on the leading issues of the day. When you arrive at your old home in Massachusetts, I want you to tell your people of us; just as you found us, from the day you came to your leaving. You have been with us about eight months; you leave us with a horse and wagon, do you? Here, take these things I have laid out for you, such as tea, coffee, cheese, butter, beef, chicken, turkey, sardines and salmon.' 'Mr. Farr, you must think I have a good horse to haul that pile over the Rocky Mountains,' I remarked. 'You have a fine horse,' said Mr. Farr. 'Yes, I am aware of it, but this is all for myself and dog, the cattle must be cared for; especially at this end of my journey. When I get into Nebraska, my cattle will not have to haul what they need to subsist on,' I said. 'Mr. Johnson, your heaviest hauling is between here and Evanston, about seventy-five miles. After you pass there, you will have a down grade. If you choose, I will put a part of it in a box and you can send it by rail,' said Mr. Farr. 'I will go and fetch my team,' I said. 'You need not go for your team, we will take it and you, if you are ready to return. Mr. Johnson, you say you are going to leave us; I regret it very much and think the rest of the citizens do. I hope you will be carried through this long journey safely. We will ever remember you in our prayers. May our Father in Heaven protect you by day and night on your long journey. Good-bye and success with it.' 'My dear friend, since my acquaintance with you, I have thought much of you, so much that I have singled you out of the many people of the city to discuss the issues of the day. I have learned much from you that I otherwise could not have learned. I have been one of your constant callers, and when in need of anything in your line I came here for it. Your deportment, to me a Gentile, has been such as I shall ever remember with pleasure. I am about to leave you; the probabilities are, that I shall never see you again, as I have no desire to return West. Good-bye.'" "Mrs. Andrews, your last question has brought out a lengthy answer; I feel as though justice should be rendered to the bridge that has safely carried me over, whether Jew or Gentile. I am neither, but a reader and thinker for myself; I believe in free agency every time. The Bible teaches many things, but the laws have fixed penalties of dollars and cents. This ancient history is a great hobby with the Mormons. They say if it was right in the olden times, it is right now; if wrong then, it is wrong now. Our natures are the same to-day as they were years ago, but we are more particular about the veil, whether it is thick or thin. Mrs. Andrews, do not think I am in favor of polygamy, for I am not. I would like to see a big fire made of some of our ancient records. If Christ and his apostles in their day, had put their feet on these ancient records, we should not now be contending with polygamy. But our natures would be the same, only we should be more particular about the veil, and wear a thick one every time. The Mormons say that we down East wear heavy veils. I told them if strong drinks were to be sold and drank, I preferred them veiled with thick boards. Well, Mrs. Andrews, excuse me, but I must make ready and move onwards, so good morning." "Good morning, if you come this way, don't forget to call," said Mrs. Andrews. "No, I will not, my fare has been too good to be forgotten."

Des Moines is the capital of Iowa, and a fine city for its age. It is situated on the Des Moines river, in the southern part of Polk county, and boasts a population of about thirty-five thousand.

On the morning of August 1st, I left the city of Des Moines, crossing the river Des Moines, by a fine bridge into East Des Moines. On the left is the State Capitol, with her golden dome, a handsome building. About seven in the evening I made Colfax.

About four o'clock on the morning of the 2nd, we left Colfax, making Newton in haste. About eleven o'clock I saw in the north a heavy cloud. As it came up it looked terrible, and having heard much about cyclones, I concluded that this might prove one. I crowded onward as fast as possible, hoping to reach town before the storm overtook us, but I fell short, as rain began to fall on our entering the town. It was not a cyclone, but a terrible thunder-storm; such lightning and thunder is seldom witnessed outside of Nebraska, but this happened to get outside of the line. I think, however, that the ammunition of Iowa is as good as that of Nebraska, perhaps not quite so sharp. I went into the town and about its centre, came to a house in front of which stood two fine trees, here I stopped. The rain was pouring down in torrents and any quantity of electricity was being discharged. While standing under the trees, a man came to the door and said, "Stranger, don't stand under the trees, yourself and the animals may be killed by the lightning." "Friend, my time is not yet come," I replied. "Lead your cattle around to my barn," said the man. "I prefer to stand under these trees, rather than be in your barn," I replied. The storm soon passed over. "Stranger," I said, "this storm has stopped my travelling for one day, at least." "Come in, stranger," said the man, "our dinner is ready, come and have some." "I will obey that order every time," I replied, "but this retreating to a barn in a thunder-storm is what I never intend to do." I went in to dinner, which was a fine one; comprising roast lamb, all kinds of vegetables, green corn, cucumbers, puddings, etc.; when through dinner, I said "Stranger, I have had a good dinner, now I want my cattle to have as good; I think much of my cattle." "I have hay, old or new, also all kinds of grain. Now, sir; you can have your choice, or you can turn your cattle into this rowen," said my host. "I will turn them into this grass, I think they will prefer the grass." "Stranger, where are you travelling to?" asked the man. "I am on my way to Massachusetts," I replied. "East, to Massachusetts; where are you from?" he asked. "I will come directly to the point; I am from California." "What! with that outfit. Stranger, you must be the very man I have heard spoken of this morning, in a Des Moines paper. It tells of a man travelling from California, going East, to Massachusetts; are you the man?" "I suppose I am. Stranger, can I stop with you until I am able to travel again?" I asked. "Yes, you can stop as long as you wish, we will feed you and your cattle as long as you stay."

Newton.—On the morning of the 4th I left Newton and reached Grinnell the same day. Newton is the county town of Jasper county. It stands on the Rock Island Railroad, about the centre of the county. It is more than an ordinary town, and few equal it.

Grinnell.—On the morning of the 5th I left Grinnell, making Ladora the same day. Grinnell is not only a fine town, but a smart business place. It is situated on the Rock Island Railroad, and is a junction of railroads from Poweshiek county. Had its location been more central, it would have been the capital of the county. A destructive cyclone which passed over this town was said to have been the work of Providence, but I would as soon think that Des Moines had more to do with it than Providence.

Ladora.—On the morning of the 6th I left Ladora and reached Homestead that day. Ladora is a town situated on the Rock Island Railroad, in the county of Iowa.

Homestead.—While in Des Moines I was informed that in this town oxen were used for many purposes, instead of horses, and no doubt I could get my cow shod, and on my arrival I ascertained I could, so I went into camp for the night with good cheer, giving the cattle grass and grain and took a cold lunch myself.

On the morning of the 7th I arose early and got the cow ready for shoeing. I went to the blacksmith's shop and asked for the proprietor, when a man said, "I am the proprietor, what can I do for you?" "I have a cow I want to have shod, can you shoe her?" I asked. "I have never shod a cow in all my days, but I have shod many oxen. I suppose a cow can be shod as well as an ox. Yes, I will try to put shoes on her. Stranger, I have been looking for you for several days. I saw in a Des Moines paper an account of your being in that city. It spoke of your route of travel, which explains why I was looking for you. How is the cow in the brake, will she shake it down?" inquired the blacksmith. "No, indeed, she is good in the brake," I answered. I led her into the brake and went to my wagon for a rope, which I made fast to her rear legs, bringing her feet directly under her, then I put the sling under her and lifted her slightly, so as she could just stand on her feet. This being done all right, I then took up one of her front feet and made it fast to the stanchion. "Blacksmith," I said, "remove her old shoes, but be careful that you do not break the shell of the hoof." While this was being done she made a great effort to get loose, but while the shoes were being put on she did not make any struggle. "Blacksmith, how much shall I pay you for this job?" I asked. "Stranger, when you get to your journey's end, you must write a book of your travels and relate what you have seen, heard and done, all the items, even to the shoeing of the cow this morning in the town of Homestead. After the book is complete, send me a copy, it is all the pay I ask," said the blacksmith. "I will, sir; with many thanks," I replied. Homestead is in the county of Iowa. About eight o'clock on the morning of the 7th I left Homestead, making Coralville at five o'clock, where I stopped for the night.

Coralville.—At eight o'clock on the morning of the 8th I left Coralville, making Iowa city. This place is a town situated on the Iowa river, about four miles from Iowa city. It is quite a place for the making of flour. I entered this town on Sunday morning. Many people gathered around me and many questions were asked on one side only, I having none to ask. I was presented with two bags of grain for my cattle and a first-class dinner for myself and dog.

Iowa City.—On the morning of the 10th I left Iowa

city, making West Liberty that day. Iowa city is situated on the Iowa river and Rock Island Railroad, in Johnson county. Formerly it was the capital of the State and now it is merely the county seat; it has a population of about seven thousand.

West Liberty.—On the morning of the 12th I left West Liberty, reaching Cedar River. This town is situated on the Rock Island Railroad, and is a junction of railroads, in Muscatine county. About twelve o'clock I came to Cedar river, a large stream of water; no bridge to cross over and too deep to ford. I called out for the Ferryman. The boatman got aboard his boat and began crossing the river; coming to a sand-bar, he labored hard for an hour or more to get his boat over the bar but did not succeed. He returned to the wharf and I went back a short distance and went into camp for a time, not knowing how long. Several teams came to the crossing, but turned back. A two-horse team with two gentlemen drove up to the river, and on turning back I hailed them, asking what they intended to do? They replied, "We shall go round through Muscatine, crossing the river there, over a bridge." "What is the distance?" I asked. "About twelve miles; where are you travelling to?" they asked. "I am going to Davenport," I answered. "If you cross the river here, you will reach Davenport in a day; if you go by Muscatine it will take you three days," they said. "But can I cross?" I asked. "No doubt you can, some time," they replied. I concluded to wait until morning and take my chances.

On the morning of the 13th, on the banks of Cedar river, I got up early and made ready for crossing the river. I drove down to the river and sang out for the boatman, who soon came down and pulled his boat across the channel, to where yesterday's sand-bar was, and came directly across to the landing where I was. I drove on the boat and was soon across the river. I said to the boatman this delay is expressly for my benefit; had I gone around to Muscatine, I should have had to travel three days to have made Davenport, now I can travel the distance in a day and a half; a saving of at least forty miles. I went on and reached Fulton where I stopped for the night.

Fulton.—On the morning of the 14th I left Fulton and reached Davenport at four o'clock in the afternoon. Fulton is situated on the Rock Island Railroad, in the county of Muscatine.

Davenport is situated on the western bank of the Mississippi river, opposite Rock Island, in Scott county. It is a fine enterprising city of about twenty-five thousand inhabitants.

About four o'clock on the morning of the 16th I left Davenport, making Creek river the same evening. On leaving the city I crossed the river on the finest iron bridge I had as yet seen, into Rock Island, passing directly by the Fort. The next place reached was Moline. A fine town, everything about it was excellent, nothing seemed out of tune. I travelled along with the river on the left and about nine o'clock in the evening I met a team, in which were a lady and gentleman. I stopped them and asked the road to Geneseo. I was told to go on a little distance further and turn sharp to my right, cross the railroad, and after crossing turn again short to the right and onward to Rock river ferry. On my arrival I found a suitable place and went into camp for the night.

Rock River I left on the morning of the 17th, making Geneseo the same day. Here I crossed the river on a ferry-boat, after staying four days; a longer time than I expected.

Geneseo I left on the morning of the 21st, reaching Mineral the same day. Geneseo is situated on the Rock Island Railroad, in the county of Henry. It is one of the most progressive towns in the State. I was compelled to stop over three days; I will tell you the reason. About thirty years ago, a man by the name of Dwight Freeman, went West from Webster; he was a special friend of mine. He made a wife of a fine young lady, that I thought much of. Before leaving Des Moines, a programme of my route was made out and reported in the papers; stating that I, Warren B. Johnson, from California, going East, to Massachusetts, would follow the Rock Island Railroad to Davenport, from there to Joliet and on direct to Cleveland, Ohio, thence to Buffalo, and from Buffalo on to Albany, N. Y. Mr. Freeman was on the look-out for me; he intended to catch me if possible on this route. He said to his wife, "Sarah, Warren will come from Rock Island direct to Geneseo. He will come either this or the west road, one of the two." Well, I had travelled that road and went directly past his house, camping directly in front of it, and did not know that I was within tens of miles of him. In the morning, early as usual, I broke camp and went into the town. Mr. Freeman, that morning, went to his pasture early, but not as early as I start when I am travelling, to see if his horses were safe, and saw where I had just left camp; which he learned by the tracks of the cow, she having on iron shoes. He returned to his house and said to his wife, "Sarah, I am going up town. Warren is there; I am sure he is. Last night he went into camp directly opposite us; I know by the marks of his cow. I am going up town; I will know surely and not let him pass me by." He harnessed his horse, put her in the carriage and drove to the town. When he came up I was milking the cow in front of the hotel. Quite a large gathering of people were around watching me milk the California cow. They were sure that I was the man the papers spoke about. Mr. Freeman did not wait for me to finish milking, but came directly up to me, saying, "Warren, I have caught you this time; I have been looking for you many days. I knew of your arrival in Davenport, the papers mentioned you. I said to my wife yesterday, that you would come through the town on the eastern road, or the west, sure. I was right, you came on the east road, directly by my house, but we did not know it at the time. Well, Warren, finish your milking and go back to where you camped last night." "Dwight," said I, "I will go back with you, expressly to see your wife; I have not seen you nor your wife since you left Webster, nearly thirty years ago." At this time a large number of people had gathered around. The inhabitants would tell one another that the man from California had arrived with his outfit, horse, carriage, cow and dog, "Come quick or you will not see him. He is going to stop with Mr. Freeman for a short time." Many questions were asked, and I remarked that if they would come to Mr. Freeman's, I would answer all the questions that they could ask me from California to Geneseo. I went back with Mr. Freeman; he kept with me and in order to surprise his wife he called her out as he sat in his carriage, and said, "Sarah, I have got him; I found him up town milking his cow. "Why, Warren B. Johnson, is that you? can it be you! Yes, it is; you look as you did years ago. I have not seen you since leaving Webster, twenty-eight years ago. It is that length of time, surely. Warren, I shall weary you out, having so many questions to ask of you," said Mrs. Freeman. "I can stand all the questions you may ask; I am tough and hardy. I have not seen a sick day since I left California; no, not an hour," I answered. "Warren, how many miles have you travelled since you left Eureka?" asked Mrs. Freeman. "I have travelled about three thousand miles; I think it will over-run that number." "And that poor cow has come all that distance?" said Mrs. Freeman. "Yes, we all have come that distance, and we are good for the remainder to Massachusetts," I answered. "I hope you will get home safe and sound," said Mrs. Freeman. "Sarah, to-day is Saturday and to-morrow will be Sunday. I want to have a good wash-up. I do not care to do it on Sunday and will put it off till Monday; how is that, Sarah?" I asked. "Warren, what are your intentions, I would like to know, and then I will come to time?" she answered. "I would like to make a long stay with you, but that will not do. I must get home before winter sets in; I can travel if it is cold, if the snow will only keep off; but should we have a heavy fall of snow, it would wind up my travelling for a while at least. Sarah, I would like to leave here on Monday, but perhaps it will be best to stay over Monday and prepare for the future, and leave you Tuesday morning early."

Mineral.—I left Mineral on the morning of the 22nd, making Wyanet the same day. This town is situated on the Rock Island Railroad and in the county of Bureau.

Wyanet.—I left Wyanet on the morning of the 23rd, reaching Princeton the same day. Wyanet is a smart, active business town, situated on the Rock Island and Burlington and Quincy Railroads.

Princeton.—I left Princeton on the morning of the 25th and made La Salle the same day. Princeton stands central in Bureau county and is the county town. As a town, I must say, it stands ahead of all on my line of travel. It is beautifully laid out; her streets are graded and paved with the best of material, and the gutters are tiled with the best of tiling pipes. The streets on either side are lined with the finest of shade trees; this makes the town look grand and imposing. She has two railroads in town, but it is a mistake that they are so far from its centre. Having a friend in this place, formerly from the East, I stopped with him, H. A. P., for two days.

La Salle.—I left La Salle on the morning of the 26th, making Ottawa the same day. This town I passed after dark, going directly through the town and into camp, not learning anything about it.

Ottawa.—I left Ottawa on the morning of the 27th, making Morris the same day. Ottawa is the capital of La Salle county. It is one of the largest towns I have passed through. I entered the town on Sunday afternoon, Monday was a rainy day, so we stayed here till Tuesday morning.

Morris.—On the morning of the 29th I left Morris and reached Joliet the same day. Morris is the capital of Grundy county, and is situated on the Rock Island Railroad.

Joliet.—This town I left on the morning of the 30th, reaching Dyer the same day. Joliet is the county seat of Wills county; it is a large city, boasting a population of about seventeen thousand, and is a large railroad centre. Here also, are located the State prisons. Just before reaching the city I passed a granite quarry; this was something novel, after travelling hundreds of miles and not a stone to be seen, then coming to a quarry of fine granite, it was worthy of note. I went on and coming to the city, I passed down Main street until coming to a fruit store, where they were unloading a wagon of watermelons. I stopped, saying, "What is the price of those melons?" "From ten to twenty-five cents each, according to the size," answered the proprietor. "Here is one badly broken, what is the price of that?" I asked. "It is worth twenty-five cents, but you may have it for ten cents. If I mistake not you are the California man. If so, put it in your wagon and pick the best one you can find, and put that also in your wagon," said the proprietor. "I think you are well posted on this California man," I replied. "I think the papers ought to keep us posted; it is not often they get a chance to post people on that subject. Are you the man that has travelled from California to this place? I know you are, without asking that question. The papers say, a man is travelling through the State from California, with a horse, carriage, cow and a little dog, en route to Massachusetts. You seem to represent those members; if you had not a cow, I would have thought you were not the man, but the cow is the prompter." "Well, sir; I am the man, there is no other person would have been so foolish," I replied. "There is no other that would have dared to be so foolish. No, emphasize the word dare; there is nothing foolish about it. Why, sir, you have a chance to see the kingdoms of this world and the kingdoms of the other world we know nothing about. Stranger, go inside, perhaps you will see something you would like on your journey; if so, take it and put it in your wagon; you shall be welcome to it," said the proprietor. I went into the store and looked around, I saw a cheese that had just been cut, I tasted it and found it was just to my liking. I said to the proprietor, "You have a fine cheese, I know nothing that would suit better than some of that cheese and crackers at some midnight hour when on my travels." The proprietor took the knife and put it on the cheese. I moved the knife back about half the distance, telling him to cut it there, but he moved it a little further on. I remarked that "I had a good horse; she would draw it, but would not care to eat it." I took the cheese and a small bag of crackers, thanking him for his generosity and went on out of the city about a half mile. Coming to a fine looking plat of grass I detached the horse from the carriage, removed her harness, turned her loose and the cow also. I seated myself on the grass, the broken melon beside me, and went into it right smart. I sat there at work eating the melon and on looking up I saw a man opposite, in the road, watching me steadily. "Stranger," he said, "you seem to be doing well, but if you will go with me a short distance, to the top of yonder hill, I will do better by you." "Sir, can you do better to my cattle than they are doing. I think much of them," I answered. "Yes, sir, I can give you a grass that has more sweetness than that they are now eating. Stranger, I think that you are the man that I have just read about in this very paper. It speaks of a man that has travelled from California thus far, and is on his way to Massachusetts. I was satisfied as I was sitting in this very wagon that you were the very man." "Yes, sir; I am the man," I answered. "Now, stranger, put your horse in your wagon and come up to my house, we will entertain you the best we know how. I don't wonder you think much of your cattle, coming all the distance they have. Why, sir, if that horse and cow were mine, I would refuse their weight in gold for them." I got ready and went with him to his house, a fine mansion. "Now, stranger, turn your cattle loose and let them romp wherever they choose, they can do no harm. Come into the house, it is our tea-time, your cattle are doing well." We went into the house, he introducing me to his wife, saying, "This man is from California with yonder horse and cow. He has led that cow in the rear of his wagon all that long distance. Our tea is ready, take a seat." I took a seat at the table and while eating many where the questions asked, which I freely answered, from my start to the present time. "Stranger," said my host, "yonder is my grain, help yourself to all your cattle will eat; if they are not in the habit of eating corn be careful not to give them too much." "What is a ration of corn to a horse?" I asked. "From ten to eighteen ears is a ration of corn for a horse," he replied. "Friend, on the morrow, I will leave you early; I thank you for your hospitality and bid you good night," I said. "Stranger, you are welcome to what you have received from our hands. Undoubtedly, you are, and probably will be the only man of the kind that we shall have the chance to entertain. Good night; hope you will have a good night's rest." "Thank you, good night," and I retired.

Dyer.—I left Dyer on the morning of the 1st of September and made Valparaiso the 2nd. Dyer is a town of small note. The Michigan Central and Louisville Railroads form a junction. The Michigan Central comes through here, crossing nine trunk roads that lead to Chicago, which makes what is known as the Joliet cut off.

Valparaiso.—I left Valparaiso on the morning of the 3rd, making Laporte on the 4th. Valparaiso is the capital of Porter county, and a fine town of about five thousand inhabitants. Have travelled about thirty miles, I should have made it in the distance of twenty-four. Owing to deep, heavy sand, I could not travel more than four to six rods before I had to stop, such hard pulling for my horse. My average travelling has been two and a half miles to the hour, but these two days it has only been one and three-quarter miles to the hour. I continually inquired how long before I would get rid of the sand. "Where are you travelling to?" they asked. "I want to make Cleveland, Ohio," I would answer. "You will have sand and deep sand all through the State. The nearer the lake the more sand you will find. I think you had better go to Laporte and from there to South Bend; from there to Elkhart, then to White Pigeon and so on," said my adviser.

Laporte.—I left Laporte on the morning of the 5th and made South Bend on the 6th. Laporte is the seat of Laporte county. It is situated in the centre of the county; several railroads enter the town. Lake Shore and Michigan Southern are the most prominent. In making South Bend, I had to travel thirty-six miles. I would travel on one road a while and coming to some place, then they would tell me to take a certain road, where I should meet with less sand and I would go for that road. Perhaps, I would travel for about one mile, sometimes two miles. Here I will state for the information of my readers that in the Western States, the Government has laid out the roads one mile apart. You travel as it were by the compass, east, west, north and south, no less angles than squares. There are roads that run parallel with the railroads, from depot to depot, which roads are the best every time. I am travelling on a flat surface. Indiana is not Iowa; I wish it was. Iowa has good roads and good hills, but Indiana has the sand hills such as no other State has. So far it is the poorest State for soil I have travelled through. Ohio I know nothing about, but should I succeed in reaching that State, and I pray that I may, I will know what I don't know at this time.

South Bend.—I left South Bend on the 8th, making Goshen the same day. This town is the county seat of St. Joseph county; it is a large, noble town, I will call it such, but I think it is a city. The Lake Shore and Michigan pass through. This has a tendency to build the town up rather than pull it down. Here I found many warm friends.

Goshen.—I left Goshen on the morning of the 10th, making Lagrange on the 11th. Goshen is the capital of

Elkhart county, situated in the centre of the county. It is a fine town. Last night was the first frost of the season. On making Goshen my travelling has improved and I hope it will continue.

Lagrange.—I left this place on the morning of the 12th and reached Angola on the 13th. Lagrange is the county seat of the same name. It is centrally located and a fine town, but does not come up to others I have passed through. On making Lagrange, my road has been very uneven; hills and valleys with plenty of sand. This variety of travel wears heavily on my horse. The cow stands it remarkably well, but the horse; oh, how I pity her.

Angola.—I left Angola on the morning of the 14th, making Bryan the same day. Angola is the capital of Steuben county. Its location is central of the county. It has a fine court-house, this was in the best part of the town; but its surroundings were not as good as many that I have passed through. On my arrival I found the place was full of people and on inquiring the cause, I found there was a circus in town that day. I drove along to a hotel, in rear of which was a small barn, and behind that a fine plat of grass. I turned my cattle loose that they might eat of the grass, and laid myself down for rest, being very weary. Soon the cow laid down, but I thought nothing of this, as it was a common thing, and soon after the horse also laid down. This was a surprise to me; I never saw her lie down in the day time before. She must have been very tired. Poor horse! I began to think, and in my mind travelled back to Dyer station, over again the long distance we had come—through the long sand-road, up hill and down, first on one side and then the other of the road, in the ditch and out trying to find something solid to step on. She would stop and look around; then I would tell her to go on, which she would do every time, without any hesitation; she was at all times ready to do as bidden. She must have rest or she would take it in another form. About ten o'clock I heard music and went down to the hotel and watched the circus procession pass down the street on their parade through the town. After it had passed I returned to my camp and found the animals still lying down. I did not disturb them. I spoke to them, however, but they made no reply. I went to my wagon and laid down again. We were all most worn out for want of rest. I had an interview with the hotel proprietor and related my travelling through the State and the advice given me to keep to the north instead of the south roads where I should find less sand. He said, "They told me wrong, and that they knew nothing about the roads. Had I travelled further south I should have had much less sand. On crossing the Baltimore and Ohio Railroad, you should have followed the road. I now advise you to go from here to Bryan and then follow the railroad. One day more will take you out of the sands. When in Ohio you will find good roads."

Bryan.—I left Bryan on the morning of the 16th and made Wauseon the same day. Bryan is the capital of Williams county. It is a fine town, situated on the Lake Shore and Michigan Southern Railroad.

Wauseon.—I left Wauseon on the morning of the 17th and reached Maumee city. Wauseon is the capital of Fulton and is situated on the Lake Shore and Michigan Southern Railroad. It is a thriving town.

Maumee City.—This place I left on the 18th, reaching Freemont on the 19th. Maumee city is but a small town, situated on the west side of the Maumee river, where we cross into Perrysburgh. From Perrysburgh to Bellevue is one of the best roads in the State of Ohio. A good macadamized road.

Freemont.—I left Freemont on the 20th, making Bellevue that day. Freemont is the capital of Sandusky county. It is a fine, large town of ten thousand inhabitants and a great town for business. After leaving Freemont my first stop was at Clyde, where we took dinner. As I sat eating my dinner I saw a monument on my left and went to it. It was a square block of very fine Quincy granite, about four feet at its base and three feet at the top, with cut corners. On the top of this block was a statue. This statue was of Gen. McPherson, one of the most noted in our whole army.

Bellevue.—I left this place on the 22nd, making Norwalk the same day. Bellevue is more than an ordinary town. It is situated on a junction of railroads which makes it a smart thriving town.

Norwalk.—I left Norwalk on the 23rd, making Wakeman the same day. Norwalk is the capital of Huron county. It is one of the high-toned towns in the State; its aristocracy stands out strong.

Wakeman.—I left Wakeman on the morning of the 24th, making Elyria the same day. Wakeman is more than an ordinary town. It is situated on the Michigan Southern Railroad. My stop here was unexpected and was on account of a severe thunder-storm.

Elyria.—I left Elyria on the morning of the 25th, reaching the city of Cleveland the same day. Elyria is the county seat of Lorian county, and is as smart a town as they make out West. It is not a large, but a clean, enterprising town. I left very early in the morning, in order to make Cleveland the same day, and did; but it was a smart day's travelling. I had a fine road which helped me much in making it.

CHAPTER IX.

From Cleveland, Buffalo, Albany, to Marlow. New Hampshire.

Resuming my journey after a day's rest, I left the city of Cleveland early on the morning of the 27th and made Painesville the same day. Cleveland is the largest city I have passed through since leaving San Francisco. On leaving the city, I came out on Superior street; I should have taken the left street, by doing so it would have saved me pulling through deep sand and four miles of travel. Leaving so early as I did, I travelled the whole length of Superior street without meeting a person. I made Painesville late in the evening.

Painesville.—I left Painesville on the morning of the 28th, making Ashtabula the same day. It is the seat of Lake county and a first-class town; situated on the Lake, and has two railroads passing through, the St. Louis and Lake Shore and Michigan Southern.

Ashtabula.—I left this place on the 29th and made North Kingsville. Ashtabula is situated on the lake, but unlike Painesville is not a county town. It has the same railroads, but still does not come up to Painesville as a town, for some reason I know not.

North Kingsville.—I left North Kingsville on the morning of the 30th and made Avonia. North Kingsville is simply a small town, like many other towns with railroads. I made Avonia in haste, being driven in by a terrific thunder-storm, with copious showers of rain, hail and fire mingled. I succeeded in getting under cover as the storm burst upon us. Such thunder and lightning I only saw back in Nebraska. Well, I got out of the hail and rain. I expected more, but thanks be to God, that lightning did not hit me or any of my family. When a streak of lightning starts from a cloud one mile high, coming down so quickly, it does not turn to the right or left to hit this one or that one. I do not believe in the doctrine that God intends to hit one person in particular and not the other. Well, where am I? In Avonia, under a shed out of the storm. The storm has passed and gone and now I can't travel. So much slipping will injure my horse, so I must wait awhile.

Avonia.—I left Avonia on the morning of October 1st, making Erie the same day. Avonia is a town situated close on the shores of Lake Erie, and has a full view of the Lake for many miles. I am now travelling on a broad road, known as the old Erie turnpike. It is much worn out. This road after a smart rain will hold quantities of water, and the water of yesterday's rain lays deep on the road, making any quantity of mud to go through, and it is of that consistency that would make fire-brick; you may judge how my boots looked about this time. As I was about entering Erie city, I saw on my right a splendid field of grass. I was undecided whether to go on and enter the city or stop here; however, I went into the city, but after entering the city and thinking the matter over, I decided to return to this field of grass and camp, asking no permission whatever. After my cattle had eaten what I thought essential, I brought them in and gave them their grain and secured them for the night, made up my bed and laid down to rest. I had not laid long when two men came up to me and said, "Stranger, are you not trespassing here?" "Gentlemen, I think I am. I have become so accustomed to doing so on my long journey. I think that had I been strictly honest, I should not have been so far on my journey as I am now," I replied. "Stranger, what am I to understand by your being on a journey?" was asked. "I will explain, I have travelled a long distance; the distance is as long as from California to this place, about four thousand miles. Strangers, I have been doing about as my mind has led me. Coming through Nebraska, I would let my cattle eat the grain while they would be standing in the road, with two wheels of my wagon in the growing grain, but the cattle were not." "Stranger, a man was passing by you and saw your cattle feeding and called and notified me of it, so we came down here to see. We have read in the papers about a man from California, travelling East to Massachusetts, with a horse, carriage, cow and dog; are you the man?" "I am the man," I answered. "Stranger, if you will go with me I will give your cattle a place in the barn and all the hay and grain you wish them to have, and yourself a good bed in the house," they said. "Gentlemen, my cattle have had all they need to-night; they ate heartily on grass, and then I gave them a feed of grain and there they are resting, as for myself, I would as soon lie on this ground, and sooner, than take a bed. Gentlemen, I thank you for your invitation, please allow me to remain here through the night, to-morrow I shall feel so much better than if I had taken a bed inside." "We have no objection to your remaining here over night, under the circumstances. We would not allow any one to turn in their cattle to feed, but you are welcome to stop over night." "Thank you, gentlemen." "Good night, stranger." "Good night, gentlemen."

Erie City.—On the morning of the 2nd I left Erie City, making North East the same day. Erie City is situated on the Lake, mid-way of Erie county, Pennsylvania. It is an old town and looks old, and is as old as it looks, but has little enterprise. It has a very fine cemetery, I had occasion to pass through it.

North East.—The morning of the 3rd I left North East and reached Brockton the same day. North East is a town situated in the most north-east extremity of Erie county. It is one of the finest towns in the county and has two railroads, the Lake Shore and Michigan Southern and New York and St. Louis Railroads.

Brockton.—On the morning of the 4th I left Brockton, making Silver Creek. Brockton is situated on the railroad in the town of Portland and my first stopping place in New York State.

Silver Creek.—I left this place on the morning of the 5th, making Lake view the same day. Silver Creek is a railroad station for the town of Hanover, it is a fine village with a good view of the Lake.

Lake View.—I left this place on the morning of the 6th, reaching Buffalo the same day. Lake View is a railroad station in the town of Hamburgh. It is a very pretty village, situated on a high elevation and overlooks the Lake for a great distance.

Buffalo.—On the morning of the 7th, about six o'clock, we entered the city of Buffalo, near the Lake, this being the most northern part of the city. We travelled directly through Genesee street to the New York Central Railroad, where we stopped some three hours. I really saw but little of the city, which is the largest I have entered since leaving San Francisco. On my left, about sixty rods distant, were many people standing. While eating our breakfast they learned that the man from California had arrived with his outfit, the people came around us by the hundreds and completely surrounded us. I did not attempt to retreat, in fact I could not; I was their captive. The people were quite familiar in asking questions, some of which were difficult to answer. After a while a squad of policemen arrived, and one of their number came to me and said, "Old man, what are you here for?" This you see was a question for authority. "Sir, your honor; I am simply passing through your city, and merely stopped to get breakfast, I will soon move on," I answered. "Move on at once, or we will take you up town," said the officer. "Oh, don't detain me. I am anxious to get home to vote for old Ben Butler," I said. When I was about leaving, I remarked to the people, "Gentlemen, I am simply passing through this extreme part of your city quietly, and have had no disturbance as yet, nor do I fear any. I have come a long distance, about four thousand miles, and no where have I received such an ovation as this." Many questions were asked and answered satisfactorily and when I was about to move on, two men came up to my wagon with a basket and said, "Stranger, take this basket and when you get a short distance, look in and help yourself." "Thank you," I replied and went on. As I was moving along, three cheers were given for the man travelling from California to Massachusetts. I left Buffalo at twelve at noon on my way to Albany, travelling the old Genesee turnpike, and made Batavia at ten o'clock on the morning of the 8th.

Batavia.—I left Batavia at one o'clock in the afternoon of the 8th, reaching Le Roy the same day. Batavia is the capital of Genesee county. It is situated on the New York Central Railroad. To its left is the city of Rochester. Here the New York Central with its four tracks, leaves Batavia to the left. Two of the tracks run due east to Syracuse.

Le Roy.—I left Le Roy on the morning of the 9th and made Avon the same day. Le Roy is situated on the railroad in Geneseo county. It is a smart, active business town.

Avon.—I left this place on the morning of the 10th and made Canandaigua the same day. Avon is situated on a junction of railroads in the county of Livingston.

Canandaigua.—I left this place on the morning of the 11th, making Geneva the same day. Canandaigua is the principal town in Ontario county.

Geneva.—I left Geneva on the morning of the 12th and made Seneca Falls the same day. Geneva is situated on the railroad and on the northern part of Seneca Lake. Soon after leaving this place it began to rain lightly. I continued on and found it improved my road, it being a deep, heavy sand. I passed directly through the town of Waterloo. The rain kept increasing, my travelling was becoming heavy, and coming to a fine-looking barn I turned in. As I did so, I met two young men to whom I said, "Gentlemen, I am a traveller, and have become quite noted in this department. I have travelled from Geneva through this rain; my horse is very weary and so am I. I should like to get under cover for the night." "I think you must be the man the papers speak of, who is with a horse, wagon, cow and dog from California, going East to Massachusetts; are you the man?" asked the stranger. "I am the man," I answered. "Lead your horse in the barn and stay till the rain stops. I want to ask you a few questions," said the stranger. I drove in the barn, removed the horse from the wagon and the cow also, making all right for the night. "Stranger, our supper is about ready, we will go in and see." We went to the house the young man introducing me to his father and mother, as the traveller from California they had read about in the papers, he telling me to take a seat, and saying, "Mother, give the stranger a good dish of tea, we will say nothing about the rest." "Is it possible you have come from California with that horse and cow?" asked the father. "I suppose you have seen all that we read about, coming across the plains; the wild beasts, the Indians, the Mormons, the tramps, the cow-boys, and I know not what?" "I have seen all you have spoken of, but there is one I have not seen, that is the elephant; he I saw not. But the Mormons, the tramps and the cow-boys, I became very familiar with, especially the Mormons, with whom I was eight months. You will be surprised when you learn what I know about them." "Well, friend, we will go to the barn and see how the California cow is, and learn if she is in want of anything in our line." We went to the barn, giving the cattle more hay and grain, then returned to the house and retired for the night. "Friend, stranger, before retiring, allow me to say a word; Massachusetts is having a very warm time at the coming election for Governor, I have interest in that matter, having the right to vote on my arrival home." "What town in Massachusetts is your home?" he asked. "The town of Webster is my home. Now, sir, I have quite a walk to get home in time to vote. I suggest that you get me away in the morning as early as you can. But I do not want to go before I get my breakfast, you understand. I am a Yankee, every time; please excuse me." "I see you are a Yankee. I question whether there is another man, Yankee or Yorker, like you. You have done that which would trouble the boys to do. Well, we must go to bed or we shall not get up early in the morning."

On the morning of the 13th I was up early, prospecting. I decided to stop over the day as it was not safe to travel, it being so slippery it would wrench my cattle. I was cordially welcomed to stay at will and thought it best to stop over the day.

Auburn.—On the morning of the 14th I thought it best to travel and make Auburn if possible. I went on and found it to be a hard day's labor.

Syracuse.—On the morning of the 15th, about six o'clock I left Auburn for Syracuse, where I arrived about midnight. I drove under a shed, giving my cattle water and grain, spreading my blankets on the ground, laid myself down, soon dropping asleep.

Oneida.—I left Syracuse on the morning of the 16th, making Oneida the same day. On making East Syracuse we were invited to take dinner by the proprietor of the hotel; such invitations we never decline. After dinner we went on, crossing the railroad and continuing about two miles, crossing the canal. We are now on the right of both canal and railroad. The day having passed and gone, I concluded to travel some time in the night and about ten o'clock camped. I was uncommonly sleepy, so much so that I was compelled to lie down and I at once fell asleep, but not for long. I was awakened by my little dog. The dog was with me under the blankets. A man in passing, being more or less drunk, came along to my cow, which was lying down and gave her a hard kick with his boots. At once the cow got up and went as near the horse as she could get, and at the same time the dog bounced out of bed and went for the man. The man's attention was now with the dog. I was still lying in bed. The man was looking for something to slay the dog. I told him to go on and let the dog alone. Then he came to me where I was lying and said, "Who in h—l are you; get up or I will blow your d—d brains out." I was up in no time, you bet, and quickly went to my wagon, having a hand-axe where I could have easy access to it at such a time as this. The man was too drunk to fear the axe. I did not want to strike him, as I might have killed him on the spot. I retreated and at the same time called out, "Murder." Nearly opposite was a house. The man had been awakened by my cry and soon had a light. I retreated towards the house and called on the man to come out; he knew the man and commenced talking to him. While they were talking I went for my wagon cutting the halter, not stopping to untie it and went on. I continually looked back, expecting the man to follow me. I think I got out of this well. On my arrival in Utica I related this incident. One man in the crowd said, "Why didn't you split his d—d head open. I would have done it." I remarked, "Had I struck the man I might have killed him, which would have detained me, and I should have gone and complained of myself, then a coroner's inquest would have to be called. I should have been detained and I would not have been here to-day, perhaps not for several days, and more, I would not reach Massachusetts by election day so that I could vote for grand, old Ben Butler; so friends, really my way was the best." "Yes, you are right; but there is no other man left like you. I don't think there is another man living that would have done as you have done."

Utica.—I left Oneida for Utica on the 17th, making the

city limits and went into camp in front of a fine residence. About midnight it commenced raining. I packed my bedding that it might not get wet and remained awhile, hoping it would stop raining, instead of that it kept increasing. I thought it best to go into the city and get under cover. I got ready and went on, not knowing the time. Coming in sight of a long row of gas lights we journeyed on, turning to my left, going further some twenty rods, turning to my right. It was raining quite smart. I came to a stop as I could see no one except my own family. While standing I saw one man; he was out of the rain of course. I was sure he must be a policeman. The old proverb is, "They don't know enough to get under cover when it rains." This was an exception; he was under cover and proved to be a watchman. I went up to him leaving my horse; but mind you the horse would not be left, she followed me, making a turn and coming up to me. As I approached the watchman he came out and met me. "You are a watchman?" said I. "Yes, sir, I am a watchman, and have been watching you for some time." "You have, I have been looking for a watchman for information. You are the first and the last man I have seen since I entered the city. It commenced raining and I thought it best to make the city and get under cover, I am a stranger, will you direct me to where I can get out of the storm." "Yes, sir; keep on down this street, turn to your right and you will come to the Mansion stables." I went on and came to a street, but did not know whether it would take me to the stables or not; I turned down it, however, and soon came to the stables. I went to the door and rang the bell, and soon we were admitted to a good house for a stormy night. The cattle were well cared for, and myself and the dog took the hay-mow and had very comfortable lodgings. In the morning I went to the Mansion House and called for the proprietor. I said to him, "I came to the city early this morning in the rain. I am a traveller, but not a tramp, a common tramp at least. I have come a long distance with a horse, carriage and a cow. My horse is a fine Morgan, a native of Massachusetts; my cow is an Ayrshire and Jersey, a native of California, and a fine cow; both are in your stables. My cow needs milking, please come and look at them." "I will, sir, with pleasure. You are evidently the man the papers tell about, who is with a horse and carriage, leading a cow from California, going to Massachusetts; are you the man?" I told him I was and we went to the stable. "If the papers told the truth, and I have no doubt they did, that horse and cow have walked more than four thousand miles. Can that be true? It is a big story, but a bigger thing to accomplish. Well, stranger, take good care of your cattle; milk the cow, I will put it on ice and test it in our coffee. Perhaps I can trade for her, how is that, stranger?" "I will milk the cow and test the milk with other fixings," I answered. This being done it was decided that I had a remarkable cow. The rumor went around that the man from California, with his horse, carriage, cow and dog were at the Mansion House. A large crowd soon gathered around and many questions were asked on one side and answered by the other.

About midnight, of the morning of the 19th I left Utica, crossing the canal, river and railroad. I am still on the old Genesee road; canal, river and railroad on my right. I was advised to continue on the same road that I had been travelling, although the south road was the river road and the most level, but I would find more mud at this time. My first four miles was deep sand, but the rain had made the sand quite hard, which made it more comfortable travelling. Further on I found clay; this clay soil is very disagreeable, causing continual slipping when wet. About seven o'clock we made Herkemer, here we took breakfast. After breakfast we journeyed to Little Falls, where we made a short stop and then went on; after a time coming to a fine-looking ranche. Here I concluded to stop for the night, if I could be permitted to use part of a shed. By simply removing a wagon I could have good accommodation for the night. I went to the house and rang the bell, which was answered by a fine-looking young lady, to whom I said, "Madam, I am a traveller and have come a very long distance and still have not reached my home." "Where is your home?" she asked. "Massachusetts is my home," I replied. "You say you have come a long distance, where have you come from?" asked the lady. "From California, madam," I replied. "I have just read in the papers of a man arriving in Utica from California, with his horse and carriage, leading a cow all that distance, are you the man?" asked the lady. "I am, and have come from Utica this day. I left about midnight this morning." "You have come from there to-day? Mother, this is the man that I was reading about in the paper; he has travelled from Utica to-day. Where is your horse and cow, I would like to look at them?" said the lady. "They are at the shed," I replied. Mother, daughter and a neighbor, who was invited by the young lady, all went to see the California cow. "Stranger, take your horse out of the carriage and put her and the cow in the barn. You are not going to sleep in the shed to-night," said the lady. "Madam, I prefer to sleep with my cattle. I have done so with two exceptions; I am dirty and not fit to get into a clean bed," I replied. "My dear sir, water and a little soap will soon make them clean. I really wish that you would comply with my request," she answered. "If you insist I will comply with your wish." "I do, my brother will be home soon, he will look after your cattle. Father I have none; we buried him some three months ago. Oh, that he were living, he would dearly love to entertain you.

What a loss we have sustained. Dear Father. Stranger, the papers say that your name is Johnson, W. B.," said the lady. "That is my name; I have but one." "Stranger, our supper is ready, I hope you will not decline to take tea with us?" she said. "Why should I decline this?" I replied. "I did not know but that you would like to be excused from coming to the table, as you look as if you had seen some mud, travelling the long distance," said the lady. Soon after, the brother came home and the young lady said to him, "William, this stranger is the California man, that we have read of in the papers. He came in to see if we would allow him to stop under the carriage shed for the night. I told him that we would do better with him and give him a clean bed inside. He seemed to discard this invitation, preferring rather to sleep with his cattle." After tea I said, "My dear friends, about sleeping with my cattle; I think much of them and they of me, I am sure of it. I will go back four thousand miles, having travelled that distance already. When I left California, I left behind me all the family I ever had; wife and one daughter, who are still living. They were opposed to my coming the way I have come. They told me all they could and got others to dissuade me from my project. They said I whould be confronted with the wild beasts of the forests; the Indians; the cow-boys; the tramps; and last, but worst of all, the Mormons. All of these I should have to contend with. I have had to do so, but not one insult have I received from any of them, with one exception, leaving out the wild animals. This exception was near Oneida, by a man too drunk to know what he was doing; this was the first and the last. Many times I have been told to look sharp after my cattle, which I have done. Many nights I have slept between them; the horse fastened to one wheel and the cow to another. While in Cheyenne I fell in with a comrade of the Grand Army, who invited me to stay with him while in the city. He remarked that I must look sharp after the cattle at nights, especially my horse, the cow he thought no one would attempt to take. The horse was a strong temptation for the cow-boys. Most of my way through Nebraska I was filled with continual fear, lest I should be overtaken by some one or more that would want the horse or trade for her. I have passed such and met them at the stations, but no insult whatever have I received from them. Well, friends, it is past my bed time. If you insist on my sleeping inside, I will go to the barn and see if the cattle are all right and then return and retire, as I would like to get a good night's rest. I am strongly inclined to think that a bed under the shed would make a better night's rest than one inside. We will try it on; it is the only way to test the pudding by eating." "What time will you leave in the morning?" asked the young lady. "About six o'clock," I answered.

St. Johnsville.—I left the ranche near St. Johnsville on the 20th, making Johnstown the same day. I arose early and got ready to leave, and as soon as the breakfast was ready, I was ready for it. Our breakfast consisted of fresh fried pork and sausage, hot potatoes, hot biscuits and coffee, all well-cooked, topping off with cranberry sauce and mince pie. This with its surroundings, was the best breakfast I had from California to Massachusetts. I did ample justice to the meal. After breakfast, and as I was about to leave, the lady came out to me at my carriage with a bundle, saying, "I would like you to take this with you; it is simply a lunch, you may get faint on your way. Take, eat, and remember us all; we will ever remember you, the man that travelled across the continent." I well knew its contents, and on parting I remarked, "Dear friends, your hospitality exceeds all others on my journey; particularly the way it has been given, with sympathy, love and affection. Oh, that I could do something in return; but I must leave you. Good morning." "Good morning, we hope you will succeed and arrive safely at your journey's end. Should you ever be permitted to come this way again, please be sure to call on us," said the lady. "I will, thank you, good-bye." I reluctantly left them and went on my journey. About twelve we stopped for dinner. Here I broke the seal of the bundle; its contents were cold meats, like our breakfast, a mince pie and some doughnuts and cheese; a good dinner was the result. I thought much of it, but much more of those from whom it came. At one o'clock we again moved forward and at five o'clock we reached a fine looking farm-house and barn. I thought it best to stop here for the night. I went to the house for a permit to use the shed for my cattle. Just as I was going to ring the bell a man came in sight, I asked him if he was the master of the ranche? He answered he was. "What will you have?" "I would like to use your shed for the night. It is going to be a cold, frosty night and I would like to get under cover, I have not been under cover, except two nights, for months. Some nights I have been so cold that I could not sleep and then travelled the rest of the night to keep warm." "Where have you come from and where going, to be travelling for months?" he asked. "Well, sir; I have but one story to tell and I have told it many times, twice in a day, and some times I have seen no one to tell it to," I replied. "I think I know who you are, through the papers. They say that a man from California is travelling to Massachusetts, with a horse, carriage, cow and dog. Are you the man that is doing such a wonderful thing?" "I am the man," I replied. "Well, well, I want to see what you have got for a horse and cow that have travelled all that distance, stranger," he said. "They are at your shed," I replied. "And you have travelled from California with that horse and cow? Take your horse and lead her inside, and the cow too. They shall have a good bed to-night. Will your cow stand beside the horse?" he asked. "She will." "She won't injure the horse, think you?" he asked. "Oh, no, they think much of each other," I replied. "We will go into the house, our supper will be ready soon; I suppose you won't decline to take a bed inside?" "Oh, no, last night I was well cared for; I think the best on my whole journey," I said. As we were sitting around the stove, the man took up the newspaper and said, "Your name is Johnson it seems, that is what the paper says. This is a Utica paper, and it speaks of a man by the name of W. B. Johnson, from California to Massachusetts, as having passed through that city; you are the man. Mr. Johnson, take a seat at the table and make yourself at home; I suppose you have one or you would not look as well as you do." I took the seat and answered, "I have not been sick a day since leaving California; no, not an hour. I have seen some hard times in crossing the Rocky Mountains. I was out on the plains in a bad snow storm, that made me think of home, you bet." "What time was that storm?" he asked. "It was the 5th and 6th of June last." "How much of a snow-fall?" "The snow fell from eight to twelve inches on the level. It commenced raining about eight o'clock in the evening, turning to hail, from hail to snow and continued all night. I was alone with my cattle and was very cold. I brushed the snow away on the ground, then I poured kerosene oil on the ground and set it on fire. This kept my hands from freezing. This I did at intervals until I had consumed nearly two quarts of oil. My feet became very cold, I could not get them warm. I went to my wagon and took from it an old blanket, putting it over the ground where I had been burning the oil, I took off my boots and stood on this blanket. It was not long before I began to feel the warmth and my feet soon became comfortable."

Schenectady.—I left the ranche, near Fonda, and the pleasant family connected with it on the 21st, reaching Schenectady early on the morning of the 22nd. On the morning of the 21st I was up early, getting ready to move on. Soon after the breakfast bell rang, the gentleman of the house came out to me and said, "Good morning, stranger." "Good morning," I replied. "You are driving things, it seems, you are going to get home to vote for old B. F., I suppose, or some one else?" "Yes, sir; that is my intention." "Have you fed that California cow; she is all right, I suppose?" said my host. "She is." "Our breakfast is ready. I suppose you are ready and waiting?" he said. "I am, sir; I could have taken breakfast in Amsterdam, but I thought you might never forget me, you might forgive." "Yes, I could readily forgive you, but I should not be likely to forget you, for a time at least." "Friend stranger, I do not wish to insult you by offering to pay for your hospitality," I said. "No, sir, you had better not; that would be an insult and a crime. I would not be guilty of taking one cent from you, not a cent; I would like to have you stop longer. I have been much interested in listening to your travels across the plains," said my host. "My friend, I must leave you, and thank you kindly for your hospitality," I said. "You are welcome, sir; I would like to entertain another man under the circumstances; good morning, and success to you." "Thank you," I replied, and I started on my journey and just at twelve o'clock I made Amsterdam. Here we took dinner, leaving Amsterdam at half-past one o'clock and about half-past five came to a small farm-house. I stopped and asked the man of the house if he would sell me some hay for my cattle. "How much hay do you want for your cattle?" he asked. "Only enough for their supper; I am going to travel to-night. I want to make Schenectady to-night or early in the morning." "Yes, you can have some hay, sir; will you put your cattle in the barn, or shall I bring it out here?" "Bring it out here, if you please," which he did. "Can I make me a dish of tea?" I asked. "Yes, if you wish. We will go into the house, perhaps my wife has some already made. It is our tea time; come in, stranger." I went in with him and he said to his wife, "This man seems to be travelling. I have given his cattle some hay and he wants to make a dish of tea. I told him to come into the house, perhaps you may have some already made." "I have some already made; perhaps the man would like some supper, he can if he wishes; will you take supper with us?" asked the wife. "I will, if you have no objections, I ought not," I answered. "Take a seat at the table." I seated myself and the wife said, "You seem to be travelling, how far have you come?" "I have come a long distance, as far as from the Pacific Ocean to this place." "Are you the man the papers of yesterday speak of as travelling from California to Massachusetts, with a horse, carriage, cow and a little dog?" "I suppose I am." After many other questions had been asked and answered, I asked, "What is the distance to Schenectady?" "About twelve miles," was answered. "I would like to see Albany about this time to-morrow." "How many miles do you travel in the day?" "I travel two and a half miles per hour, all day and night when I travel. Friends, I thank you for your hospitality, good night." "You are welcome, good night. Stranger, one word; soon you will be travelling close by the railroad. It is dangerous to travel at night. There are many trains the first part of the night, all from the West, and mostly freight. The engines throw out streams of fire, which in the night look horrid, especially to the horses." I went on and came to a place where the carriage road was close to the railroad. I had but just got to the place, when a train came along in our rear. I stopped; the horse turning partially round; the cow had left her position and stood sideway of the wagon, as near me and the horse as she could get. I was not afraid of the horse but I was of the cow. The cow has always been afraid of an engine, while the horse would stand perfectly still. On this occasion, I thought the cow would upset the wagon, but I spoke to her, keeping her quiet and when the train had passed I said, "Bessie, I told you it would not harm you." We went on and not long after another train came in our rear. I stopped as before until the train had passed and then again went forward. But one train did we meet, while seven overtook and passed us. Going further we came to a railroad bridge, which we went under instead of over. We are now travelling on the right of the railroad and about midnight came to a signal station; here I stopped for a time and went to see and learn the workings of the station. When a train arrives the number of the train is signalled to Albany. Number ten, on time; number eight, behind time twenty minutes; number fifteen, behind time thirty minutes, and so on. Going on we made Schenectady about ten in the morning. I drove under a shed and gave my cattle grain, spread my blankets and laid myself down; I was very tired, sleepy and weary and soon dropped to sleep. I was awakened by a team coming into the shed. I got up, made ready and went on to the city; coming to a fine, cozy ranche, I stopped for the day. After making known my presence the gentleman and lady of the ranche were much interested in me and my cattle, and entertained us with much pleasure, and made me acquainted with A. B. and C. as they passed by. For example; a gentleman and lady is passing, my host says, "Mr. Adams, please stop a moment." Mr. Adams stops. "I am entertaining a man who has just arrived here, who says he has travelled from California, with that horse, carriage, cow and dog. They are all well, eating their breakfast. If we can rely on his word, which I think we can, it is the biggest thing out. That cow, travelling over four thousand miles, think of it; she speaks for herself. She is a fine looking cow, bright and handsome. Oh, she has shoes on, and iron at that, that tells her story." "I saw some time ago an account of a man travelling from California to Massachusetts, with a horse and carriage, leading a cow. I think this must be the man, no doubt," said Mr. Adams. "You have come from California, how could you travel that distance? Did you cross over the Rocky Mountains?" asked the wife. "I did, ma'am," I answered. "Did you come alone?" asked the wife. "Yes, all alone." "How dare you come alone; did you see any Indians on your way and were you not afraid of them?" she asked. "I was at first, but I found them Americanized. The young Indians could speak good English quite well; the older Indians I had nothing to do with, I did not like their looks, not one bit. They looked ugly, like the pictures of all Indians, painted up, decked with rings in their ears and nose." While we were talking, others came up and a like introduction took place. Others came and stopped to see what is the matter, until a large congregation had gathered round. Two teams came along and stopped. "What does this mean, so many gathered here; have you a show here?" asked one of the men. "Yes, we have a show, hand over your money. The man from California has arrived; there is his outfit and a good one too." The men that came in last, were direct from the city; one of them I learned later was a reporter. He was anxious to know all that was worth knowing. The two teams returned to the city and reported what they had seen. This brought out many more. I was at dinner when these came and when I had finished I loaned my services for one hour, answering all the questions they could think of, from California to my present place.

Cozy Ranche.—I left Cozy Ranche, two miles east of Schenectady, at four in the afternoon of the 22nd, for Albany, arriving on the morning of the 23rd, at nine o'clock. On entering the city I was much annoyed by the boys. It seems they had been informed of my coming and came to meet me in large numbers. They were armed with pistols and fire crackers. My horse cared but little for these, but the cow became frantic; I could do nothing with her. I tried to reason with them, but in vain. I travelled as far as I could with safety and then stopped. Here I remained until I could have assistance from the police. A street car was passing by and I spoke to the conductor, asking him to send me a policeman to assist me in passing through the city. The officer soon arrived, saying, "Stranger, what is the matter, that you are obliged to send for me?" "The boys are having more fun than I can stand; the horse stands it, but the cow has become frantic," I replied. "What can I do for you; where are you going?" asked the policeman. "I am on my way home to Massachusetts; I do not intend to stop in the city. I wish to pass directly through and cross the river into East Albany; will you see me to the bridge?" I asked. "I will, with pleasure," answered the policeman. We went on and the boys' fun was all cut off; no more crackers were heard from them. On reaching the bridge, I asked him, "How much shall I pay you for this favor?" "Not anything, sir," said the policeman. "Thank you, sir," I answered. I crossed over the bridge into East Albany and here I stopped for dinner. About two o'clock we resumed our journey and on reaching East Greenbush we stopped for the night.

East Greenbush.—I left this place on the morning of the 24th, making Nassua the same day. It was early in the morning as I left, I did not stop to take a breakfast. About nine o'clock I came to a small ranche where I stopped, fed the cattle and myself and then went on. A change in the weather is about to take place, the clouds threatening a storm. A given time had been set for crossing the State line, therefore, I would have to make a given place in order to come to time. About eleven o'clock it commenced raining, so I pushed onward and soon came to a house, and opposite this house was a carriage shed, which we went under. It continued to rain and the wind had changed its quarter into the north-east. My quarters were good for a north-easter. About twelve at noon, a man with a horse and carriage drove up to where I was. I said to him, "Stranger, I have taken possession of your shed; it commenced raining and I was anxious to get under cover, out of the storm, so I took the liberty to drive in here and would like to remain until the storm is over; with your consent I will remain." "All right, sir, you can remain," said the man. "Will you sell me some hay for my cattle?" I asked. "I have no hay to sell, I will give you some," said he. "Thank you; that is a saving of time in counting your money," I answered. "Where are you from; excuse me for asking the question?" he said. "That question has been asked me many times. I can answer it by night as well as by day; I am the man that has travelled almost across the continent. I presume you have seen me mentioned in the papers," I said. "I have read in the papers of a man travelling from California to Massachusetts; are you the man, with that horse, carriage, cow and little dog; where is the dog?" was asked. "He is in the carriage, under the blankets," I answered. "I must go into the house and inform my wife of your arrival. No longer than yesterday, we were reading of your arrival in Utica. We had no idea of seeing the man and his cattle; you have come to us and you can stop as long as the storm lasts, and longer should you wish.". "I am anxious to get home." "Where is your home, by the way?" "Webster,

Massachusetts. I am almost home." "Come into the house, our dinner is ready and waiting." We went into the house, he saying to his wife, "Here is the very man with his horse and cow that we saw mentioned in the paper of yesterday; I asked him in to dinner, is it ready?" "Yes, and has been waiting some time," said the wife. "I don't care for any dinner; I ate my breakfast between nine and ten o'clock, I am not in want of any dinner," I said. "Have a dish of coffee and a piece of pie, we will have supper early," said the wife. "I may have to stop here several days waiting for the storm to pass over, or travel in the storm," I said. "Don't trouble yourself about the storm; I have never known but one storm that did not clear away soon, and this will, I think," said my host. After dinner we went to look at the California cow. "Is that cow a native of California?" asked the man, looking me straight in the eye. "Yes, sir; she is. I am no fraud. Some think she has not travelled half that distance, but you can see that she has marks that belong to the far west. I say, and repeat it, that cow has travelled more than four thousand miles and she has been shod four times on the journey. Her first shoeing was at Reno, Nevada; up to that time she had travelled seven hundred miles; her next shoeing was at Ogden, Utah; the third was in Weber, Utah; the fourth time was in Homestead, Iowa; the fifth will be at Lebanon, to-morrow, should the storm pass over so soon." "Stranger, would you not prefer to have your cattle in the barn, if so, you can as well as not?" "They are comfortable as they are, as the storm is in the east and it is much more comfortable to lie on the ground than on timber." "We can give the horse a good bedding." About five o'clock I milked the cow and carried the milk into the house and handed it to the lady, who seemed much pleased with it. About this time supper was ready and on the table. "I have been reading about your arrival in Utica. It says that a man from

California, by the name of W. B. Johnson, is in the city, on his way to Massachusetts. I have learned your name by reading the paper," said the lady. "That is correct, my name is Johnson." "Our supper is ready, Mr. Johnson, take a seat at the table." After supper my cattle were well cared for, and when the time for retiring came, I remarked, "That it was my custom to retire with my cattle and I had strictly adhered to it with two or three exceptions. These were since travelling in this State. There have been times when I would not leave my cattle by day or night. While in Cheyenne, I was invited by a comrade of the Grand Army to take my meals with him, and he told me to look sharp after my cattle at nights or I should loose them, especially the horse. The cow there is not so much danger of. The cow-boys are fond of swapping horses and are sure to get the best every time."

It was late on the morning of the 4th when I got up and found it still raining. I went to my cattle and found them all right, I gave them some hay and returned to the house. My host, John, called out, "Go back to bed, you will not leave here to-day." "I will, if you say so," I answered. "I do say so," said John. I went back to my bed and remained there until I was sure they were all below. When the bell sounded for breakfast, I reluctantly got up; it was just ten o'clock and breakfast was waiting. After breakfast I went to the barn and gave my cattle more hay and returned to the house.

Nassua.—I left Nassua on the morning of the 27th, making Pittsfield, in Massachusetts, the same day. This morning I was up early, making ready to move onward. It was a fine morning, but cold. After getting all ready, I returned to the house. The lady of the house was up and had made a good fire. I sat near the fire warming my fingers, which were very cold. "You intend to leave us this morning?" said the lady. "I do; I have made a long stop, one day more than I really could afford. I must take it from some one else." "Come, John, get up, my breakfast is about ready," said the lady. "Yes, John, get up and see me off," I said. "I will, stranger," said John. After breakfast, I left them with a good-bye all round. "Should you come this way again, call and see how we are getting along," said the lady. "Yes, call. If you should get into a storm, we will try and keep you warm," said John. "Good morning and success to you." I left them and went on until coming to two roads, one to West Lebanon and the other to Lebanon. Here I inquired the best road to Pittsfield. I was told the best road was to my right, over Mount Lebanon. I went on until coming to the latter place where I made a stop, inquiring the distance to the State line. A lady told me it was but a short distance up the mountain. She was dressed in the Shaker fashion. I said to her, "You are a Shaker, I think, by your attire?" "I am, sir," she replied. "I am a traveller on my way home to Massachusetts, which is my home. Can I know when I step over the line into Massachusetts?" I asked. "I can not answer that question," said the lady. Opposite where we were standing was a stable, and two men were standing near. The lady spoke to one of the two saying, "Please step here a moment; this gentleman has asked me a question that I am unable to answer. His question is, can I know when I step from one State to another, or cross the line?" "Yes, sir; you can. It does not require a long step to decide the question. When you come to the State line, you wlil find a post, the centre of which is supposed to be the line. Stranger, why are you so particular to understand the exact line?" asked the man. "I will tell you if I have time. What is the time of the morning?" "It is just ten o'clock," answered the man. "I first remarked to the lady, that I was a traveller; yes, I am one on a large scale. **I have** almost crossed the continent, from the Pacific to the Atlantic; from California almost to Massachusetts. Now, sir; when I make the line, I want to know it, **as** I propose as I step into Massachusetts to give three cheers for the Old Bay State. Do you now understand?" I said. "I do," said the man. As I was about to go on the man said, "But, stop, stranger, I wish to ask you a few questions." "If you begin to ask questions and I attempt to answer them, I shall not be able to cross the State line to-day. Why, just look at it, more then four thousand two hundred miles of questions to ask and answer; it will cover more than three hundred pages on paper. I want to step into Massachusetts just at twelve o'clock. Now, sir, I will contract with you. It is this, if you will give my cattle grain; myself, bread and hot coffee; my dog a bone, with no meat on it; (be careful about the meat, as it might hurt him,) I will stop and listen to your questions for one hour; will you agree to this contract?" "I will," said the man. "Begin with my cattle," I said. "Lead them into the barn, here is the grain," said the man. I led them into the barn and they had their grain, not in small quantities by no means, but in large quantities. The last part of the contract, I am not particular about, but the first part I am. Had I not well cared for **my** cattle, they would not have been here to-day. "Well, stranger, I will listen to your questions, begin." "You gave me to understand that you have travelled with that horse and carriage, leading that cow, more than four thousand two hundred miles. Now, sir, where did you start from to make that distance?" he asked. "I started from Eureka city, Humboldt bay, three hundred and three miles north of San Francisco, with that horse, wagon, cow and **dog**. I followed the Central Pacific Railroad to Ogden; from Ogden, I fol**lowed the Union** Pacific Railroad most of the way to Omaha. From Omaha, I followed the Rock Island Railroad through Iowa, Illinois, Indiana, Ohio, and a small bit of Pennsylvania to Buffalo. From Buffalo to Albany, and from there here. Now, sir, it has taken many days to travel that long distance. I have seen all that was worth seeing except the elephant; he had just slipped out, I could not get a sight of him." "When you left Eureka, that cow left at the same time and place?" he asked. "We all left at the same time and place." "Well, well, she is a wonderful cow; it is all most wonderful. You have only about one hundred miles more and you will be at home, which I hope you will safely reach. Will you ever regret that you undertook the journey?" asked the man. "I can not answer that question. I think not; however, I can not tell. If I reach home safely, there will be no reason to regret," I answered. "It is eleven o'clock, come in and get a lunch, you will have time," said the man. I went in and got a lunch, then returned and made ready and went on. I came to the State line and crossed into the Old Bay State, with three cheers. Going on and just before reaching Pittsfield city, we came to a fine plat of grass, I stopped and gave the cattle a chance to eat of it. Opposite this plat of grass is a large Monumental Manufactory. I called at a house for permission to make a pot of coffee. Both the lady and gentleman were at tea. I asked the lady if she would permit me to make some coffee. "Oh, yes; with pleasure," she answered. I went for my coffee pot and on returning I was asked into the house. "Are you travelling?" asked the gentleman. "I am, sir," I replied. "I see you are feeding your cattle opposite, and I thought you might be travelling. Where are you travelling to?" he asked. "To Webster, Massachusetts." "Wife, put a plate on the table for this man. I think I have heard about you through the papers. They tell about a man travelling from California to this State; are you the man?" "I am," I replied. "Take a seat at the table; you are welcome to what you want to eat or drink." I took a seat at the table and after supper I asked him if he could accommodate me and my cattle with barn room?" "Yes, I have plenty of barn room; I will accommodate you. I will be well paid for it, without money or price, as I think you can tell a story that will be interesting to us; such a story as is not often told, if ever. We have stories, but they are all fiction; you can tell us what you have seen, something that is worth telling. First, we will go to the barn and see what is wanted." We went to the barn. "There is a stall for your horse, the cow can stand beside the horse; how is that, stranger?" "All right, sir." I led the cattle in and made them fast to their allotted places. "My hay I call good, we will see what your cattle say about it." They pronounced it good. "Now, we will go into the house, as I am anxious to hear from the West. I have many questions to ask; you must take it easy," remarked my host. "To-morrow will be Sunday and I do not care to travel. I have travelled on Sundays, however, not knowing it at the time. All the days seemed alike. Days and days have I travelled and would not meet a living being, but wild animals." "You have had something to do with the wild animals?" asked my host. "I have seen them, but never cared to make close acquaintance with them. There have been times when I would break camp and leave them; I disliked their deportment. They were always cross and crabbed." How about the Indians?" he asked. "The Indians, I have seen many of them and I have travelled with them many miles; conversed with them many times, and have asked them to put me on the right track frequently. They would do it; one time in particular, I had lost my trail and was returning to Carlin, about eight miles distant, when a cavalcade of Indians came down the bluff. I signalled them to stop, and two of them rode up to me, saying, 'What's wanted, friend.' 'I have lost my trail to Elko,' I answered.

'Follow me,' said the Indian. I followed him and was soon on the right trail. I thanked him and went on to Elko." "How was it with the cow-boys; did you ever come across them?" asked my host. "I did, I saw many of them; they were gentlemen to me; they offered me no insult whatever. Having heard much about them, I was afraid of them at first, but that soon disappeared. Many times I was reminded of the cow-boys; my first day out from Cheyenne, I saw two men on horseback; I was a little excited; they were in my rear, coming towards me. I had about twenty-five dollars about me; two ten dollar bills, one two and three dollars in change. I dropped the bills into my boots and went on; soon they overtook me, passed to the right and went on. I was more scared than hurt; after this I was afraid of no man. I was insulted by no one until I had travelled more than four thousand miles, and that man was so badly drunk, that he feared not the weapon I was swinging around his head. I could have laid him out with one blow."

On the morning of the 28th, Sunday, I arose about seven o'clock. I went to the barn, finding all right, I fed the cattle and returned to the house and to bed. About nine o'clock I was called for breakfast, which I answered. As I entered the dining-room, I was received with "Good morning, friend Johnson." "Good morning," I responded; "you are ahead of my time. You have been reading the morning's paper." "I have not this morning's, but I have the papers of several mornings back. I learn from them that your name is W. B. Johnson; do you answer to that name?" asked my host. "I do, sir. Well, friend, how am I to learn your name; what paper shall I find it in, please tell me?" "I think, sir, that you will not find it in any paper, but I will give you my name. My name is Hungerford." "Mr. Hungerford, where will you attend church to-day?" "I think, sir, I shall not attend church to-day," he replied. "I think I will take to the bed, it will do me more good than going to church. Mr. Hungerford, is this lady your wife?" I asked. "She is my wife," he answered. "Mrs. Hungerford, last night as I was about to retire to bed and turning down the bedding, what do you think I found?" "I don't know, I am sure; what did you find?" asked the wife. "Find? I found a clean bed. It reminded me of home."

Dalton.—I left the Monumental Works, near Pittsfield, on the morning of the 31st of October, arriving in Greenfield about midnight of November 4th. On the morning of the 31st, after a recess of three days, caused by the falling of snow and rain. I made an attempt to travel. My road was heavy with mud; I continued on, however. On making Dalton I concluded to stop over for the night. On coming to a livery stable I stopped and went into the office. There were several persons sitting round a good, comfortable fire. "Is the proprietor in?" I inquired. "He is, what will you have?" he asked. "Could I stop under your shed to-night, I am travelling and have been stopping in Pittsfield the last three days on account of the storm. The storm has made it heavy travelling and I am anxious to reach home as it is getting late in the season. I am liable to get snow-bound and will not be able to travel." "Where is your home?" asked the livery-man. "My home is in Webster, Massachusetts." "You say you are travelling; where are you from?" asked the livery-man. "I have come through from California," I replied. "I have heard about you through the papers. Where is your team?" asked the livery-man. "Under the shed, sir." All hands went to the shed. "Ah, a cow; yes, yes, you are the man the papers speak of. Stranger, back out of this place and lead your horse in the barn, it will be much more comfortable than under this shed," said the livery-man. I led my cattle into the barn and they were well cared for. "Come to the house with me and get some supper," said the livery-man. I went with him, he introducing me to his wife, as follows, "Wife, this is the gentleman that we were reading about in the papers, travelling from California to Massachusetts." "You have come a long distance. Where in Massachusetts is your home?" she asked. "In Webster, Worcester county." After supper we returned to the stable and fed my cattle with grain. "If you have no objections I would like to spread my blankets on this hay, it will give me a good bed for the night." No objections being raised, I made me a bed of hay and laid down for the night.

Windsor.—On the morning of November 1st, I left Dalton, travelling over the mountain through Windsor. While on the mountain I was struck by a snow squall, snow falling some six inches. Having passed Windsor and descending the mountain, about mid-way, I came to a house and barn. I stopped, and at the house I asked permission to use the barn. I was told by the lady that the floor of the barn was filled with corn and I would not be able to get my wagon in, but the cattle could get in, no doubt. I took the cattle to the barn, removing the snow from them and giving them their blankets, made them comfortable. By this time I had got wet and very cold. I went to the house to warm my hands as they were very cold. As I was about to enter, the lady met me at the door and said, "Come in, I have a good fire; you must be cold." I went in and the lady said, "Your cattle are comfortable, I hope." "They are; I have removed the snow and have given them their blankets, which makes them comfortable. Madame, will you allow me to bring in my lunch basket?" I asked. "Oh, yes, certainly," said the lady. I carried in my basket, made a pot of coffee, boiled some eggs and made a dry toast of crackers, making a good supper. After eating my supper I went to the barn, giving my cattle their grain, made me a bed of hay and went to sleep. After a time the man of the ranche returned from market and I explained to him my taking possession of the barn by a permit from his lady. "It is all right," had I been in your boots I would have done the same. You had better come into the house and take a bed, you are welcome," said the man. "Thank you, I shall be very comfortable here; it is not very cold. I prefer to remain here; I have matches but only use them for lighting my lantern. I am not a smoker, I never made but one attempt, that sickened me so much, that I never made the second attempt. I have fed my cattle with your hay, how much shall I pay you?" I asked. "Not anything; not a dime will I take. I may want the same favor some time," said the man. "I may leave early in the morning, before you are up," I said. "Stop and get your breakfast before you leave. Good night." "Good night," I replied.

Early on the morning of November 2nd, I was up making ready to leave, and left the ranche mid-way of the mountain at six o'clock. I went on down the mountain, coming to the road I should have taken at Dalton. This road would have taken me around the left side of the mountain, instead of over it and through Windsor. The map told me that Windsor was in the right direction. Therefore, I went over the mountain, and several miles out of my way; and a more disagreeable road I have not found on my long journey. Now I am on a good road. Had it not been for yesterday's snow, I should have had a good day's travel. My last few miles have been free from mud and snow; to-morrow I hope to find it still better. About half-past four o'clock I came to an old-fashioned New England farm house. I went to the door and rang the bell, which was answered by an elderly lady.

"Madame," I said, "I am travelling; it is about time that I should know where I am to stop for the night. It is going to be a cold, frosty night, and I would like to get under cover; your shed will answer my purpose. I would like some hay for my cattle, I carry grain and my own grub; all I wish is hay for my cattle?" "My husband is in the barn taking care of his cattle; he will be in soon. Perhaps I had better sound the horn, it will hasten him along." She took down the old tin-horn giving it a couple of blasts, which brought the old gentleman to the house. "Richard, this man wants to stop over night under the shed, and wants some hay for his cattle," said the lady. "Travelling, are you; where are you from and where are you going? Why I ask these questions is, you represent the man that I saw an account of in the newspapers, travelling from California to Massachusetts." "I am the man." "Do you belong in Massachusetts; what town?" asked the man. "I do; the town of Webster," I replied. "I have plenty of room in the barn for the cattle, which will be much more comfortable. It will cost you no more," said the man. I concluded to have them in the barn; they were well cared for. "We will go into the house and see what the woman will do for you. She ought to do as well for you as I have done for your cattle." We went into the house, he saying, "Wife, this man has done a great thing. We will never have another opportunity to show our hospitality." "I can give the man a good supper and a good bed, and in the morning a good breakfast and lunch for his dinner. I will do so much," said the wife.

The morning of the 3rd I was up as usual, getting ready to leave the old New England farm-house, which I left at seven o'clock, with good mornings on both sides; with success on one side and a thank you on the other. It was a fine morning, a good road and every thing in harmony. About twelve o'clock I made a factory village. Here we stopped for dinner, which was just one hour, and then went on and came to a railroad, which we crossed, and onward to a river which we crossed on a suspension bridge. Here was a fine plat of grass. I stopped and allowed my cattle a grass supper and while they were eating I gathered fuel and made a fire, boiling water for coffee, and ate my supper. Having a good road and a fine evening, I concluded to travel a while. Here my stop was two hours. I went forward and about midnight reached Greenfield. We went under a shed, I made up my bed, laid me down and had a good night's rest. While in Pittsfield I had not fully decided on my direction to travel, having two sisters, one in Marlow, New Hampshire, and one in Webster, Massachusetts. The one in New Hampshire I did not positively know that she was there. I wrote the Postmaster at Marlow, asking if Mrs. A. Emerson was in Marlow, and please write me at Greenfield, Massachusetts. Leaving Pittsfield, I took my directions to Greenfield. Greenfield lay to my left and Northampton to my right. Had I known positively which place to travel to, I should have gone to Northampton, for Webster; had it been Marlow, I should have gone direct to Keene. On my arrival in Greenfield, I went to the Post-office, but it being Sunday it was not open. I called upon the Postmaster, who, not being at home I was delayed in getting my mail, as there was one.

Turners Falls.—On the 4th of November I left Greenfield about two o'clock in the afternoon for Marlow, where I arrived on the 7th, about seven o'clock in the evening. On leaving Greenfield, my direction was east to Turners Falls. Here I crossed the Connecticut river twice, on two suspension bridges; one to get into the city and one to get out. The one above the Falls is much larger than the one below; both are very fine bridges. I passed directly through the town, making no stop. I found it difficult to get through, as the boys were under no restraint whatever, but I succeeded in crossing the bridge and went on, coming to the town of Gill. Here, on the 3rd of April, 1880, Sunday, I stopped with a friend on my way to California. I thought it not more than right that I should stop on my return. On my arrival I was received with much pleasure and we were all well cared for. Many questions were asked and disposed of, which made a lengthy evening. I was strongly urged to remain a few days, but I was anxious to get to my journey's end, that I might get a rest.

Winchester.—On the morning of the 5th, about eight o'clock I left Gill, and about eleven o'clock came to the Connecticut river. Here we crossed the river on a boat into Northfield, where we took dinner. After a stop of two hours we went on, but our good road was left behind. I am about leaving Massachusetts, by simply slipping over the line into New Hampshire. I am now travelling in that State, what a change in the roads from one state to another; such a change ought not to be. About four o'clock we passed through Winchester, where we made a short stop, feeding my cattle with grain and then went on; I concluding to travel a while the first part of the night and make Keene early in the morning. I continued my journey until I could not travel any further, I was so weary and sleepy that I would drop to sleep while walking beside my horse. I stopped and made my horse fast to a post and laid myself down on the ground, without spreading my blankets. I was so weary and sleepy that I at once went to sleep. A passing team awoke me and I got up, feeling as well as usual and went on. It was not long before I commenced to feel sleepy again. On ahead I saw a light and I spoke to my horse, "Fanny, we will make that light and then stop for the night." I turned in and went to the house. A man was sitting in front of a pile of turnips and was cutting off the tops. I spoke to the man, saying, "Good evening. I am travelling and intended to have made Keene tonight, but something peculiar has come over me. I am so sleepy that I drop to sleep while walking beside my horse. I stopped a short distance back and laid down, and I at once fell asleep and was awakened by a passing team. I got up and came on, but soon the sleepiness came upon me again and your light brought me here. Can I lay down under your shed awhile, I am in want of rest. I have been travelling continually since last May, by night and day." "Where did you start from last May?" asked the stranger. "From Ogden, Utah," I replied. "That is a long distance from here," he said. "About three thousand miles," I replied. "Stranger, give me your hand," he said. I gave him my hand. "Stranger, I will call you comrade as you have given me the signs of the Grand Army. I thought I saw your badge, had I seen it sooner I would have given you my hand at once. Comrade, what department do you belong to?" "I belong to the Massachusetts department, Post 61," I replied. "Have you the countersign?" he asked. "I have the National countersign, but not the Post. I have not met with my Post for several years; I suppose I have been suspended for non-payment of dues; you understand its workings," I replied. "Comrade, I have room in my barn for your animals, hay and grain, and for yourself a good bed in the house; so much I can do for you, and it is with pleasure that I do it." After my cattle were in the barn and well cared for, we went into the house. "Wife, this stranger is a great traveller; he says he has come from Ogden here, a distance of three thousand miles," said the comrade. "I think I read in the paper of a man travelling from California to Massachusetts with a horse and carriage, leading a cow," said the wife. "Comrade, I have said nothing about California, but I will, under the circumstances. When I relate the whole story it makes a long one, and should I ever write it on paper it will make a book of many pages. As I have just said, I will give you the long story. One year ago last June I left Eureka, Humboldt Bay, California, for Massachusetts. Came down to San Francisco, three hundred and three miles, on the overland road, so called. From San Francisco to Ogden. When in Ogden I footed up one thousand four huundred and thirty-seven miles that I had travelled. In Ogden I remained nearly eight months, leaving there May 14th. From Ogden here, about three thousand miles. My travelling road is many more miles than the railroad. Remember, stranger, I could give you the items on this long journey if there were time. To-morrow I hope to make Marlow, about eighteen miles from here. In Marlow I have a brother and sister, with whom I intend to stop over Thanksgiving, then turn back to Keene, and on to Webster, Mass." "Comrade, my wife has made you a dish of tea; sit at the table and take some, and also eat of what is on the table; help yourself." I took the seat and made myself acquainted with such as I desired. "Comrade, it will be morning by-and-by, and I would like you to help me away early. I carry tea, coffee and sugar—yes, and milk. I have not been without milk since leaving California. I will get up and feed my animals, make a fire and cook a pot of coffee; you need not get up." In the morning the lady did not wait for me to make the fire; no, she was up and dressed and ready for my departure.

Keene.—On the morning of the 6th, after being entertained and cared for by a Grand Army comrade and lady, I left for Keene. On entering the city I was met by a marshal and his assistant in an open buggy. We passed the compliments of the day, and the marshal inquired,

"Are you the man that has almost travelled across the continent with that outfit?" "Yes, sir; I am," I replied. "We were notified of your coming to the city; go on up to the park; we would like to meet you there," said the marshal. I went along, coming to the park, which was filled with people, eager to see and hear. More than four thousand three hundred miles of questions were asked and answered. While I was entertaining the people, a friend of mine, an old acquaintance, came through the crowd to me and said, "Warren B., is this you, all the way from California?" "Yes, Charlie, it is I." "As soon as you can leave these people come up to my house. Should my wife learn that you are here she would be here before you could get to them." About eleven o'clock I left the people and went up to my friend Charles' house, where I remained the rest of the day.

Marlow.—Eight o'clock on the morning of the 7th I left Keene for Marlow. About twelve o'clock we made Gilsum. On my arrival I found many people waiting for me. "What does this mean?" I asked. "Friend traveller, we received a dispatch from Keene this morning, saying the man from California, across the continent with his outfit, left Keene this morning for Marlow, and would arrive in Gilsum about twelve at noon. This telegram being circulated, has brought out this gathering. Stranger, we were anxious to see you—the man that has travelled across the continent with a horse and carriage, cow and dog. Yes, stranger, we have assembled here for this purpose, and to congratulate you on your arrival. You have accomplished a great undertaking; we are not able to grasp it. Stranger, come down to the hotel and get some refreshments; you are heartily welcome." We went to the hotel and took dinner. After dinner, in fact, even while at dinner, many questions were asked. I disposed of them satisfactorily. About two o'clock I asked to be excused, as I was anxious to reach Marlow that day. As I was about to leave three cheers were given to the man from across the continent. I stopped and said: "Ladies and gentlemen, I thank you for this ovation; it was wholly unexpected. In a few days I will return and see you again. Good afternoon." "Good afternoon, and success to you," was the reply. I left just at two o'clock. About six o'clock, as I was about to enter Marlow, I was met by a delegation, who asked for a short delay, so that the band, with a delegation of citizens, might have the time to come and escort me into the town. "Gentlemen, this is wholly unexpected. This will call out some remarks from me which I am not prepared for at this time, but as you are wanting something, I know not what, I will cheerfully comply with your request." Not long, however, before I saw a procession coming towards me with torches. I fell in their rear and soon found myself in the town, directly in front of my brother and sister's house. "Stranger," said the marshal, "for several days we have been looking for you. We thought, should we omit the holding of this reception, we would never have another opportunity of the kind. You, a stranger, travelling across the continent as you have, have accomplished no small thing. We will not call on you to-night for any remarks, but at some future time, before you leave the town, we would like to listen to you in regard to the many things that must have transpired or come under your observation while on your long journey." "Strangers, I thank you for this reception; it was wholly unexpected; I have had no such dreams on my way. When I first started on my journey I made up my mind that I would take things as they came and dispose of them to the best of my ability. I have done this, and have accomplished that which I was told could not be done. Strangers, you have surrounded and captured me and my family; we surrender and ask for a parole." Three cheers were called for the stranger from California who has crossed the continent; which were given, and the company dispersed to their homes.

CHAPTER X.

FROM MARLOW, NEW HAMPSHIRE, TO WEBSTER, AND WEBSTER TO LYNN, MASSACHUSETTS, AND RETURN.

On the 7th of November, 1883, I arrived in Marlow, New Hampshire. It was my intention to stop here four weeks, to pass Thanksgiving with my sister, and then return en-route to Webster, Massachusetts. As the time was expiring and just as I was about to leave for my home, the first snow-storm of the season set in, so I was compelled to remain until the first of May, 1884. My stay here was four months longer than I intended; being completely snow-bound that length of time.

Marlow is a town situated in the most northern part of Cheshire county, in a delightful valley, surrounded by lofty hills, that are visible for miles. It has two churches, three stores, a post-office, a hotel, a flouring mill and a mill for cutting lumber, and a very extensive tannery, which consumes two thousand cords of bark annually. I was told that the celebrated calf-skin, known as the Wesson Calf, was made here. This tannery gives employment to many people. The citizens of the village are enterprising; their houses show this. In painting their buildings they use white lead, instead of red, with a shading of green, which I admired much.

Gilsum.—On the morning of the 5th of May, 1884, I left Marlow for Webster, Massachusetts, and made Troy the same day; distance, twenty-eight miles. In making Troy, I passed through the town of Gilsum and the city of Keene. Gilsum is a manufacturing town with much enterprise. In 1880 I passed through this place, when on my way to California, and in 1883 on my return, I again passed through. I knew the village, by some old landmarks, but a great change had taken place and many new marks were to be seen, that showed plainly that the villagers were up early to work as well as early to rest.

Keene is a beautiful little city, with a population of seven thousand, situated in a valley, surrounded by the hills of the old Granite State, midway of the county, and is the county seat. Entering the city from the south you cross the railroad; in your front is a fine park, not large, but lovely. It is the beautiful shade trees that make it lovely.

Troy.—On the morning of the 6th I left Troy, making Gardner the same day; distance, twenty-two miles, passing through the towns of Fitzwilliam and Winchendon. Troy is situated in the southern part of Cheshire county, near Monadnock mountain, on the Cheshire railroad, about ten miles from Keene. It is a very respectable town, with a fine hotel, called the Monadnock House. I can speak well of the house, and more so of the landlord, because I and my family were well entertained there without money and without price.

Fitzwilliam is a much larger town than Troy. I passed directly through, making no stop. I noticed that it pretended to support two hotels. I went on as I was anxious to get into Massachusetts, knowing that there I should have good roads, which New Hampshire did not have. About ten o'clock I made the town of Winchendon where we took dinner. After a rest of two hours we moved on, having a splendid road, and at four o'clock we entered Gardner, making only a short stop, and then made South Gardner, where we stopped for the night; making myself known as the man who had travelled almost across the continent. Quite a crowd of people gathered around me to learn the particulars, which consumed much of my time. The landlord said, "Stranger, our supper is ready; you must be in need of something about this time." I answered, "I never refuse. I have had many such invitations, but never refused. Could I have had such when crossing the Rocky Mountains; but no, nothing of the kind was offered me; not even a house for hundreds of miles." "Stranger, you must be a brick, well burned, to have accomplished such a journey across the continent, and all alone at that. I don't think that we have a correct idea of what you have accomplished. Stranger, go to the barn with my hostler and give him directions how you want your cattle fed, and give them a good bed. Come in and we will give you a good bed, we will never have another opportunity to do so under the same circumstances," said the landlord. "No, sir; there is not another man that would be so foolish," I answered. "Not much foolishness about it, you bet. Stranger, would you travel the same road over again?" asked the landlord. "Landlord, it would take some money to have me return the same road," I replied.

Holden.—On the morning of the 7th I left South Gardner, making Holden the same day; travelling through the towns of Hubbardston and Rutland, arriving in Holden at four o'clock in the afternoon, in a rain-storm. From Gardner to Hubbardston my road was good, and from Hubbardston to Holden it was not as good, as it was hilly and rough over the cut-off. On my arrival in Holden I stopped with an old friend, formerly of Webster, for the night.

The morning of the 8th dawned on a rainy day, which continued throughout the whole day, yet the day passed by with much interest. So many questions to ask and to answer that consumed much time. Some of the time was passed on the hay mow, fast asleep, and some in cleaning the harness and other needed things.

Webster.—On the morning of the 9th I was up and around early, anxious to see my old home again. I fed my animals, greased the wagon axles and was all ready to start onward, with twenty-five miles between me and home and much mud to encounter. I left Holden just at six o'clock and was advised to take the old road to Worcester, eight miles distant; more hills, but less mud. I took the old road and went on. About nine o'clock I was within the limits of the city, and on coming to the Boulevard, I stopped to consider whether I should go through the city or around it. I reasoned thus: If I made an attempt to go through the city, I would not be able to reach home; if I go around, I would not be detained by the people, and I would be able to reach home. So I turned into the Boulevard and went into the city; on coming to the cemetery I stopped and fed my cattle with grain, myself and dog with cold boiled ham, brown bread and hot coffee. After a stop of one hour we went on, passing on to North Auburn and on to Oxford. Here we stopped, because we could go no further, as we were surrounded by many of my old friends and acquaintances, who had been looking for us for weeks. Some of these were from Webster. While in Oxford a dispatch was sent to Webster, saying, "The man from California, across the continent, with horse, carriage, cow and dog, is now in Oxford, on his way to Webster and will arrive there about seven p. m." I went on, amid cheers that were being given for the man from California, across the continent. About two miles from Webster, an escort of carriages was in waiting, and a little further, an escort on foot was in waiting. On my arrival in the town, before I reached Main street, I was surrounded by hundreds, I could scarcely move. I remained on Main street for a long time. Salutations of all kinds were given me, shaking of hands; "How are you, Johnson; you have arrived, you old hero; Johnson, you beat the d—l all hollow; we knew you would make it; we said you would come through, and you have." "Gentlemen, please give way and let the man pass on up to the Joslin House," said a voice in the crowd. I went on to the Joslin House and stopped. "Gentlemen," said the same voice, "he has arrived; look at him, do you know him? It is Warren B. Johnson, he is one of our old citizens; he helped to make this town of Webster. He went out to California, but a short time ago and has returned home, not the same way he went, by rail, but on foot. He has crossed the continent with that horse and carriage, leading that cow more than four thousand five hundred miles. On foot, remember, not by rail; how does he look?" "All right," said another voice from the crowd. "Yes, gentlemen, he looks all right. I do not think there is another man living that could have done what he has. Gentlemen, I will make you acquainted with Warren B. Johnson, the man that has almost crossed the American continent, from California to Massachusetts." "Gentlemen, friends and strangers, the remarks friend Shumway has made, were most of them correct. Where he says there is not a man living that could have done this, we will strike out. Gentlemen, I wish to be excused from saying much to-night. I have travelled from Holden to-day, eight miles beyond Worcester and am not in tune to play the music, but can say this much, that the reception given me to-night, is no small reception. I have not the language to express to you my feelings. This ovation was wholly unexpected. I will say, however, at some future time, I will give you a history of my travels, which no doubt will be interesting to you all." Three cheers for the man that has crossed the continent from the Pacific to the Atlantic, was called for and given, after which I drove into H. I. Joslin's stables and put up for the night. For several days after my arrival at home, the people came long distances to see me and the animals, that had travelled almost from ocean to ocean. All kinds of questions were asked and I entertained them with pleasure. The question was asked, "Did you keep a daily record of your travels, if so, make a book of them, it must make an interesting book." Some would add, "There is money to be made in the book, and you are the man that should be benefitted by it." This prompted me not to stop at Webster, but go on and make the Atlantic ocean. Then I could truly say, that I had crossed the American continent, from ocean to ocean. Before leaving Webster I had fully decided on the place I would make the ocean; some of my friends desired me to make it at Plymouth, as Plymouth was an historic place. My desire was to make the ocean at Lynn, as I could reach it in two day's less travel.

On the morning of June 11th, I left Webster for the Atlantic coast. After travelling about two miles I came to two roads; to the right was Plymouth, and to the left was Lynn. I stopped and hesitated which of the two roads to take. I did not stop long, and took the road for Lynn. I went on to West Sutton and stopped directly in front of a blacksmith's shop. "Can I get that cow shod?" I asked. "No, sir," replied the blacksmith. I went on about three miles and coming to the town of Sutton, stopping again in front of a blacksmith's shop. I asked, "Will you shoe that cow for me?" "Yes, sir; I will," said the blacksmith. I led the cow into the brake and made her fast to the stanchions. "Will she let me shoe her?" asked the blacksmith. "Yes, sir, she will; she will behave like a lady," I replied. "Did she ever have shoes on her feet before?" asked the blacksmith. "Yes, she has worn shoes many miles. Perhaps you don't know that that cow has travelled almost across the continent," I remarked. "Is that the cow the papers said so much about?" asked the blacksmith. "That is the California cow," I answered. "Where are you going with her?" asked the blacksmith. "I am on my way to Lynn," I replied. I left Sutton about twelve o'clock and about three o'clock I passed through Grafton.

Grafton is a fine town, one of the leading towns in the State, with much wealth and enterprise; the towns are scarce that can come up to it. About seven p. m., I made Westborough. Here I stopped for the night, with an old New England Farmer. Every thing free as usual, costs nothing to travel; that is, it costs me nothing.

Westborough.—On the morning of the 12th, after breakfast, we went to the centre of the town and I made a call on friend "Judd," formerly of my own town. Westborough is a fine town, none in the county a head of it; none in the county is equal to it in beauty and enterprize. There are towns much larger, but they always fall behind the smaller towns. Stand in front of the Whitney House, where do you find another that is equal to it in the county? I did not find it on my long journey; I have passed through hundreds of towns. Coming through Illinois, I passed through the town of Princeton, it was prince of princes. I am on my way to Lynn. If I find a town that surpasses Westborough, I will give it notice. About nine o'clock we went on, it was a very warm morning and about eleven we came to a fine shade, where we stopped, it being too hot to travel. A little distance above was a house; the man of the house came down to where we were resting. "Stranger," said the man, "you are travelling, it seems. A very hot day to travel with that cow." "Very hot indeed," I replied. "Stranger, move up to the house, I have a good shade for your cattle. I will give them some dinner, and yourself also," said the man. "Thank you, I will," I answered. We went to the house and a good dinner was the result. About two o'clock we went on, it was very hot, almost suffocating. About four o'clock we passed through Southboro. This is a fine town, with some very fine shade trees; but it is situated too far from the Boston and Albany Railroad. All towns and parts of towns that stand on the Boston and Albany Railroad do grow wonderfully. About five o'clock we passed through the town of Framingham. I merely stopped to give my animals water and then went on. Framingham is an old town, no older than others, but when a railroad cuts through a portion of a town like this, it's gone up to rise no more. About eight o'clock we made Cochituate and stopped for the night. This was a rational stop; it was at the right time and at the right place. My regards to my friend Lyon and lady, for their hospitality. Cochituate we will call a fine town. I only know it from reputation; I entered late at night and left it early, therefore, I can't judge, personally. I can and do say, that friend Lyon and lady has the finest house, inside, that I have entered, and I have entered several, but not with false keys.

Waltham.—On the morning of the 13th we left Cochituate, but not until we all had breakfasted. The lady, Mrs. Lyon, insisted on my staying to breakfast and I was obliged to comply with her request; I could not consistently decline. Our next stop was at Waltham, the day being so exceedingly hot that I could not travel, yet I was able to make the town and go into camp. While in camp I was reminded of a gentleman that went from my town to Waltham, by the name of Graves. I made inquiries and found that my camp was but eight rods from his house. I called at the house, finding no one at home, I went to the next house, and was informed that Mr. Graves' place of business was down town and his lady had not returned from a ride. As soon as Mrs. Graves returned, she was informed of my calling and made haste to meet me; we both were glad at the meeting. "Mr. Johnson, sir; can this be thee?" said Mrs. Graves. "It is I," I replied. "And where are you going with your animals?" she asked. "I am on my way to Lynn; to make the Atlantic Ocean. I started from the Pacific and am anxious to make the Atlantic, so that I can give my book the title, 'From the Pacific to the Atlantic.'" "And you are going to make a book of your travels, are you?" asked Mrs. Graves. "I am," I replied. "Mr. Johnson, I want a book, it must be an interesting book," said Mrs. Graves. "Where is your husband, Mrs. Graves?" I asked. "He is down town; he will be home soon; it is time for him now; here he is. Mr. Graves, come here, quickly!" said Mrs. Graves. He came, and after the usual greeting, he said, "How are you, Mr. Johnson?" "I am well, thank you," I replied. "And here is the California cow. Mr. Johnson, where are you going?" asked Mr. Graves. "I am on my way to Lynn, to make the Atlantic, so as to give my book the title, 'From the Pacific to the Atlantic,'" I answered. "I see. Wife, how about your supper?" inquired Mr. Graves. "I came here as soon as I returned from riding; I did not even go into the house, and have been here ever since that time," replied Mrs. Graves. "I think, Mr. Johnson would like some supper," said Mr. Graves. "I will go in and get the tea ready," she answered. It was not long before the bell sounded for tea. "Mr. Johnson, the bell says tea is ready; we will go and see what the lady has to say about it," said Mr. Graves. We went in and Mrs. Graves said, "Come, husband; come, Mr. Johnson, and please take that seat." I took the seat, a fine chair, in the centre of the table. On the table stood a dish of fine strawberries, with cream. In the rear was a plate of bread and a dish of butter. The strawberries' left and right flanks were supported by two batteries of cake, which did excellent service. When through supper, I said to Mrs. Graves, "You have given us a good supper, well done." "Thank you, Mr. Johnson, I think you are deserving of as good as you have had."

Lynn.—On the morning of the 14th I left Waltham for Lynn, travelling through the towns of Watertown, Brighton, Cambridge, East Cambridge, Somerville and Everett, arriving in Lynn at two o'clock in the afternoon. On my arrival, I travelled directly to the beach. I could not get over the breakwater, down to the Atlantic's waters. I returned to the Ocean House, receiving permission to pass through the gate and down on the beach, and into the Atlantic's waters. While this ceremony was being performed, there was but one person that witnessed the performance. I returned to the city, feeding my cattle and left for Webster, returning to Everett where I camped for the night, and ultimately reached Webster all right; thus finishing my journey from the Pacific to the Atlantic, without any serious mishap or accident to make me regret my long and perilous overland journey.

www.ingramcontent.com/pod-product-compliance
Lightning Source LLC
Chambersburg PA
CBHW030355230426
43664CB00007BB/608